Following Rabbi Jesus

Following Rabbi Jesus

The Christian's Forgotten Calling

Phil Needham

Foreword by David P. Gushee

WIPF & STOCK · Eugene, Oregon

FOLLOWING RABBI JESUS
The Christian's Forgotten Calling

Wipf & Stock
An Imprint of Wipf and Stock Publishers
199 W. 8th Ave., Suite 3
Eugene, OR 97401

www.wipfandstock.com

PAPERBACK ISBN: 978-1-5326-3607-3
HARDCOVER ISBN: 978-1-5326-3609-7
EBOOK ISBN: 978-1-5326-3608-0

Manufactured in the U.S.A.   JANUARY 19, 2018

This book is dedicated to a host of people who have turned my heart and mind to Jesus. Altogether they have done this by loving him, resembling him, following him, obeying him, teaching him, and living him. Because of them I have been compelled to return again and again to the New Testament Gospels to study this Rabbi, the true Founder of the Christian faith, God-in-the-flesh teaching us how to live in this radical kingdom of God he announced, showing us the ropes, surrendering his life to empower us for it, and overcoming death forever to seal it. I dedicate this book to all my Jesus influencers—my parents who were my first Jesus informers, all my family and friends who have loved me by both accepting me and calling me to account, my teachers and mentors who have in their own individual ways helped to mold my heart and life, and above all my wife Keitha, who has given me space to complete this book and grace to bless my life again and again.

Did Christ aim too high? Was he too idealistic? Was his faith in the possibility of the kingdom of God on earth a fanciful dream? Or have people been too slow to believe? Has our lack of faith caused us to be earth bound and prevented us from mounting up with wings as eagles? Have we been unwilling to submit ourselves to the kingdom discipline and consequently failed to receive the kingdom power?

CLARENCE JORDAN, *SERMON ON THE MOUNT*

Contents

Section II—Jesus on Loving: Finding Our Center in the Great Commandment

Our Beloveds

The Art of Loving

Section III—Jesus on Witnessing: Finding Our Calling in the Everyday

The Cultivation of a Life

Foreword

CHRISTIANITY IS ABOUT JESUS Christ, but for many centuries Christians have had a remarkable ability to show only passing familiarity with their Lord's actual ministry and teachings.

It is not too much to call this a pattern, a pattern of evasion. We have evaded Jesus' teachings and ignored his example while fixating on personal salvation and theological disputes. This pattern of evasion has badly misdirected Christianity, malformed Christians, and harmed our witness in the world.

In *Following Rabbi Jesus*, Phil Needham takes his readers on a visit to go see Jesus. In a series of thoughtful and unhurried brief essays, Needham brings us into contact with every important aspect and implication of the actual ministry and teaching of Rabbi Jesus.

In Section I, we encounter "Jesus on Becoming." Here we sit at Jesus' feet learning about what it means to be truly human and what kind of character leads to true flourishing. In Section II, "Jesus on Loving," we are reminded that Jesus established love of God and neighbor as the heart of true religion. This section is especially valuable in offering much concrete content about what that elusive word "love" really meant for Jesus. Finally, in Section III, we engage "Jesus on Witnessing," which focuses on witness through a certain kind of lifestyle in the world, and then through a certain set of practices in relation to self, others, and God.

Most of Christianity's historic renewal movements have involved a return to the life and teachings of Jesus. Though Christians are always tempted to stray into cold dogmatism, or worse, the Gospels remain ever ready to teach us about what Jesus himself actually said and did, how he carried himself, treated people, and served God.

"Following Rabbi Jesus" has the potential to contribute to much-needed Christian renewal in our time. Awash in Gospel texts, always accurate and fair-minded, "Following Rabbi Jesus" takes us by the hand and moves us into the presence of the God-Man who transformed the world and who calls to us today. Suitable for private, church, or academic use, this book is an essential guide to Christian discipleship.

Rev. Dr. David P. Gushee
Distinguished University Professor of Christian Ethics, Mercer University
President, Society of Christian Ethics
Pastor, First Baptist Church, Decatur, Georgia

Preface

A FEW YEARS AGO I decided to study Jesus more closely. I am a believer in Jesus. I believe him to be the Son of God in human flesh, the Christ and Savior of the world. I wanted, however, to learn more about Jesus the Palestinian Jew who lived 2,000 years ago and set out at around age thirty to gather disciples and announce the presence of a new reality he called the kingdom of God. Jesus invited people to enter this kingdom, and he made it clear that doing so required a departure from their current lifestyle and the adoption of a radically different way of life. There were other religious teachers around at the time, instructing their students in the their particular take on Jewish practice. None of them taught and modeled what they taught in exactly the way Jesus did. What Jesus claimed was shocking, and the strange way he lived was stunning. Most people didn't know what to make of him, nor could they finally bring themselves to follow him at the time.

I have a suspicion that today even many who identify themselves as Christians are not interested in coming to terms with the extraordinary teachings of this down-to-earth Jesus, much less actually live by them. Many of us prefer to have discussions about faith than to practice a living faith. As long as we keep talking about our gospel beliefs, we won't have to pay attention to our gospel living. And the living is what the Jesus of the Gospels seems most interested in. I suspect many Christians have consciously or unconsciously avoided Jesus himself, and in doing so have chosen to become Christians who don't follow their Leader very well. It's not surprising; following him goes against the grain of the world of our day, as it did against the world of his day.

Is it easier to follow Jesus today? Certainly not. The way of life he taught is still countercultural, still demanding, still almost impossible. To make him more acceptable, his profile has been softened and his teaching diluted. He has been reconstructed as a God more conveniently handled and more suitable to our tastes. The strong Jesus of dusty Palestine has been overshadowed by the polished Christ of our creeds. The Rabbi Jesus by the Christ of abstract doctrine. The radical ethics of Jesus by the cheap grace of a ritual God.

There is deafening dissonance between this compromised Christian culture and Jesus' radically different way of living. This is why I set out to 'learn' Jesus better and to discover what being his follower really means.

I knew the place I had to begin was the four Gospels—Matthew, Mark, Luke, and John. I decided to read, re-read, and continue to read them. I tried to read with an open mind rather than preset opinions. I paid attention to context and content. I was surprised to see many things I had never really noticed or taken seriously before.

The Gospels are the primary source for and witness to the story of Jesus. Phyllis Tickle makes an interesting comparison of the four Gospels and the Acts of the Apostles to the Torah (the first five books) of the Old Testament. She notes that for Jews the Torah is foundational for the entire Old Testament. Without the Torah the rest of it has no legitimacy and makes no sense. Tickle suggests that the first five books of the New Testament are similarly foundational for the entire Testament. Without them, the rest has no basis. They are the Christian's 'Torah,' and to study the rest of the New Testament—and the Christian faith, for that matter—without beginning there and reading other passages in relation to them is to miss the whole New Testament witness (Phyllis Tickle, *The Words of Jesus*, 51–54).

The Gospels are four voices, each one adding uniquely to the rich fabric we call the gospel of Jesus and its transformative effect on people. Each of the four Gospels presents different facets, different insights into Jesus. Each facet offers new details, new insight, new mystery, all of them together comprising a whole gospel. Long before beginning this search I had read and studied the Gospels, and done so to my benefit. This time, however, I have tried to look more carefully at Jesus—how he interacted with people, what he said and did, what was important to him, what his priorities were, what his mission was and how he carried it out, and what he expected of those who took the risk of following him. My goal was, and continues to be, to grasp better how I can be his disciple, his imitator.

When I say this I am not ignoring the importance of Jesus as the incarnate (literally, 'enfleshed') presence of God. I am not buying into the so-called Enlightenment view of Jesus as a great moral teacher worth emulating, but not the very embodied presence of God in human form, as the apostle Paul claims in Philippians 2:7. I am affirming what the New Testament and the classic Christian creeds claim: that Jesus was as fully human as any of us—and I would add, *more* human, more *truly* human, than any of us.

This book is a product of my search, a search which continues for me, as I will never be finished in this life with learning Jesus. It is written as an invitation to other professing Christians and other seekers to look honestly and carefully at the Gospels and ask some hard questions about what their findings mean for them personally. Questions such as: Are there crucial aspects of following Jesus I have skimmed over, or intentionally avoided, or never really known? What is Jesus *really* calling us to be and do? You will most likely be surprised to discover a Jesus that defies many of the stereotypes of the church and the culture that shape our views and our actions.

In order to discover what following Jesus (being a disciple of Jesus) looks like, we must begin with the man himself, not doctrinal concepts about him. We must look at the story of Jesus, see how he lived, ask why he lived—and discover how he is inviting us to live. What we know about the man Jesus is basically that he gathered a band of disciples around him, taught a new way of life he called the kingdom of God, modeled that way of life before his world, and accepted the consequences. Importantly, he expected his disciples not only to learn this new way of life but also to *live* it! In other words, *Jesus was a rabbi.*

There are many names and titles Christians use to refer to Jesus: Christ (Messiah), Lord, King, Savior, Son of God, Good Shepherd, to name only a few. These are scripturally based, apt, and important. When Jesus first emerged to pursue the life that defined his calling and mission, however, he was called "Rabbi" (literally, our Master or our Teacher). The rabbis of Jesus' day were mostly learned laymen with no official appointment who acquired students and taught them how to live righteously. The students or disciples were to carry on the teaching of their rabbi and live as he taught and modeled for them to live. In the case of Jesus and his followers, the term 'disciples' was most often used in the New Testament to designate all of Jesus' committed disciples, not just the inner circle of twelve. In our day the term should have the same reference. All followers of Jesus are called to imitate his way of life.

Gregory the Great (ca. 540–604) described Jesus' mission as our Rabbi in these words: "He [has] come in the flesh to the end that he might not only redeem us by his passion [suffering] but also teach us by his conversation, offering himself as an example to his followers" (*The Book of Pastoral Rule*). In other words, as our Rabbi, Jesus is both our teacher and our model or example. Jesus did what rabbis of that day did: he taught and showed his disciples how to live righteously before God and in their communities.

If someone wants to be a disciple of Jesus—which is what being a Christian means, if it means anything!—he must see Jesus as his Rabbi, or he will fail to get the whole point. To call Jesus our Savior, Redeemer, Lord, Incarnate Son of God means little if we are not living the actual life he makes available to us, the way of life he taught his disciples and modeled for them.

He called it life in the kingdom of God. He devoted his life to showing us how to live in this kingdom, this new reality, and he laid down his life to empower us to do so.

The great tragedy of settled Christianity is that it largely gambles on the efficacy of Jesus' death on the cross and subsequent resurrection, while it conveniently ignores the very life his death and resurrection make possible. It is absolutely right for Christians to sing, "Nothing in my hands I bring, simply to thy cross I cling"; it is sadly off the mark to return from the cross disempowered by a mistaken conviction that God has not really begun, or intended to begin, a new and good work in us (Phil 1:6).

This book is written with the conviction that Jesus came to bring us life in all its God-given fullness (Eph 3:19), to invite us into a new reality called the kingdom of God where we come to know that fullness (John 10:10b). It is an invitation for us to meet and embrace Jesus as our Rabbi, to become intimately acquainted with him, and to learn and practice the very different way of living to which he calls those who decide to follow him. It is the same invitation that Jesus extended almost 2,000 years ago to everyone who saw and heard him.

Extended to *everyone*. You and me, and everyone else. The good news is this: Jesus' call to be his disciples is the most appallingly open invitation on the planet. There's a reason why the New Testament records go out of their way to spotlight Jesus welcoming the most sinful, or low-class, or marginalized, or self-righteous people into his kingdom. There's a reason why around his banquet table are seated somebodies who are willing to confess they are nobodies, and nobodies who now know they are somebodies. They are all qualified to be there by saving grace, ready now to start acting like they belong there, acting like sons and daughters of God, acting like disciples of Jesus.

This is a book for anyone who is seeking to follow Jesus, or who wants to follow Jesus, or who is curious about what that all means. It is not for those who think they have already attained spiritual perfection—that is to say, those who have excluded themselves from the real journey of growth in discipleship. My intention has not been to write a book of New Testament scholarship, although I have not hesitated to consult New Testament scholars when I needed their insight. Rather I have sought to make this more a devotional study. One cannot fully engage the Jesus of the Gospels without worshiping. The work of the Gospel writers is not a collection of cold facts to be analyzed; it is a witness to the story of salvation, a story to be received, entered, and prayed over. This book seeks to open as many doors as possible for entrance into the life of Jesus and living in his kingdom of God.

The four Gospels will help us understand what it means to follow Jesus. Only occasionally will we look at passages from other books of the New

Testament. Our concern is not the history of the early church, or doctrines *about* Christ (Christology), as important as these are to Christian faith. Our concern is to study Jesus of Nazareth, a Jewish rabbi who came on the scene in early first-century Palestine and shocked his listeners and students with the announcement of a kingdom that turned on its head many of the current expectations. Today his words continue to startle us, his life to challenge us, and his calling to beckon us.

(Note: The appendix at the end of this book seeks to build a more extended case for the relevance and importance of studying the Jesus of the Gospels. Readers who are interested in exploring the matter further before beginning the study that follows, may want to take the time to read the appendix now.)

Overview and Approach for the Reader

OUR STUDY OF JESUS will look at many aspects of his life and teaching. We have organized them under three main sections.

The first section will bring together Jesus' message about who he is inviting us to become. Quite simply, he is inviting us to become who God created us to become: fully and truly human. Contrary to some popular opinions, sin is not an expression of our humanity; it is a violation of our humanity. And holiness is not an achievement by which we transcend our humanity; it is the realization of our humanity. Jesus invites us to become holy by becoming human. This is the calling of every disciple.

The second section will bring together Jesus' message about who and how he is inviting us to love. Here we meet the radical center of Jesus' life and mission. It is radical because of how broadly he defines our beloveds and how he calls us to love in such uncommon ways. We will see how Jesus' way of loving is the heart of our humanity, the most genuine expression of human holiness, and the most all-encompassing requirement of our discipleship. All disciples come under Jesus' command to love God and neighbor.

The third section will bring together what Jesus teaches us about our witness in the world. We will consider what he says and models about keeping fit spiritually and being prepared wisely for the mission to which he calls us. And we will explore the rich opportunities and ways he gives us to advance his liberating kingdom in the personal and public spaces of our lives. All Jesus' disciples are called to the Great Commission.

The relevant passages and verses from the Gospels (along with a small number of biblical citations outside the Gospels) are referenced throughout the text. The reader is invited and encouraged to consult them. This book will be helpful if it is read alongside an open Bible. Indeed, the whole point of the book is to help readers take the life, teaching, and example of Jesus seriously. This cannot be done without engaging the Gospel texts directly.

Otherwise, the reader is only taking my word for it, and I, like everyone else can only see imperfect reflections in a mirror and know only partially (I Corinthians 13:12). On the other hand, the reader may be interested in catching the flow and direction of the studies by first reading through a chapter of the book without the constant interruption of "checking out" references. If this is the case, please be sure to go back and then engage the referenced texts, or any other texts that come to mind as relevant to the matter being discussed. What is important is that you, the reader, engage the Gospels—and through them—Jesus our Rabbi, our Teacher.

As a resource for helping the reader to engage each or any of the subjects of the book on a more personal level, a companion *Guide for Reflection and Response* is available. It can be used for both personal meditation and prayer, and as a stimulus for group discussion and reflection.

Jesus on Becoming

Finding Holiness in Our Humanity

THE STUDY WE ARE pursuing is the study of a man named Jesus. This man, a Jew, was born in a small town in Judea called Bethlehem and grew up in another small town in Galilee called Nazareth. Following in the footsteps of his father Joseph, he became a carpenter. He attended the local synagogue and learned both the sacred Scriptures of the Jews and the teachings of the rabbis.

And then, at around the age of thirty, everything changed. The carpenter left his trade and his home town to become an itinerate preacher and teacher. Following the pattern of Jewish rabbis he gathered disciples, twelve of them, who stayed with him so that he could teach them—and change them. This band of thirteen, at times supplemented by other followers, traveled in Judea, Galilee, Samaria, with a few brief forays into more outlying areas, and finally back to Judea, to the city of Jerusalem, where the carpenter-become-rabbi was killed, leaving it to the band of twelve and others who had become his disciples to carry on his work.

This is the man we are studying. The Christian faith says he was also fully God. But this was a conviction his followers came to gradually, and Jesus was slow to admit it, one of the reasons certainly being it would have exposed him to the charge of blasphemy and precipitated his death before he had concluded his mission. I imagine he also wanted his followers to come to this confession on their own rather than because he forced it on them.

It is extremely important to Christian faith, however, that Jesus was fully human. Saying this takes us beyond simply saying he was a human being and specifically a man. All of us, from time to time—some more frequently than others—exhibit traits and behaviors that show us to be men or women, but not humanity at its best, not fully human. The witness of Scripture is that the human race was created "in the divine image" (Genesis 1:27), in the very image of God himself. Scripture also tells the story of a human race that has managed to defy this God-given nature. Human beings decided, and still decide, not to be fully human. Christian faith calls such decisions sin. Created as human beings, we are free to be less than fully human, and we often are.

Then Jesus appears on the scene, a person who fully embodies what it means to be fully human. He becomes the teacher and model of it to those who follow him. He invites and empowers them to be like him, to imitate him, to begin to become fully human.

Whatever else we say about Jesus—and there is much more to say—it is crucial that we see and affirm him as the embodiment of full humanity. God the Father has placed him before us so that we can begin to discover who *we* are and what *our* lives are about.

This movement toward our true humanity is what many Christians call the pursuit of holiness. A holy life is not a life for a select few who are spiritually superior to the rest of us. If human is what we are, what God created us to be, then for any of us to be holy is for us to be *fully human*, or moving in that direction toward Jesus our model. Jesus invites us to become like him. This is our calling as his disciples: to follow him and, in doing so, to discover where the human meets the holy, to realize that holiness *is* full humanity, and from there to come to know our true selves. This is the new place where Jesus invites us to stand and the new way he invites us to travel, on the way to becoming who we are meant to be.

A New Place to Stand

Chapter 1

Holy Ground

Moses is alone at the edge of a desert—rather, he thinks he is alone. He comes to a mountain called Horeb. In front of him he sees a bush in flames that keeps burning without being consumed. He hears a voice calling his name and telling him to remove his sandals. The ground is now holy with God's presence. Moses soon hears what God has in mind. It has to do with a mission that will change his life—for the rest of his life. God has made a desert place Moses' holy ground, a life-transforming, holy ground (Exod 3:1–12). Joshua has a similar encounter on a Jericho road, where "the commander of the Lord's heavenly force" meets him, and Joshua not only removes his sandals but also falls prostrate. He is on holy ground, and his life is changed forever (Josh 5:13–15). As is the life of Isaiah, worshiping in the temple when the worship suddenly becomes an overwhelming vision of God's holiness and a prophetic call that redefined and redirected Isaiah's future (Isa 6:1–8). A desert place, a road, a temple sanctuary—all become holy ground, a place of beginnings, calling, transformation.

For Paul of Tarsus the holy ground is found on a trip to Damascus where a bright light blinds him and he hears the voice of Jesus (Acts 9:1–20). After his sight is restored, he tries to understand this holy ground, this new place where he now stands. He eventually finds the perfect name for it: grace (Rom 5:2).

Jesus at twelve stands in the Jerusalem temple teaching elders, baffling them with hints of a new way, perhaps a kingdom of God emerging (Luke 2:41–48). At thirty he stands in his hometown synagogue and announces that this new kingdom of God, foretold by the prophet Isaiah, is now fully present, being fulfilled before their very eyes. Its location, however, is quite different from where they expected it to be, its primary beneficiaries not whom they assumed. (Luke 4:16–21). Three years later he stands in the court of state government, and when Pilate tries to get him to identify his kingdom, Jesus describes a very strange kingdom not of this world. He is standing at the center of government power, powerless before Pilate, yet sure that behind his weakness is the power that can save the world (John 18:33–36).

Wherever Jesus stands is holy ground. His presence confers holiness. His words and actions define it. His life is an invitation to join him on the holy ground of wherever we are. His name for this everywhere-place is the kingdom of God, and it's here and there; it can be anywhere. Anywhere can be a place of new beginnings. Anywhere can be holy ground, any moment can be holy time. Jesus says to his disciples, "Look, I myself will be with you every day . . ." (Matt 28:20).

How do we locate this everywhere kingdom? Jesus says it's here among us (Luke 17:21), hidden like yeast in a loaf (Matt 13:33) or treasure buried in a field (13:44). Sometimes, however, it makes itself known through such miraculous events as healings (Luke 10:9). It may be as difficult as a tiny seed to see, but the kingdom will reach maturity, just as the seed sprouts and grows into a mature plant or tree (Mark 4:30–32).

Jesus says the kingdom of God is valuable far above what any other kingdom or allegiance is worth, like the hidden treasure discovered in the field worth so much the finder sells everything he has to buy the field and claim the prize, or like the pearl of greatest price discovered by a merchant who does the same with his possessions to be able to buy the precious jewel (Matt 13:44–46). The price paid, however, is not what qualifies us to enter the kingdom; it is only the first step in making us suitable. We can't enter with the baggage of our idolatries; we must give away our presumptions. The apostle Paul has a graphic way of putting it: "Flesh and blood can't inherit the kingdom of heaven. Something that rots can't inherit something that doesn't decay" (I Cor 15:50). It is the Father himself who qualifies us (Col 1:12–14), and it is through Jesus that we gain entrance (John 14:6). Our job is to seek the kingdom above all else (Luke 12:22–31) and to be ready when the kingdom breaks through (Matt 25:1–13).

The kingdom of God turns the kingdoms of this world on their heads. It sabotages all power-based kingdoms as it is grounded in the grace of God now appearing (John 1:14; Titus 2:11), the love of God now given (John 3:16), and the salvation of God now available to all (John 1:12–13). It is enough to make a person dizzy as it calls him to reassess and reorient his whole life. Jesus confuses a lot of people because he disassembles the systems of our social, religious, and economic order by teaching a kingdom both disarmingly simple and radically counter-cultural. He disorients us because we have come to accept that society, religion, and the economy must operate by self-interest, exploitation, and exclusion; and he offers us instead a kingdom of compassion, justice, and inclusion.

The inclusion of everyone is one of the shocking claims about the kingdom (Matt 24:13; Luke 13:29). If anyone is in an advantageous position for getting in, it's the poor (Luke 6:20). Why the poor? Maybe because they have so little to hold on to or surrender. Or because they have fewer illusions about themselves, less to prevent them. Or perhaps God has a very special place in his heart for those treated as insignificant or lesser. The Letter of James underlines the strong position of the poor even further: "Hasn't God chosen those who are poor by worldly standards to be rich in terms of faith? Hasn't God chosen the poor as heirs of the kingdom he has promised to those who love him?" (James 2:5).

This brings us to another shocking thing about the kingdom: looking at it from our point of view, it is *counter-intuitive*("Love your enemies" [Matt 5:44; Luke 6:27]); *counter-cultural* ("God's kingdom belongs to people like these children" [Mark 10:14; Matt 19:14; Luke 18:16]); and *upside-down* ("Whoever wants to be great among you will be your servant. Whoever wants to be first among you will be the slave of all" [Mark 10:43–44; Matt 20:26–27]). It's not hard to see why Jesus' announcement of such a kingdom upset the power structures—and still does when not sugar-coated or idealized.

What does Jesus say about how life is lived in this radical kingdom? He speaks of living in the kingdom as a farmer putting his hand to the plow and not looking back (Luke 9:62). Living in the kingdom requires a focused commitment that allows no dabbling. The focus is obviously on Jesus, but how can we locate him? Not surprisingly, given what we have pointed out so far, in the parable of the sheep and the goats (or the judgment of the nations) the message is quite clear. We find him in "the least of these": the hungry, the thirsty, the stranger, the sick, and the prisoner—in other words, the vulnerable and marginalized. Importantly, Jesus says that in some decisive way we meet *him* in *them*, and that relationship ushers us into eternal life (Matt 25:31–46).

To what extent does this radical kingdom ushered in by Jesus inform and guide the mission of the church today? Unfortunately, we have learned to be "realistic" and accommodate our Christianity, to lesser and greater extents, to the present world order. Often we are confused about where we draw the line of accommodation. When we read the Gospels and hear what Jesus actually teaches and how he calls us to live, we find ourselves in one dilemma after another. How can we take this kingdom seriously when it goes up against both the present world order within which we must live and the personal compromises we consequently deem to be necessary?

Many Christians have taken one of two very different approaches to the extreme behaviors and radical ethics of the kingdom of God taught by Jesus in the Gospels. The first approach is simply to consign them for life in the hereafter on the assumption they are wonderful but impossible ideals by which to live in the present fallen world. At best, this approach is driven by fear of attempting a perfectionism that hides the truth and inevitably fails. At worst, it reveals a willing laxity of the spirit, a failure to take the teaching of Jesus seriously.

The second approach is indeed to pursue the very perfectionism rejected by the first approach. It is taken by the legalistic Christian who does claim to take all the teachings of Jesus seriously and to be living by them. He is extremely attentive to his behavior, careful not to appear to be un-Christ-like in any way. He is therefore embarrassed or even defeated when someone finds a chink in his armor of righteousness.

A third approach has also been taken. Some agree that the radical lifestyle of the kingdom of God *was* intended by Jesus for his disciples in this present world. They also, however, approach it in humility, confessing their personal inadequacy, their reliance on the grace of God, and their openness to admitting their failures and learning from them. As far as I can tell, this is the approach to the kingdom of God Jesus invites us to take. He would certainly not preach a righteousness at which he knows his disciples are destined to fail, and yet he never sees their failures as disqualifications for his kingdom or for continuing the journey with their Rabbi-Lord. The apostle Peter fails his Lord time and again, but he is not banned from the kingdom each time. He receives the grace of forgiveness and the empowerment of another chance. The kingdom is always within our grasp, says Jesus. The problem is, we don't always see it, or risk the grasping of it. The kingdom of God is a place where we stand in persistent faith, even with all our stumbles along the way.

We stand on kingdom-of-God holy ground. As believers in Jesus we're in a new place, a new place not just co-existing with the old place, but a new place intending to insinuate itself into the old and take it over, kick it out, make it irrelevant (Revelation 11:15). The kingdom of God is among us, around us, within us, and to ignore it is to deny the reality that stares at us in the face of Jesus. The only way to see Jesus for real is to see in him an invitation to receive him, follow him into this new kingdom, and start living the way he shows us.

The presence of the kingdom of God in our midst is Jesus' invitation to stand with him on the ground he makes holy. Here we see him proclaiming hope to the hopeless, and we are on holy ground. We see him curing the sick and healing cripples, and we are on holy ground. We see him standing alongside the poor and oppressed, and we are on holy ground. We see him refusing to take the mantle of worldly power, and we are on holy ground. We see him looking into the hearts of men and women, calling them to their true humanity, and we are on holy ground. We see him confronting the power structures and the powerful people of this world with the power of strong love, and we are on holy ground. We see him on a cross, paying the full price of this improbable reclamation project of his, and we are on holy ground. Wherever Jesus was—it became holy ground, kingdom-of-God turf, a place of transformation. Some who were present saw and entered; others didn't. Holy ground is scary. Moses, Joshua, Isaiah, Paul, Peter and a host of other disciples can confirm that. The kingdom of God will turn you upside-down if you let it. Disciples of Jesus are those who take the risk because the upside is the prize of God's gracious presence and the loving fellowship of his inclusive family. And this is more than enough.

Chapter 2

Fullness of Grace

It's a week for Keitha and me to take on some extra grandparents' responsibility. Dad is in London on business for the week so we need to help Mom (our daughter Heather) with their three sons, each of them in a different school. One of my responsibilities is to drive Ryan, age 9, to his elementary school each morning. I do well the first day, get him there in plenty of time. The second morning is another matter. I didn't sleep late; I'm an early riser. I just got deeply into a book and completely forgot. Ten minutes after I should have been at their house to get Ryan, I get a call from Heather, who is by now getting concerned and hoping I'm on the way. I'm not.

I'm sure you know that unpleasant feeling when you forget something important and it adversely affects someone else. Especially a grandson, who you assume is still not old enough to be able to grasp and accept any serious flaw in his grandparent. I get to their house quickly, apologize profusely to both Heather and Ryan, and get Ryan to school as fast as I safely can.

When we finally pull up to the school, I give Ryan very firm instructions to tell his teacher that his lateness is the fault of his grandfather forgetting to pick him up. Ryan gets out of the car, and before he closes the door, I see a small smile and a look of gentle defiance on his face as he says to me, "I'll tell her the traffic was heavy." And he closes the door.

What has just happened? I think you know. One word says it.

THE APOSTLE PAUL IS particularly fond of the word grace. It makes frequent appearances in his letters. In the last chapter we saw how he speaks of it as a place or environment in which we stand through Christ, having come there through faith (Rom 5:2). Standing in this place of grace, "we boast [rejoice, NIV] in the hope of God's glory." Sounds like a great place to be!

Is he talking about what Jesus calls the kingdom of God? Are entering the kingdom of God and coming into this environment of grace through faith the same thing? I think so. These two different metaphors approach the same wonderful reality from different angles. Combined, they speak of a very unusual kingdom—one whose leader leads with a gracious heart rather than a strong arm. Grace trumps law. Love trumps power.

"The Word became flesh . . . full of grace and truth" (John 1:14). Full of *grace*. Grace-full. If the apostle Paul tells us that grace is the Christian's new living environment, the evangelist John tells us that the environmental change came through Jesus. We don't know if Jesus was a "graceful" person in a physical way, like some of us are, and some of us aren't. What we do know is that he was grace-filled, full of grace. The evangelist John is saying this complete implantation of divinity into human life has the glory of grace as well as truth (John 1:14).

The apostle Paul goes even further in his Letter to Titus (Titus 2:11–12). He sums up the coming of the incarnate Christ in Jesus of Nazareth as the appearing of God's grace—and he adds, first, that none of us is excluded from receiving this infusion of grace, and second, that "it *educates* us so that we can live sensible, ethical, and godly lives right now . . . " (italics added).

What does it mean to let grace be our educator, our teacher? Well, Jesus—suffused with grace in human form—will show us.

As we read the Gospels, we see grace-filled Jesus repeatedly coming up against the legalism of a religion that has lost its centering in grace. It's a legalism that says one's righteousness is proven by strict obedience defined by the practices of a particular religious culture, or by a minutely detailed list of dos and don'ts (and especially the don'ts).

What is so confusing to the legalists is that Jesus affirms the Old Testament law, but without digressing into the trivia of certain scribes and Pharisees. In fact, Jesus claims that the purpose of his mission is not to overturn the Law and the Prophets of the Old Testament but to fulfill them! And then he goes on to suggest that the righteousness of the scribes and Pharisees must actually be *surpassed* by those who wish to enter the kingdom of heaven (Matt 5:17–20)!

Surpassed? So is Jesus preaching an even *greater* legalism? How do we "surpass" the legalists? (Perhaps we should also ask: how do we surpass our *own* personal legalisms? Let's not pretend we don't have them!) Certainly we don't surpass them by becoming more legalistic. Nor by trading in one form of legalism for another. (A fundamentalist Christian may have a theological legalism, for example, and a liberal Christian may be extremely legalistic about his social and political ethics.) Legalism paints us into a corner where we force ourselves to judge actions by their righteousness according to the precise rules of *our* version of Christianity.

We shall see that Jesus' gracefulness flows with a spirit of freedom from a heart of compassion, sometimes willing to pass by the rules when doing *real* good is the object. Grace primarily seeks what is *good*; legalism primarily seeks what is *correct*. The contrast comes to life in Jesus' parable of the prodigal son. After the son has left with his part of the inheritance, we wonder what the father is going to do if the son ever has the nerve to return after squandering everything. The father's response is extraordinary:

"While [the son] was still a long way off, his [ever-waiting] father saw him and was moved with compassion."

> He ran and embraced him, stopped his son's lips before he could finish his confession. *Bring the best robe, the family ring! Get the feast ready! Let's celebrate!*
>
> Then the father said, *Where's my first-born? Oh, there he is, coming in from the fields—what a faithful son he is. Someone I can really count on. . . . What's wrong, son?*
>
> The firstborn son shot back his reply: *This profligate son of yours . . . I've served you faithfully all these years, and he gets the royal treatment.*

The first-born son understands nothing about getting what you don't deserve. Or perhaps better said, he believes the only things of value in life are what you earn. It's the difference between a grace-filled life and a rules-based life. It's the difference between Jesus and law-driven Pharisees (Luke 15:11–32).

Jesus clearly understands the intent of the Old Testament law: love of God and love of people (Matt 22:34–40). He knows the kind of life that nurtures this outcome, and he himself embodies it. He doesn't embody it by carefully watching his step: in fact, he gets himself in trouble time and again. He doesn't set out to do it; it's simply inevitable. When the grace-filled life of Jesus meets the nervous, contrived life of legalism, there is push-back and something has to give. Jesus is maligned as a law-breaker, pressed again and again to justify his actions, physically attacked, dragged into both the religious and the civil courts, and crucified, partly because he observes the Sabbath—but in a very different way! He observes the Sabbath with compassion as well as commandments. He is willing to break the rules if doing genuine good requires it. For some of the Pharisees the rules are absolute borders: Yes, do good, be compassionate—so long as you do it without crossing the borders and going beyond what our rules permit on the Sabbath. It's interesting that Jesus does not seem to have to go through some ethical dilemma or strained internal debate before he concludes he can heal this or that person on the Sabbath or allow his disciples to pick some grain to satisfy their hunger on the Sabbath. He does these things naturally, with grace, as a normal part of a daily course of compassion.

Another reason Jesus is attacked is because he calls God his Father and even accepts the title Son of God, as we've already seen. This is blasphemy. But look at the gracious way he does it. He doesn't gather people on a hillside to announce this startling claim to the world; he simply teaches them the way to live in the new kingdom of God. He doesn't force his identity. He's almost shy about it. It emerges over the course of his ministry, as the time ripens and as events pave the way. He doesn't make it an issue; others do: If you are the Christ, for heaven's sake, tell us! When these challenges are made, Jesus is either silent or slow. Gracefulness even here: the love of God not forcing this doctrine down our throats, but letting us discover it as we get to know Jesus more deeply.

Jesus is also attacked because he preaches and, most importantly, demonstrates *radical forgiveness*. Now this is an interesting subject. It's very hard, if not impossible, to figure out where the bar *is* for Jesus when it comes to forgiveness. Honestly, the excessive forgiveness of Jesus is an outrage. It's grace released in an uncontrollable torrent. The legalists see very quickly that this radical forgiveness will overwhelm the order of their righteousness. They understand very well that if Jesus is truly speaking from the heart of God, they themselves will drown in the ocean of their now unsustainable legalism. They *cannot* accept it. If Jesus is allowed to teach this fullness of grace, grace so full it welcomes the worst sinner with an open embrace, and if he succeeds, their own religion has no real future, their kind of righteousness no legitimacy. Like the elder son in Jesus' parable of the forgiving father, they refuse to join the party and celebrate the God who overlooks what our past deserves. They turn away from the God who embraces us with forgiveness and then invites us undeserving souls to the kingdom banquet. Rather than allow this divine conspiracy to undermine their brand of righteousness, the religious leaders plot to stop him dead, literally.

A Pharisee invites Jesus to dinner at his home. When Jesus takes his place at the table, a sinful woman from the city steals in and finds her way to him. Kneeling before him she begins to cry. Her tears wet his feet with her sorrow, and her hair wipes them clean and dry. She then pours on the expensive perfume of her love.

The dinner guests are thinking to themselves: *Jesus, don't you recognize sin when you see it? You let this disreputable woman touch you and anoint you. I thought you were a holy man. . . .*

Jesus decides it's time to tell a story: A lender had two debtors who evidently couldn't make the payments on the debt. One of the men was in very big trouble; he owed 10 times what the other man did. The lender does something rare for someone of his profession: he forgives both of them their debt. Which one, says Jesus to his host the Pharisee, will love the lender more? The one who owed the most, of course (Luke 7:36–48).

I must say, it does seem that Jesus rubs it in when, after concluding his story, he then points out that the host did *not* greet him with a gracious kiss or fulfill the host's obligation of seeing to the dust of the road being washed off the feet of his guest—as the "sinful" woman *did*. In fact, *she* even perfumed my feet, says Jesus, and anointed my head with oil. Where does all that love come from? It comes from a woman whose sins are forgiven. Forgiven much, she loves much. It all adds up to the God of, and in Jesus—the God of all grace. The sinful woman was "graced" out of her sin—forgiven, like the thief on the cross. Perhaps on that day the hosting Pharisee was "graced" out of his sin, as well.

Again and again we Christians need to return to the unlimited grace of our forgiving Father, and come to terms with it. We need to deal with our own temptation to civilize it with conditions and reduce it to contracts. Before we know it we may distort grace and package it our own way so that we can draw lines between the sinners and the righteous—"them" and "us"— those that don't belong in our camp and those of us who do.

Perhaps the most common enemy of a grace-filled life is the view that a person should always get what he has earned or rightfully deserves. Actually, it is deeper than a "view"; it seems to be a conviction embedded in our emotions that have been shaped and strengthened by every instance that we've been treated unfairly or without appreciation. We fight all the more to get what we think we deserve because of hidden hurts that reside in the deep recesses of our hearts and that call on the justifying arguments of our minds. To be controlled by this drive to get what we rightfully deserve is, tragically, to lose the fullness and beauty of grace.

A grace-filled life says thank-you to what is given rather than what is deserved (Matt 20:1–15). It's the only way we can take God's generosity seriously. If we can see Jesus' parable of the workers in the vineyard only as so far removed from the reality of our lives as to not be taken seriously, we are opting for a God who will give us what we think we've rightfully earned rather than a God who truly loves us as his children and is forever generous toward us beyond our deserving. The workers who have toiled all day and cannot believe the landowner is paying the part-day workers the same wages do not know who the landowner really is. To be sure, he is a terrible employer, and in our day could be taken to court in most states. But this is a parable of God, from whom everything we receive is a gift from the heart. What we have earned is irrelevant. What we have received stands alone as more than we deserve, and with it comes the presence and goodness of God. Happy are those who live in the fullness of this grace!

Centuries before Jesus, a man named Jacob flees his father's land because of the wrath of Esau, the older brother he has tricked out of his birthright. Esau has a right to be angry, but Jacob is able to escape. Years later, Jacob returns and is met at the border by Esau. He fears the worst, so he brings plenty of gifts for Esau, hoping to soften him. Keep the gifts, says Esau, I have plenty. Welcome back!

Jacob is stunned; he doesn't know what to say. He expects to get what he deserves for his wickedness. Instead, he receives grace. Finally, he looks at Esau and says, "Seeing your face is like seeing God's face" (Genesis 33:10b).

At that moment Esau *is* the face of God for Jacob. Jesus, God in the flesh, is the face of God for us. When we truly see *Jesus*, we see grace. The amazing thing is this: in spite of our own imperfections—regressions, slip-ups, self-promotions, cowardices—there are moments when *we* become the face of God to someone else. Like Jacob, we have also returned and found ourselves standing in this new place called grace, the place where, having received mercy, we then begin to be a face of God. Nine-year-old Ryan was the face of God that morning of my failure, refusing to blame me for it, releasing me from the debt I felt, gracing me with all the innocent beauty of a child. We all have personal encounters with someone when *we* become grace embodied where mercy has otherwise been lacking. I think those are times when we are dangerously close to looking like real disciples of Jesus—graceful, full of grace.

Chapter 3

Purity of Heart

Perhaps we see it in boldest relief and with greatest courage when it is least typical. One would not describe the world of President Kabila, profoundly compromised and corrupt leader of the Congo (Kinshasha), as a place for the pure in heart. The year is 2002. Kabila appoints Dr. David Nku as the Governor of the city of Kinshasha to serve a two-year term. Dr. Nku worships at The Salvation Army and heads The Salvation Army's medical services in the Congo and Angola. He has now been placed where graft is the way most government business is transacted or favors bestowed.

The doctor is given an elaborate house with twenty-one servants. He declines the offer, choosing to stay in his modest home in The Salvation Army compound. His responsibility for a city of eight million people is enormous. During those very busy two years, however, Dr. Nku insists on carrying on his medical duties. He works evenings to continue to improve the much-needed medical services. Asked later about his political involvement he says:

". . . we can transform society. It's true that it's easy to become dirty in politics, but if the right person takes the place, he can change things. He shouldn't be afraid. . . . If we refuse to do so . . . it will be impossible to change things. . . . Yes, it's dangerous. That's why before every meeting of the Politburo we prayed!"

Those who try unsuccessfully to corrupt him say, "He will die poor because he doesn't take the money [the bribes]." On the day he hands over the governorship to his successor, there is a huge outdoor gathering with plenty of Salvationists represented. The Salvation Army band plays "How firm a foundation, ye saints of the Lord." When the music is over, the crowd grows silent. Dr. Nku crosses the platform to congratulate his successor. And that is when a large sign appears, lifted above the crowd for everyone to see. It reads, "Dr. David Nku, No *Stain!*" A testimony to the purity of one man's heart in a government where corruption reigns.

ONE OF THE MOST offensive behaviors of Jesus is his habit of keeping company with people of questionable habits and lifestyles (Mark 2:13–17). Jesus finds his way into a lot of places considered contaminated by the sordid people who are there and the questionable practices they engage in. In the world of his day, to be associated with such people and exposed to such behavior brands a person as sinful. Guilt by association. It is sufficient cause for the moral gatekeepers to label Jesus a person of questionable character. And yet, Jesus, undeterred, repeatedly finds his way to such places and people.

This same Jesus proclaims blessing on "people who have pure hearts, because they will see God" (Matt 5:8). Surely people so blessed keep themselves free of contaminants by staying clear of "the haunts of sin and shame." Surely the purity of their hearts prevents the association.

Evidently not. Clearly there is something here to be explained. Perhaps the example of Dr. Nku helps. The purity of his heart proves real when it holds strong in an environment of grasping self-advancement and exploitation. His insistence on continuing his medical practice in a world desperately needing competent health services suggests that a compassionate heart rather than moral posturing is his motivation. Further, he seems to understand that purity of heart is not a protected place for saints. It is a hidden power called forth, proven, and strengthened by engaging the opposite force. In fact, purity of heart unproven is weakened, and the heart withheld is depleted of compassion.

Jesus teaches us that compassion is the telling gesture of genuine heart purity. When he is asked to distill in words the essence of the law, the pure heart of his Jewish faith, he speaks of both loving God with all our heart, being, mind, and strength and loving our neighbor as we love ourselves (Mark 12:29–30; Matt 22:36–40). And when he is asked who our neighbor is, he tells the story of a traveling Samaritan who quickly revises his travel plans to go out of the way to help and heal someone he's not supposed to. He does it because compassion trumps social and religious laws of exclusion, the contrived rites of purity that pollute the heart. He does it because he has a purity of heart that two other travelers in the story have blocked, possibly in favor of religious duty or a busy schedule.

Inner purity overflows into compassion, and acts of compassion further purify the heart. The more we love others at a price, the more our hearts are cleansed of bordered religion. Purity without compassion is an isolated and lifeless existence. Compassion without purity is an indulgence that only compromises both the giver and the recipient. Purity of heart has credibility and strength where it aches and acts for an impure world. The textbook for it is the life of Jesus.

What this living textbook teaches us is that purity of heart is by nature not a condition to be treasured but a risk to be taken. Jesus, described by the evangelist John as "the light for all people. . . . [that] shines in the darkness" of the world (John 1:4b-5a), pays for the shining with his life. The shining, the illumination in the presence of human defilement, threatens the darkness (of sin) by exposing the desperate, grasping self-delusion it cloaks. The purity of Jesus again and again comes face to face with impurity, the compassion of Jesus again and again reaches beyond the confines of a safe piety.

Jesus calls his disciples to imitate him by letting their light shine brightly in the world and their salt give the flavor and zest of real life (Matt 5:13–16). If we want to be Jesus' disciples, do we dare to hang out with the riff-raff? Should we be seen with them? Should we reach out to them and engage in genuine conversation? The Jesus we find in the Gospels says: Yes. He sends us out as "sheep among wolves" (Matt 10:16a). Just as he trusted those first bumbling disciples with his mission, so he trusts us because he is purifying our hearts with love for the world. He does this even though he knows we will stumble and fall, blunder and fail. He also knows we will be refined by fire, our hearts strengthened by the risk of compassion.

Our Rabbi Jesus teaches and models a true purity of heart, a holy humanity, a genuinely human holiness. John Wesley speaks of holiness as the perfecting of love. Holiness is not a sterilizing that leaves the heart safe from exposure or injury. Without love's takeover the cleaned up heart is an empty shell. And as Jesus' parable of the "cleaned up and decorated" house makes clear, failure to pursue the life of holy compassion leaves us empty and found wanting (Luke 11:24–28, 37–52).

As we study the life of Jesus we see an extraordinary singleness of purpose, a focus on his mission to free the captives of darkness and usher in the kingdom of God. "Purity of heart," says Kierkegaard, "is to will one thing." It is the pure in heart, says Jesus, who will see God. And so this Rabbi of God travels through Galilee, Judea, Samaria, and places further afield, all the while knowing the final destination is Jerusalem, to which he is firmly determined to go (Luke 9:51). Here the "one thing" would be most fully revealed, the cost for it most dearly paid, and the power of it most manifestly released (Acts 1:8). Jesus wills one thing: to give his life for the world so that "the world might be saved through him" (John 3:16–17).

Those who follow this Rabbi-become-Savior are being purified for the same mission of compassion (I Timothy 1:5; I Peter 1:22, NIV). Jesus' kingdom of God is the place for true lovers, people who can care without hidden agendas and see without the distortion of self-serving hearts. Like Jesus, they are able to have a purifying effect on the world around them because they care deeply and courageously. They are true disciples. Perfect, no. Faultless, no. Sinful, sometimes. Lovers of God and humans, yes.

Jesus invites us into the kingdom of God, a new place to stand. This is holy ground. Not this particular place, or that, but *any* place. Any place becomes holy when we, like Dr. David Nku, stand firm with a pure heart and move forward with compassion, because we are seeing God and imitating Jesus.

Chapter 4

The Heart of the Law

I grew up in a very religious environment. There were certain rules of Christian practice, and we children were expected to abide by them. Sunday afternoons, after church and dinner, we were taught to be quiet, honoring the Lord's Day and, I now suspect, giving our parents this one and only afternoon in the week to have a nice long nap. We faithfully went to church Sunday mornings and evenings. We had devotions after dinner and said our prayers before going to bed. We attended Sunday school as well as junior church. Conversation at home was to be civil, and denigration of other people was frowned upon. These were some of the laws we lived by. By and large, such practices are good. Our Christian faith must be lived out in some disciplined way.

I did begin to think that some Christians went too far. When I was eight years old a revivalist came to our church and stayed in our home during the week. Before he arrived our parents told us the preacher believed that TV exposed Christians to too much temptation and therefore shouldn't be watched. So, we would not have the TV on that week. I was crushed at being denied the next episode of The Lone Ranger. I also remember the revivalist holding up his hand in front of the children in Sunday School and saying, "This is a hand that has never spent a nickel on a movie"—as if it were some kind of badge of honor. This testimony cast a shadow over my Saturday afternoon visits to the neighborhood theater to watch a couple of cartoons and a cowboy movie—for the price, yes, of a nickel. Was something wrong with me that I felt no guilt? I concluded the revivalist must live on a higher plane of spirituality reserved only for the hardy few. After all, he drank this disgusting thing called buttermilk with his meals (Surely a suffering only the spiritually elite could endure!), and I was determined I would never be able to do that!

I was becoming aware that different Christians practiced different laws. When it came to matters like TV, movies, and buttermilk, I wasn't sure where the commands of God came from and why different Christians had different views on such matters. Once I entered adulthood I was aware that the dos and don'ts of Christian practice could vary considerably from one Christian and Christian group to another. But the worse thing was that they were frequently also the occasions for smugness, infighting, and division within the whole spectrum of Christianity—clearly not good for the overall health of the body of Christ and the claim of all Christians to be following the same Lord and Rabbi.

RELIGIONS HAVE A WAY of building elaborate structures on top of simpler foundations. Judaism leading up to the time of Jesus was no different, and the same was to become true of Christianity. When Jesus comes on the scene the Torah of the Jews has expanded into intricate and detailed guidelines, each designed to provide a rule of conduct for just about every situation. Furthermore, there are differences and disagreements between the various rabbinic schools on certain matters. Jesus, a Jew, is aware of this, and especially of the difficulty the great majority of Jews, basically the humbler folk, have in following all these guidelines. At the same time he claims that he has not come "to do away with the Law and the Prophets . . . but to fulfill them," and that "neither the smallest letter nor even the smallest stroke of a pen will be erased from the Law until everything there becomes a reality." These commands, he says, are not to be ignored (Matt 5:17–19). Here, Jesus, the Word of God, is calling us to live and be guided by the light of the words of God rather than our own flaming torches of spiritual enlightenment.

Where, then, does Jesus part company with many of the Jewish religious leaders of his day? A thorough reading of the Gospels reveals Jesus taking the Old Testament very seriously; but as he sees it, the minute elaborations built on top of them over the succeeding centuries, while they can be helpful to some, are definitely not binding. In fact, says Jesus, these detailed additions to Old Testament law are sometimes actually used to circumvent the law itself, or at the very least they unintentionally create that outcome. For example, Jesus asks some of the Pharisees and legal experts, "Why do you break the commandment of God by keeping the rules handed down to you?" In this particular instance, Jesus is referring those who avoid the obligation of supporting one's parents by claiming that the money has gone instead to God as a "gift"—i.e., to a greater purpose. Jesus sees this as sheer hypocrisy, using the pretense of a higher act of righteousness to mask a violation of the Old Testament command to "honor your father and your mother" (Exod 20:12; Mark 7:6–13; Matt 15:3–9).

Jesus is exposing a great irony of religion: In subsequent generations after the founding of a new faith, certain descendants of that movement, for reasons sometimes good and sometimes questionable, set out to interpret, explain, adapt, or further detail the faith for their current generation. The outcome is often a collection of elaborate rules that eclipse understanding of the original purpose of the law in question. It may reduce something that is of spiritual importance to trivial prescriptions. It may even allow exceptions based on questionable, self-serving motives.

What, then, does Jesus see to be the purpose of the law of the Old Testament? What guidance does he give his disciples in discovering what the heart of the law is, what the point is, what it seeks to accomplish or help us to accomplish? Where does he stand on these matters, and where does he invite us to stand?

The most important thing we learn from the Gospels is that *Jesus locates the purpose of the law in the heart*, the place of motivation, the spring of compassion. He does not locate the purpose in the mind, the place of concepts, organization, and details. Like the psalmist who speaks of the law that resides in the heart, motivating him to do God's will (Ps 48:8, NIV), Jesus blesses those with pure hearts and says they will see God (Matt 5:8). This is in stark contrast to many of the religious elite who trivialize the law by breaking it down into endless pieces of piety while ignoring compassion toward others and love for God (Luke 11:42). Jesus sees that the center of the Old Testament law is loving God and our neighbor (Matt 22:34–40; Mark 12:28–33; Luke 10:25–27). This is *exactly* what the law intends. The law is a guide, a school teacher, a behavioral course to enable us to begin to realize this love of God and neighbor in our living. We distort this intention, says Jesus, when we focus on the mastery of details and miss this center, this one thing.

Jesus invites his disciples to go beyond the law itself to its true intention. Obey the law, he says, do not break it, but always see beyond it to its actual purpose, love of God and neighbor—and trust where it leads you! It may lead you to go beyond (not against) the law itself. The law says not to murder another person, but Jesus goes beyond the sinful act and says not to allow yourself to murder someone *in your heart* by harboring deep anger against him or her. The law says not to commit adultery, but again Jesus goes beyond the act itself and says for a married person not to allow him- or herself to commit *adultery of the heart* by harboring lust toward someone's wife or husband. (Matt 5:21–32) Jesus locates sin where it actually resides, whether or not it exposes itself in specific action.

The heart, the place where motivation is formed and intention resides, is the real key to who we are and what our spiritual condition is. The heart can be at war with itself, as the apostle Paul so vividly describes in his Letter to the Romans, chapter 7. In our heart we can be far from God, though we say all the right and religious things (Isa 29:13; Matt 15:8). The evil we act out begins in the heart (Matt 15:19). Our hearts can be hardened, thereby blocking our understanding (Mark 10:5). And our hearts can be pure. The most important way to love God and our neighbor is to love with all our heart, being (soul), mind, and strength. With *everything*, beginning with the heart (Mark 12:30–31; Luke 10:27).

Jesus understood that at the heart of the law is a great story, the story of God's love affair with us, the story of his extreme actions to enter our lives and claim his beloveds, the story of what he is now doing for us in Jesus. The more we conceptualize and systemize, embellish the law with endless rule-making, the more we remove ourselves from the love story. Jesus tells stories for a reason: They are the best way into the big story. His parables open doors of understanding and participation. The parables make no sense to those who resist the big story. The ones who get it are those who enter the story and allow it to claim them (Matt 13:10–17).

The stories of Jesus help people see the law in the context of *grace*. The parable of the grace-giving father and the grace-receiving son, in contrast to the law-abiding elder son, paints a picture of how the law of forgiveness, which can only reside in the heart, is far more precious to God than an external obedience seeking recognition and reward (Luke 15:11–23). Obedience to the law is a good thing. Obedience is a tragedy, however, when it doesn't flow from a heart answering to the grace and love of God.

The disciple of Jesus comes to understand that obedience to the law is a matter of how we come to our true humanity, or how we become a holy people. It is no accident that Jesus affirms what some Jewish teachers have already said: All the law boils down to love of God and neighbor. "I give you these commandments," says Jesus, "so that you can love each other" (John 15:17). This is our humanity distilled, our holiness explained. We neither love nor obey God in a vacuum. God is supremely near in our neighbor, the people near and far, all our neighbors. All of God's laws are finally relational and seek to unite what our sin against him and each other has broken—our God-given humanity. The heart of the law is this holiness, and if our obedience to the law misses this, it misses the heart. Jesus invites us, his disciples, to stand with him in this new place where obedience flows from a heart of love. Such obedience will save us from a dead legalism and a heartless righteousness.

Let us have the various and sundry traditions of our Christian practice. So many of them are faith practices worth keeping, and helpful for our journey with Jesus. Some, we learn after honest scrutiny and prayer, are not worth keeping. Jesus invites us to ask of each of them: is it helping me to stay in Jesus' company and live his life in the world? Does it help to situate me in a place of grace? Is it helping to form me as Jesus' disciple?

Chapter 5

A Different Way to See

A few years ago Keitha and I were in search of a place with perspective—to be specific, a small cabin with a large view of a mountain range. We wanted to see forever, with a rich carpet of trees in between and endless sky above. A big order for our small budget. Melissa, our real estate agent, tirelessly showed us place after place—some desirable, but beyond the budget.

One day she led us to a place on Walnut Mountain. As soon as we walked in we absolutely loved it. It was modest but elegant, almost fifty years old but strong. And best of all we could stand on the porch and see forever—well, at least to the Cohutta Mountains of north Georgia, stretching into Tennessee to the left and North Carolina to the right. The previous long-term owners of the cabin were Rabbi and Mrs. Alvin (Barbara) Sugerman. The place was redolent with the grace and simplicity of this extraordinary couple. The memories of their family visits and good times together seemed to linger in the very woodwork. We felt they had made the cabin a holy place. And yes, with gratitude we have kept the mezuzahs on the doorposts and the parting blessing over the door: "Shalom, y'all." (We're in the South, you know.)

Typically, we city folk call a cabin in the mountains a "getaway," a place of escape or refuge. True enough. But we discovered there's more to it. There is, of course, the overwhelming impact of being surrounded by the sheer beauty and wonder of God's creation. That is also a huge gift.

But there's still something else, perhaps the most important thing. We go there to see things differently, to get a new perspective on the world and on our lives. Freed from the press of picturing the world within predefined boundaries and copied preferences, we look out on our mountain horizon and see a world in creative flux. The sky is never the same from day to day and hour to hour. The landscape varies with the play of light and mist and temperature. When the light comes with a different hue or angle, everything changes. When thick mist concentrates in the large crevices between hills and mountains, the ridges become stark definitions of a seemingly new landscape. When the temperature or humidity goes up or down, the possibilities of weather changes are endless. There is ever more to see than we think or imagine. It's as if God is inviting us to see that there are fresh ways to see the world we haven't imagined. It's as if we're being taught by the Jesus of the Gospels, who frequently looked around him and pointed out what others had not seen before.

JESUS INTRODUCES US TO a new way of seeing. He invites us to look out on some field of beautiful, thriving flowers or a flock of birds in carefree flight. Even Solomon in all his glory wasn't dressed in such splendor as those flowers, and through all the changing scenes around those tiny winged creatures of the air, he says, in all conditions of weather, harsh and pleasant, God watches over them (Matt 6:26–29; Luke 12:24–27). Hundreds of years earlier the prophet Isaiah has a vision of "the Lord sitting on a high and exalted throne, the edges of his robe filling the temple" where Isaiah is worshiping. The Lord is surrounded by six-winged creatures who cover their eyes with two of their wings, so unbearably great is the Lord's glory. They call out to each other, "Holy, holy, holy/is the Lord of heavenly forces!/*All the earth is filled with God's glory*" (Isa 6:1–3, italics added). Isaiah sees a world filled with God's glory, Jesus a world held in the hands of a providential God.

God has something to say, a story to tell in the world around us. Through all the changing scenes of life, he is at work. Every now and then we see it. Sometimes the glory is so great we can't stand it; we're not sure we shouldn't cover our eyes. Sometimes we cry, maybe laugh, or catch our breath. Most of the time, sadly, we don't notice, like frightened seraphs protecting ourselves by covering our eyes. There's only so much we can take at once without it changing us. Allowing ourselves to see such providence gives us insane courage to live beyond our fears. Seeing the divine presence surrounding us tempts us to live like saints. Dare we open our eyes and see such burning glory and breathtaking beauty? Jesus, it seems, is inviting us to do just that.

It would not be far from the truth to say that in our fallen-ness we see wrongly. Shielded by ourselves from seeing God's world, we choose to see a different world by prejudicing and twisting our perspective. We see the world as our entitlement, a resource to be exploited rather than a gift to be received. Our skewed vision is particularly and perhaps most tragically true of our perspectives on one another. We notice appearances, we jump to conclusions, and unfortunately we sometimes (or perhaps often) suspect the worst. Fear takes hold of us and drives us to question one another's motives or intentions. We keep our distance to avoid being disadvantaged or made vulnerable by risking closeness, openness, or affection. We refuse to see and believe more than our apprehension allows. The filters of fear blind and bind us.

Jesus invites us, his disciples, to trust God's providence by standing in a new place with a different perspective. He calls this new place of vision the kingdom of God. Entering this kingdom and seeing things as Jesus does requires nothing less than a new birth (John 3:3). Our eyes now see differently because this new birth turns us upside down and inside out. It often seems we are now seeing the reverse of what we saw before. We see value and blessing, even beauty, in people we previously ignored or even shunned. We now begin to risk seeing more deeply into a person, beyond his public persona to his heart.

This new way of seeing is precisely what our Rabbi Jesus models for us. His eyesight goes beyond the surface. In doing this, he often must first unmask a person's deception. A group of legal experts and priests try to trap him into making a dangerous statement about not paying government taxes. They seem to be asking an innocent question, but their sincerity is pretense. Jesus sees exactly what they are up to and doesn't bite (Luke 20:20–26). He perceives when the voice of a person is not the person's true voice but another spirit, a demon by whatever name to whom the person is prisoner and from whom he longs to be released (Mark 1:21–26; Luke 9:37–45). These and other examples suggest that when someone says something to Jesus, Jesus determines the true motive or identifies who or what is actually doing the talking. In the former case he sometimes has to unmask the true intent hidden behind a pretense of sincerity; in the latter he confronts and expels a usurping spirit.

Jesus, however, does not go looking for the bad in a person. He looks for the good and sees the bad only as an impairment of the true image of God that shapes a person's holy humanness. He sees past the faults and failures of his disciple Peter, to the person Peter will become. Again and again Peter misunderstands what Jesus is really about and what discipleship entails. And at the end he fails the test of loyalty to his master. He denies Jesus. But at the last resurrection appearance of Jesus recorded in John's Gospel, Jesus singles out this failed disciple, looks into his heart and sees the potential for good that Peter is incapable of seeing because of his previous disloyalty. Jesus takes this broken man and commissions him to a spiritual leadership far beyond anything Peter could ever have imagined—and a martyr's death that only the most loyal disciple could ever accept.

Jesus sees in all of us a level of discipleship and spiritual courage well beyond what we can believe we're capable of. He knows what is in us, hidden as it may be. He knows our heart. (In Scripture the "heart" metaphor usually refers to the source of our motivations and actions.) Jesus says that good things come out of "the good stored up in a person's heart" and bad things come out of "the evil stored up in his heart" (Luke 6:43–45). Jesus' incredible eyesight comes out of his ability to see what is really in a person's heart, which is not something of which the person is usually aware. What he sees in the heart is the key to how he interacts with the person. We need look no further than, for example, Jesus' encounter with the rich young ruler (Luke 18:18–25) or with the woman at the well (John 4:4–30).

Are we, Jesus' disciples, capable of such insight, or at least some measure of it? Jesus clearly thinks so. It is doubtful that by their natural gifts certain people have more insight than others. According to Jesus, it is more a matter of dealing with our own judgmental nature, our sinful tendency to point out minor obstructions to the spiritual viewpoint of others, without having removed the major obstruction in our own vision (Matt 7:3–5; Luke 6:41–42). Remove the log of your own blindness, he says, before thinking you can even begin to look into another's eyes and see what is really there. Give up the presumption to judge, and confess your own sin-induced blindness. Then you may begin to see—that is, if you really *want* to see. Insight is given to those who do want to see or who care about seeing what is really there in a person's heart. (Jesus is implying that those who see splinters in the eyes of others while not addressing the log in their own eyes, don't really want to see, only criticize. Their own blindness enables them to see what they want, to see without seeing.)

Jesus invites us, his disciples, to do as he does: look beyond the surface of a person, look deeply. He challenges us to be willing to move beyond what we want to be there or what we are afraid is there and fear to find out. Sometimes we are afraid to look deeply into someone's heart. We wonder, or doubt, whether we can handle what will be revealed. Or we may be more comfortable just accommodating pretense (ignoring "the elephant in the room"). Seeing as Jesus sees means moving beyond blinding fear and opening our eyes to the good in a person, or seeing what is blocking it. We may see a distorting spirit voicing ugliness, or we may see pretense—or we may see an inkling of goodness or a taste of purity. When we see with such clarity, we are in a position to encourage, help, even heal.

Being in such a sacred place is Jesus' gift given to the humble disciple. It is not unlike watching the revelations of a changing mountain scene. We may want to capture the beautiful scene in a quick photo to define and retain what we've experienced, glance at it later, show it to someone, put it on a wall, move on. Or we may allow ourselves to be caught up in the wonder, letting it unfold before us and take us in, patient recipients of the gift of seeing what God is sharing.

Jesus invites us to see with awe and humility each God-given revelation as it is being given. For the preoccupied there is no such gift of sight, no insight into the heart of the world or another person. Rabbi Jesus teaches us a radical attentiveness born of humility, a willingness to wait to be shown who and what is really there. To be sure, none of us has splinter-free eyes. Before considering the possible sin of another, we would do well to confess our own; and in doing so we are humbled into a better and more helpful vision. A new way to see. Jesus' gift to us, his disciples, is sight with insight.

Chapter 6

A New Self-Understanding

I find myself drawn to the PBS series hosted by Henry Louis Gates Jr. called "Finding Your Roots." Well-known Americans are invited to be subjects of an all-out search for their ancestry, going back as far as family and historical records gathered from diverse sources can trace the story. In each case the search is rounded off by DNA analysis informing the subject of his or her racial makeup and the extent (identified by percentages) of each racial type.

It is often quite moving to see the effect on the person being featured of previously unknown facts and stories of their ancestral history. One of them is African American actress Anna Deavere Smith. She learns that one of her ancestors was a free man living with his family on a farm he owned in Pennsylvania when the Civil War began. One day he is warned that a large battle will probably take place near where his farm is located. He moves his family a few miles north. Following the long battle, he comes back to discover thousands of unburied and half-buried corpses of Union soldiers strewn across his farm and the surrounding fields and woods. (The Confederates have already removed the bodies of their stricken soldiers.) The United States government desperately needs to give their fallen a decent, honorable burial. They ask the farmer if he would take on the gruesome task, with the help of funding they would provide. He agrees.

It takes three months for him to complete all the burials. He does it with care and reverence. And when the task is done, a special national commemoration is held on the site. President Abraham Lincoln is the speaker, delivering what is perhaps the most remembered and oft recited speech of his presidency. The place, of course, is Gettysburg.

When she hears the story, Ms. Smith is stunned into silence. This story of her amazing ancestor, linking her to one of the most iconic events and greatest human sacrifices of that horrible war, now becomes part of her identity, her story, her own self-understanding.

LIKE THE GUESTS OF Henry Gates on PBS, we learn that a part of our identity, sometimes a significant part, is wrapped up in where we came from and what our family stories are. None of us appears out of nowhere. We each are birthed with unique DNA and an ancestral line going back centuries. But is that alone—our DNA, our family history—what defines us?

Jesus presents us with another DNA, a larger sweep of human history, and a story that takes us all in, whatever the special details and character of our individual stories. The basic DNA, we could say, is the image of God he comes to restore and revive. The history is the sad affair of our whole human race, now given hope by the presence of the kingdom of God inaugurated through Jesus. The large story is God's love affair with his people that reaches a critical mass in Jesus' life, death, and resurrection. Our individual DNA, generational history, and personal stories are all an important part of who we are. But at the root we are all sinners who are invited to enter the kingdom of God and join the inclusive race of the restored. Here is where we come to understand and better live out our individual stories. Here is where each of us comes to know who we really are as God sees us.

Jesus the Rabbi is interested in shaping lives, helping people come to a new understanding, a sense of who they can become and what their mission in life can be. He invites them to enter the kingdom of God, a "location" where they find their new identity fits them just right, even though it often makes them misfits in an outside-the-kingdom world that clings to the old truthless identities. He gathers around him disciples in whom he wants to instill this new identity, or perhaps better said, to enable them to discover their *true* identity, hidden as it may have been till now.

What about this rabbi himself? What qualifies him to do this, or even to presume to do it? How can he help others understand themselves in a totally new way? Surely he must first be a model of it himself.

Jesus was human. Completely. All the Gospel writers begin their accounts fully understanding that their main character is a human being who lives a life of about thirty-three years, and during the last three is a rabbi who gathers students (disciples) around him and travels throughout Palestine announcing and teaching the kingdom of God. He is a man, fully human, not a divine being impersonating a human. The Jesus they write about refers to himself as "the Son of Man," which means "the Human One." Like us, he is birthed by a woman, grows and learns his way into adulthood, masters a trade, is given a calling, and dies. Like us, he needs food, water, and sleep. He gets hungry, thirsty, and exhausted. He feels the whole range of emotions, from tenderness to anger. He loves. He sees himself as fully human—in fact, as a fulfilled human, satisfied toward the end of his life that he is completing the work given him by his heavenly Father (John 17:4).

Like us, he has his own calling, once described in his own words in this way: "I came so that they [we] can have life—indeed, so that they [we] could live life to the fullest" (John 10:10). His calling is forged through the particular circumstances of his life, as is ours; he owns it and follows it. He leaves his carpenter career to follow this calling no one else could have expected or requested. Even his parents cannot define him (Luke 2:41–51). He loves his mother but is not "a mother's boy" (Matt 12:46–50; Mark 3:31–35; Luke 8:19–21). And when the crowds try to make him into the messianic leader of a violent revolution, he has no part of it. His calling is not the fulfillment of someone else's expectations. He knows who he is and why he is.

Things get more complicated, however, when the Gospel writers claim that Rabbi Jesus is also God in human flesh. There is no denying that all four writers believe in the divinity of this rabbi. *Mark*, who gives no birth narrative, opens with this succinct statement: "The beginning of the good news about Jesus, God's Son"(Mark 1:1). Plain, simple, and straightforward. *Matthew* sets the birth in Jewish historical context by citing Joseph's genealogy leading up to Jesus' birth. He speaks more indirectly of the conception of Jesus by the Holy Spirit (Matt 1:18b) and identifies Jesus as "Emmanuel," meaning "God with us" (1:23b). The magi from the east come to find the star-lit child so that they can "worship him" (2:1–2). Who would they worship save who they perceived to be divinity itself? Sensitive to Jewish belief in the radical otherness of God, however, Matthew does not say up front that Jesus is the Son of God. Too much too soon. It doesn't come in words until Jesus' baptism by John the Baptist in the third chapter, not in a claim on Matthew's lips, but in the voice of God himself (3:17).

Luke sets the stage with the conception of John the Baptist, the forerunner of Jesus, by Elizabeth. Then he gives his direct account of Mary's conception by the Holy Spirit, announced by the angel Gabriel, who says, "the holy one to be born will be called 'the Son of God'" (Luke 1:35b). *John* uses very different language to describe the beginning of the gospel. He obviously wants to appeal to Greek readers by calling Jesus the *logos* (meaning word or mind) and identifying him as the Word who is God (John 1:1). Jesus is the agent of Creation itself (1:3). He is "life," God's life-giving light shining into the world's deadly darkness (1:4–5).

As we read further through the Gospels, we find Jesus sometimes referring to himself as "the Son of God" and some of those he encounters making this claim about him. At his baptism "a voice from heaven" identifies him as "my Son, whom I dearly love; in you I find happiness" (Matt 3:17; Mark 1:11; Luke 3:22).

This dual claim to which the Gospels (and the New Testament in general) witness is that Jesus of Nazareth has this unique identity as both fully human and fully divine. *Fully* human, *fully* divine—not part one and part the other. Not an intermediate being but God complete, taking on human heart, mind, and flesh—as human, more human than we are. This is Jesus' identity, God revealing and restoring our humanity, making it possible for us to be human (holy) again. By living example and empowering authority, Jesus gives us back *our* true identity, disfigured through sin. We who have lived by a twisted understanding of who we are now have a Rabbi who teaches and models a new (the true) self-understanding.

How do followers of Jesus come to a new self-understanding? The answer is by entering into a relationship with this Rabbi. Jesus' disciples hear, follow, and live out his teaching. It is not, however, simply a matter of legalistically enacting Jesus' rules of life in the kingdom of God or literally copying Jesus' behavior. Slavish imitation can be either heartlessly shallow or overbearingly desperate, and therefore lacking in authenticity. *Discipleship is primarily a relationship.* Jesus does not recruit twelve people primarily to fill their minds with Gospel gems and adjust their behavior according to his wishes. The heart of his mission lies elsewhere. His central purpose is to be the person through whom we come to know God: " . . . nobody knows the Father except the Son and anyone to whom the Son wants to reveal him" (Matt 11:27b; see also Luke 10:22b). Through Jesus we come to know God, a knowing of our heart more than our mind, a relational knowing.

In this relationship with God we come to know ourselves. As John S. Dunne puts it simply but profoundly,

> Our mind's desire is to know, to understand; but our heart's desire is intimacy, to be known, to be understood. To see God with our mind would be to know God, to understand God; but to see God with our heart would be to have a sense of being known by God, of being understood by God. . . . having a sense of God seeing us.

Dunne likens this seeing ourselves in God to "looking into the eyes of another and seeing there the pupil, the *pupilla*, the 'little doll,' the tiny image of oneself reflected in the other's eyes" (*The Reasons of the Heart: A Journey into Solitude and Back Again into the Human Circle*, 39–40). Or to use the apostle Paul's analogy, it's like progressing from seeing only an imperfect image of oneself in a mirror, to a face-to-face encounter with God, whose face reveals us to ourselves because he knows us completely (I Cor 13:12). The way to understand ourselves is to look into the eyes of Jesus, God in human flesh, giving us heart access to God, to a relationship in which God sees us in his image, and calls us to it. The regimen of the disciple life itself doesn't create this self-understanding, intimacy with God through Jesus does.

Think of the ways Jesus describes us, his disciples. We are *sheep* in need of a shepherd (Matt 9:36; Mark 6:34), lost sheep needing to be loved and found by the Good Shepherd (John 10:11–16). He calls us *children* who are able to enter the kingdom of God when we are of humble spirit, we trust him, and we are vulnerable to love (Matt 18:1–4; Mark 9:33–35; Luke 9:46–48). He sees us as his close *friends* from whom he hides no valuable secrets he's been given by his heavenly Father (John 15:14–15). He calls us *servants* of all (Mark 9:35) who humble themselves (Matt 18:1–4; Luke 9:46–48). He says we are *stewards* of all God has given us and own nothing ourselves (Matt 25:14–30; Luke 12:13–21; 21:1–4). None of this allows for pretension, hiding behind power, claiming greatness. It's a kind of naked, vulnerable identity, a humility about ourselves made possible by the gaze of God seeing through our self-made masks. It is knowing who we really are because God looks at our hearts, and in this looking he sees *us* and we begin to see ourselves in his face. It is surely such a glance directed at twelve men that beckons them to take the risk of following Jesus and to discover who they are and what their lives are about.

Two terms tell them what it will mean to follow this Jesus of whose intimate circle they are now a part. They tell us, as well. Those who love and follow Jesus are his *disciples* and his *apostles*. As his disciples we follow his teachings (John 8:31); give up our lives to follow him (Matt 16:24–25; Mark 8:34–35; Luke 9:23–24); love each other (John 13:34–35); and bear fruit for his kingdom (John 15:8). As his apostles (literally, "those sent out") we are commissioned to go out into a world ready to respond to the good news of the kingdom of God (John 4:34–37), empowered to give witness and be agents of healing (Luke 9:1–6; 10:1–11), and authorized to make disciples (Matt 28:16–20).

The metaphors of sheep and children, and the descriptions of friendship, servanthood, and stewardship give us a multifaceted picture of what it means to recover the image of God, our true humanity, our holiness. The terms disciple and apostle help us discover our calling and live out our mission. It all adds up to Jesus teaching us and modeling for us how to become who we really are. He gathers us around him so that we can see him and listen to him, so that we can learn to *be* him in our own limited, faltering but often convincing and unique ways.

Many Christians seem to think they are disciples because they've learned of Jesus and profess belief in him, as if they have then grasped the fullness of faith. The truth is they are at the beginning of a long pilgrimage, a process of *becoming* Jesus in the sense that their personal identity is being found in him. He became us so that we could become him. He found us so that we could find him in each other. A church congregation is a pathetic, purposeless social club if its members are not finding their true identity by being Jesus to each other and to the world—no matter how impressive their success, their programs, their worship, and their community service.

Jesus invites us to discover our roots in him. Each of us is unique in our DNA, our ancestry, and our stories. The God who made us all different honors that uniqueness. He set it in motion. Our individual uniqueness, however, does not push us away from each other; it is what draws us closer together in the never-ending fascination with the mystery each of us is. And as we learn each other, we also learn how profoundly we are the same; made in the image of God and given the possibility of completion. This is surely what Jesus has in mind when he announces that he has come so that we can have and live life to the fullest.

The DNA analysis of guests featured on "Finding Your Roots" usually reveals something startling. It often shows that the guest is a blend of multiple races or ethnicities, some with a variety representing much of the entire globe! This, of course, is not a huge surprise as America calls itself "the melting pot of the world." It may say something of even greater significance: Perhaps we can become more alike at our core, a rich blend of each other—this, regardless of the persistence of self-isolated cultures, many with a religious base that preaches and practices the exclusion of others with whom they claim little or no commonality. Eventually, however, our kinship as a God-created humanity must win the day.

Jesus, our Rabbi, gives us a new understanding of ourselves as human beings, as the bearers of his image. This image is why we are alike and different, and for both these reasons, drawn to one another. Our alike-nesses without our differences make us boring; our differences without our alike-nesses make us enemies. Jesus affirms the gifts of both our common humanity and our wide differences, and when we embrace both we reveal the image of God in us. It all comes together in Jesus, who taught this new self-understanding, lived it, and still invites us to risk it. Those who do, he calls his disciples.

Chapter 7

Vulnerability

The downy woodpecker who inhabits our backyard is a bundle of confident energy, an aggressive perpetual motion machine, always pecking here and there for food. And then one day I see him change his whole demeanor. He suddenly flies from our feeder to the groove between a nearby tree trunk and a branch growing off from it. He lays himself flat into that groove and is absolutely smooth and still for four minutes as if he were dead, not a single twitch. What in the world is going on? The answer comes quickly. I see a red-tailed hawk flying overhead. The downy is vulnerable, and he knows it. He has taken the only appropriate action for his survival. He disappears.

We do the same if we want to survive. We try to avoid potentially dangerous traffic situations. We don't undertake climbing a steep, rocky mountain, nor raft down a river with violent currents without proper training and experience. We don't invest a major part of our financial resources in high risk stocks. These are wise, prudent behaviors.

Sometimes, however, we're forced to take a risk because all the available choices are risks. Recently, Keitha and I were driving on an interstate highway in the middle of three lanes going the same direction. The van in front of us suddenly swerved into the left lane. Immediately we saw why. A large tangle of bent pipe lay in our lane, probably having fallen off a truck. I could have swerved into another lane, as the van had done to avoid the metal jumble, but that van was now on our immediate left, and a huge tractor-trailer truck was on our immediate right. I had two choices, both of them risks: try to swerve and possibly collide with another vehicle or stay in our lane and hit the metal pipes head-on. I chose the latter, even though I knew the pipes could end up coming through our windshield and doing us serious harm. Fortunately, we ran over the pipes, which turned out to be aluminum, causing only minor damage. Sometimes we have to choose between risks, between actions either of which could lead to unfortunate outcomes.

Occasionally we purposely choose to take a risk. Some of our most deeply fulfilling choices carry risks: marriage, having children, a challenging vocation or job, a project that stretches us but could fail, a new partnership—to name only a few. It's sad when someone is too insecure or afraid to invest themselves in such risks, though in some cases there may be good reasons for the caution. And sometimes one of those ventures seems to have great prospects for success, but for unforeseen reasons it fails or doesn't turn out well. The gift in the failure may be greater wisdom about the world and deeper insight about oneself.

Some people experience life in general as a dangerous place. They see themselves in a kind of permanent position of vulnerability. They live nervously avoiding dangers, some of them imagined. They often have been so wounded they accept their easy wound-ability and tragically live in cowering fear. Or they may decide to use their vulnerability to their advantage by finding someone strong to take care of them, like an addict finding his co-dependent. Yes, and there are many for whom someone else's vulnerability is an irresistible attraction. Every pastor, counselor, and therapist knows the lure, and not all are able to resist getting pulled in by it. Becoming someone's "savior" can be a powerful seduction.

WHAT DOES THE LIFE of Jesus teach us about dealing with our vulnerability? Quite a lot. Like us he has to deal with the everyday risks of life in the world of his day; he certainly is not spared them. The Gospel writers, however, do not give us many such details. They know that their subject is a man and therefore subject to normal physical susceptibilities, but their goal is a salvation story not a detailed biography. Jesus may well have broken an arm or a leg growing up. He may well have taken a bad fall climbing a cliff or have been roughed up by the neighborhood bullies. He really was human. He shared the same vulnerabilities we do.

His heart was vulnerable. He weeps for his now-deceased friend Lazarus (John 11:35) and grieves over Jerusalem (Matt 23:37–39; Luke 13:34–35). He releases his anger and dismay over the abuse of the worship place, the temple in Jerusalem (John 2:13–16; Matt 21:12; Mark 11:15–17; Luke 19:45–46). He opens himself to those he loves, telling his disciples to love each other as he has loved them (John 15:12). He talks about he and the Father making their home with the disciples (John 14:23). He says he is intimately tied to them as the vine is tied to its branches (John 15:5). Everything that is his is theirs, and theirs his (John 17:10).

Near the end of his life he reveals his torment. In the garden on the night of his arrest, he admits to Peter, James, and John, "I'm very sad. It's as if I'm dying." And he begs them to watch and pray with him (Matt 26:38; Mark 14:34). On the cross he exposes the pain of his abandonment to the world: "My God, my God, why have you left me?" (Matt 27:46; Mark 15:34). At the end, he cries out with a loud shout, and then he dies (Matt 27:50; Mark 15:37). Death, the final vulnerability.

There is yet a different kind of vulnerability the Gospel writers find in Jesus. It is a vulnerability arising from a position of strength. Jesus allows himself this vulnerability by saying and doing things he knows expose him to danger and invite abuse. This is not Jesus avoiding or dealing with an existing danger to which he is vulnerable; it is Jesus creating a new vulnerability. The uncommon vulnerability of Jesus is *the vulnerability of compassion*.

We first see this vulnerability in Jesus' openness to others. He makes himself available to anyone—those who admire him, those who want to be like him, those who have questions, those who oppose him, and those who hate him. He allows himself to be interrogated and attacked. When this happens he typically refuses to go on the defensive; sometimes he recasts the question or redefines the issue. He seems to feel he has no right to protection from the criticism and abuse heaped upon him.

Behind this vulnerability is what births the Gospel itself. The Gospel originates not so much in the mind of God as in his heart. His incarnation in Jesus is an extreme act of compassion more than the implementation of some carefully constructed salvation plan: "God so *loved* the world that he gave his only Son. . ." (John 3:16, italics added). The Gospel is God loving us beyond reason by entering our human life, and in doing so making himself vulnerable. Compassion (which literally means "suffering with" someone) calls a person to surrender a good measure of comfort, security, or protection to share the pain and exclusion of the marginalized other. It always has a price. Such an act often incurs the wrath and opposition of the "privileged included," who see the attention and help given to those below them as a threat to their own secure position and power. There is no compassion given that does not place us in a position of vulnerability. Charity with no risk is not compassion.

From the very beginning of Jesus' life, circumstances seem to prepare him for the risks of compassion. The stage is set by his coming into the world away from home in a dirty stable and being whisked off to Egypt to escape a paranoid ruler's infanticide. Such unusually difficult circumstances prepare the young Jesus for the position the adult Jesus puts *himself* in during the last three years of his life. For example, in his return to his home-town of Nazareth he proclaims not only that he is the fulfillment of Jewish messianic prophecy, inspiring hometown jealousy on the part of some; but also that this new era is primarily for the poor, the prisoners, the blind, and the oppressed, just as the prophet Isaiah had said (Isa 61:1–2; 58:6). *They* will be the recipients of God's love-inspired saving actions. The resulting violent action against Jesus only makes sense as the punishing action of the local power holders and brokers, mixed perhaps with the jealousy of his former childhood contemporaries (Mark 6:1–6; Luke 4:14–30). When Jesus confronts certain religious leaders with a message that does not align with *their* attitudes and prerogatives, the pushback is vindictive and harsh (Matt 12:9–14). Quickly Jesus learns the violent consequences of proclaiming and demonstrating that the kingdom of God is God's compassion in action, and as such it must begin with those who suffer and are most despised before it can be received by the secure elite. Compassion always seeks the least among us. Those who are "well" are not in need of a physician (Mark 2:17; Matt 9:12; Luke 5:31), and they won't go to one until they discover and con-fess their own spiritual sickness.

And finally, as the three-year ministry of Jesus moves to its culmina-tion in Jerusalem, his compassionate vulnerability comes face to face with the power of the state. Those who have the most to fear from Jesus' mes-sage of compassion are the rulers in Rome and their minions in authority throughout the vast empire, who have everything to lose if revolutionaries prevail. They will keep order at any cost, violence included, all under the guise of maintaining peace and the common good. Any rising leader who draws large crowds, who is driven by compassion for those at the lower end of the social order, empowering them as human beings with dignity in God's eyes, is an unacceptable menace to state power. Empire has no place for compassion, only for the preservation and expansion of the status quo. Compassion upsets every empire because it places the least first, while em-pire is sustained by keeping them last.

The Roman Empire saw political implications in everything. Roman authority in Palestine could see Jesus only in terms of the prospect of the political unrest his movement might trigger and possible disruption of the difficult balance between sustaining Roman authority and keeping peace with the Jews in that troublesome part of the eastern Empire. Pilate asks the arrested Jesus pointblank, "Are you the king of the Jews?" Jesus seems un-interested in the question, deflecting it with, "That's what you say." Pilate is utterly dismayed at Jesus' refusal to defend himself one way or the other. In John's Gospel Jesus goes on to say he does have a "kingdom [but it] doesn't originate from this world." He says further that his mission in this world is "to testify to the truth. Whoever accepts the truth," he says, "listens to my voice" (Matt 27:11–14; Mark 15:2–5; Luke 23:3–4; John 18:33–38).

Pilate is totally disarmed and can only respond, "What is truth?" (John 18:38). The only "truth" he understands is political reality. He knows Jesus is innocent, but he also knows his high-status job is on the line. The religious authorities also know it. They aim carefully at Pilate's fear: "If you release this man, you aren't a friend of the emperor! Anyone who makes himself out to be a king opposes the emperor!" (John 19:12). The sensitive nerve is hit, and for an intimidated Pilate, the die is cast. He knows he is vulnerable. Jesus is vulnerable because of his compassion, his desire to save the world, beginning with the least. Pilate is vulnerable because he desires to save his hide and keep his position. Jesus never abandons the vulnerable place to which his compassion brings him, and he pays with his life. Pilate abandons the threat of his own vulnerability by taking "realistic" action and thereby buying a few more years in power.

How does all this fit into our calling as disciples of our Rabbi Jesus? In what ways does he call us to imitate him by accepting human vulnerability, ours and others'? First, he never says his disciples are protected from danger to which others are exposed by happenstance. Discipleship does not come with that kind of insurance policy. Bad things do happen to good people. Christians who think the bad things that happen to them through no fault of their own are intended by God are sadly mistaken. They are *not* mistaken when they sense God is suffering with them. In a fallen world unfortunate things happen—to all of us. (Note: This is not to deny that some bad things happen largely because of someone's stupidity, unhealthy lifestyle, or destructive behavior.) What we *can* say about the unfortunate circumstances of our lives is that they drive us to a deeper understanding of our faith and to a more intimate relationship with our Lord, if we allow them. On the other side of an understandable sense of God's abandonment we experience at times, is a beckoning to a deeper place. There we see the face of our suffering God and hear him say, "Look, I myself will be with you every day until the end of this present age" (Matt 28:20b). We do not suffer alone.

Perhaps Jesus' invitation to us to become vulnerable is best illustrated by his saying to his disciples that they must undergo the radical change of becoming like a child in order to enter the kingdom of heaven (Matt 18:2–4). We often interpret this saying as an invitation to simplicity and humility, and it is. If we take the metaphor of a child seriously, however, we must add vulnerability. Children are susceptible to injury at the hands of insensitive and abusive adults. They are on the weak side of a power imbalance. Jesus wants us, his disciples, to be as blamelessly vulnerable as children. He wants us to be as open and woundable as he was, to come out from behind our protective walls—even if those walls are our public piety—and risk our hearts with people who are looking for someone with an honest soul and real, human emotions. He wants us to risk compassion. He wants us to move beyond our overly-cautious fear—fear of losing status, financial security, power, and respectability.

Make no mistake about it, the place to which Jesus calls us is not a protected fortress. It is a world needing disciples who are vulnerable to compassion, compassion willing to suffer. He could not have done more to lead us to this place and to show us how to take the real risks that love demand.

A New Way to Live

Chapter 8

Be Willing to Change

The world in which we live is a constant whirlwind of change. Many have even said that change has become the only reliable constant. We can rely upon the ground shifting, fashions altering, values changing, people moving—all at a faster and faster pace. We revisit a place of fond memories and find it to be a very different, and not necessarily a better place. Does anything stay the same?

Some change is good, some not. It depends on the purpose and the nature of it. If we make a change to advance ourselves over others, or to "move up in the world," or to throw our resources at the latest plaything in order to be seen and to be known as having the very latest plaything, or to capture the elusive full satisfaction we think this latest thing or accomplishment will bring—the change, the studies show, will at best result in a short-lived state of gratification, and at worst leave us persistently dissatisfied and hungering for the next step up.

What if there were a very different kind of change, where we were not the subject of it but the object? What if the way to fulfilling our true humanity (our identity in God's image) is through *being* changed rather than chasing change?

JESUS ADVOCATES A LIFE of continual change, but it is a far cry from the endless change cycle of consumerism. Put simply, he comes to change the heart, the core of our self, the source of our motivation. His kingdom of God is a place of ongoing deep transformation, preparing and equipping us for a new way of living. It is where we live as pilgrims on the way to becoming who we are in God's image. It is a place of deep change, which is change that only takes place in the humble of heart. It transforms motive rather than fortune. It does not offer status, it offers life.

Real change, change that goes deep, is never easy. The call of Jesus to become his disciple is a call to radical (literally, down-to-the-roots) change. It begins with seeing our image, our true humanity, in the life and teachings of Jesus. This leads us to take a hard look at ourselves and to face up to how we may have evolved into something quite different from what Jesus has in mind, then to repent, and then to have our lives reshaped in obedience to Jesus.

The Gospels of Matthew, Mark, and Luke record an incident when some people ask Jesus why his disciples do not fast, as do the disciples of the Pharisees and of John the Baptist. Fasting is a time-honored tradition. Who is Jesus to excuse his company from following suit? Jesus tells a parable about wine and wineskins, moving the conversation from the specific issue of fasting to the broader matter of how his disciples—those who take the kingdom of God seriously—must make changes. Old wineskins which once were able to expand and hold the new wine can no longer do so. They have outlived their usefulness. New wineskins with the capacity to expand and not break are what the new wine now requires. Jesus seems to be saying that in him a new kingdom has arrived, and it calls for us to change if we are to live in it and live for it. This kingdom is centered in him and not in a temple and not in a complicated set of laws. In everything related to this kingdom, he is the way, the truth, and the life. Are we now to live out this new life in the same old ways, pouring the new wine of the new kingdom into the old, now unsuitable wineskins? Jesus' answer is clearly: No, " . . . new wine must be put into new wineskins." Be ready to scuttle whatever is irrelevant or not in keeping with the new kingdom (Mark 2:18–22; Matt 9:14–17; Luke 5:33–37).

Even when we desire it, change is usually not easy. Radical change is especially difficult, and often painful. (Think about the rich young ruler whom Jesus tells to sell everything and give the money to the poor.) When Jesus speaks of changes his disciples must make if they are to be his follow-ers and enter his kingdom, he is not speaking of altering window dressing or improving one's position. Nor is he speaking so much of changing habits or traditions or the way we do things, although the change he is talking about will undoubtedly impact and lead to some changes or adaptations in these practices. What he is talking about is deep change that transforms the heart—making new wine, if you like—and by doing so alters our whole approach to life—like adopting new wineskins. Radical change, change that goes to the heart, to the roots, is a threat to our Christian complacen-cy—so much so that Luke also includes Jesus' follow-up comment to the parable: "No one who drinks a well-aged wine wants new wine, but says,

'The well-aged wine is better'" (Luke 5:39). Sadly, some choose to remain unchanged, clinging to what they know and enjoy, unwilling to risk the new.

Every disciple of Jesus is called to be changed and to make changes. For each of us, among those changes is usually one that addresses a key personal issue, blind spot, or sin that particularly besets us. The apostle Thomas must move beyond a faith based only on clear evidence to a faith willing to trust what the heart knows even though the mind does not fully grasp it. The apostle Peter must expand the reach of the kingdom of God beyond the boundaries of his own more exclusive ethnic religion. The apostle Paul must take the radical leap from religious legalism to spiritual freedom, from a law-based to a grace-based faith. Francis of Assisi must shed his wealthy inheritance and walk naked into the world, armed only with the compassion of Christ. Martin Luther must move from his felt inability to please God to the serendipity of God's loving acceptance of him as his child. John and Charles Wesley must open themselves to the miracle of God's sanctifying love.

Jesus calls us all to be radically changed and to make radical life changes as citizens of his kingdom. The kingdom is within us, he says, and if we want to discover it, live it, and advance it in the world, we will have to change—and continue changing. The apostle Paul describes an ongoing process of being transformed into the likeness of Jesus (II Cor 3:18). That is a very good place to start, and to live. The invitation to change and the ways we can be changed call out to us from just about every page of the Gospels. The place to start is where we are, and our Rabbi Jesus leads us step by step, change by change, as we forever seek and forever find.

Chapter 9

Embrace Life Fully

The call from Brenda informs us that Jim has passed away. Would we come to participate in his funeral? Of course we would.

We served together with Brenda as Salvation Army officers in St. Petersburg, Florida where we were pastors at the local Salvation Army church. During Brenda's time with us she met Jim, who had successfully come to sobriety and faith through a special alcohol and drug treatment program operated by The Salvation Army. Eventually they became engaged and married. They worked together for the Army, until Jim was also commissioned as an officer. They served as pastors and social workers for a period of time, and then as administrators of a number of adult rehabilitation centers before retiring a few years prior to the phone call from Brenda.

Jim's funeral is a fitting celebration of God's grace in his life. During the service opportunity is given for anyone who wishes to express gratitude for Jim's influence on their life. The words that draw my attention in that part of the service come from a lady named Debbie. She stands and shares a story from her own daughter's wedding a few years before. Jim and Brenda are present at the wedding; they're the parents of the groom. At the reception people are dancing to celebrate this exciting new beginning of two people's lives. Jim is doing his fair share of dancing. He's good at it, poetry in motion. And then he spots Debbie standing alone. He comes over to her and asks her to dance with him. Debbie grew up in a church that frowned on dancing. "I can't, I don't know how," she protests. Jim coaxes and cajoles her. He'll teach her if she'll trust him. She lets him lead her onto the dance floor. That day she begins to learn this new grace in motion.

Debbie tells that story at Jim's funeral to thank God for Jim gently pulling her onto that dance floor and to let us know that those few moments were a kind of personal triumph for her. She danced. That was Jim's gift to her. She goes on to say she has come to realize that what Jim did for her that day was very much like what he had done for hundreds of men trapped in the prisons of their own addictions; he invited them to step onto a dance floor called the transforming grace of God. Jim, the recovered addict himself, became a personal invitation to the dance from the Lord of the Dance.

The calling God gives us and what our Rabbi Jesus teaches us, is a dance. We dance to the music of God's kingdom, and our dance partner is the grace of God. It's a life we can trust and embrace fully, without or in spite of our fear.

JESUS IS LIFE-AFFIRMING. HE is so life-affirming, death is no threat for him. "No one takes [my life] from me, but I give it up because I want to" (John 10:18a). He wants his disciples to have a similar confidence about their lives. If God takes care of birds in the air and lilies in the field, he will certainly watch over the creatures he made in his image (Matt 6:25–34; Luke 12:22–31). When gale-force winds and violent waves buffet the boat occupied by Jesus and his disciples, Jesus asks his terrified company, "Why are you frightened? Don't you have faith yet?" (Mark 4:40; Matt 8:26; Luke 8:24-25). I am reminded of a story about Dwight L. Moody, who at the time is crossing the Atlantic. The ship is entering a terrible storm. Moody is standing on the deck, rather enjoying the excitement. Some of the passengers come looking for him. They want him to join them in a meeting to pray for deliverance from the storm. Moody respectfully declines. "No thank you," he says, "I'm prayed up."

We find many examples in the Gospels of Jesus' courage. Whether he is facing storms, the ruling elders and teachers of the religious establishment, the strong arm of the government, or the unpredictable violence of the crowds, there is a peace and a calm about him. To say that he is a brave man does not adequately explain it. To say that he embraces life fully takes us much closer to the truth. For him, life is not something that can be taken from him by a storm, or a person in a power position, or a dangerous mob. It is something not even death can rob him of.

Jesus invites his disciples to life without fear. Fear robs us of our ability to embrace the life Jesus comes to give us. Fear keeps the disciples terrified, huddled in fear behind closed doors after Jesus' crucifixion. It keeps Peter, a very devout Jew, hesitant to trust what the Spirit of the resurrected Jesus is doing among Gentiles, those who do not live by all his Jewish laws. It has kept millions of would-be followers of Jesus from fully embracing and imitating the way of life Jesus taught them. Disciples of Jesus need not diminish their lives with cautionary rules that make them feel safe and secure. If we don't risk life, we risk losing life (Mark 8:35; Matt 10:39; Luke 9:24).

One day some of the Pharisees jump all over Jesus because they see his disciples eating food without having done the ceremonial washing of their hands. They challenge his failure to require his disciples to live "according to the rules handed down by the elders." In response Jesus recalls the words of Isaiah (Isa 29:13), "Their worship of me is empty since they teach instructions that are human words." The insecure create more and more rules to build walls of protection around themselves. The legalism kills life and replaces it with dead scripts, and we who try to live by those scripts miss so much of the life Jesus comes to bring. Jesus "came so that [we] could have life—indeed, so that [we] could have life to the fullest" (John 10:10). And our small rules, when we make them more important than they are, take away life. We get caught up in pettiness, and real life, life in Christ, passes us by while we are hiding behind our self-made fortresses of carefulness. Jesus calls and empowers us to embrace life, not to brace ourselves against it.

Jesus does not promise us all roses on our earthly journey. He knows sorrow and tears personally (John 11:35). He assures us that at times we will "cry and lament" while the world rejoices (John 16:20a). He also assures us that these times when he seems absent will be followed by the joy of his presence (Matt 5:4; Luke 6:21b), a joy that cannot be taken from us (John 16:20b, 22). We must receive the sorrow in order to enter the joy. If we risk embracing life fully, we will walk both heights and valleys. The alternative is not to live, but to shudder and withdraw, which is to die. We affirm life through sorrow as well as joy.

There are times when living fully calls for tears of repentance. We value life at these times by asking for forgiveness or removing an impediment in our lives—all this so that we can now move forward on our journey with Jesus. Repenting of our sins or shedding distractions and diversions for a better obedience positions us to embrace life in Christ more fully. Jesus sometimes withdraws from joy, as when he fasts in the wilderness for forty days, because he is then ready to emerge "in the power of the Spirit" (Luke 4:14a) and spread the joy of a new kingdom. His disciples disappoint him again and again, but he knows the time will come when he and they will fill each other with joy (John 15:11). Jesus calls us to repentance so that his already-there forgiveness then becomes accessible to us as we own up to our sins and blunders and move forward in newness and joy. Furthermore, as we receive God's forgiveness in full, we can also affirm others by forgiving them when we are wronged, and they may also extend forgiveness to us when we need it (Matt 6:12; Mark 11:25; Luke 6:37c; 11:4).

Jesus says to us, his disciples, that at the end of our struggle is peace, at the end of our sorrow is joy, and at the end of our death is life. He faces the extraordinary self-abnegation of his last days on earth, says the writer to the Hebrews, "for the sake of the joy that was laid out in front of him. . . " In doing so he invites all of us to "throw off any extra baggage [and] get rid of the sin that trips us up" and "run the race that is laid out in front of us"(Hebrews 12:1–3). Yes, he says to us, we will know sadness and grief, but it will turn to a joy which can't be taken away. It is not a postponement beyond the grave, it is reality today: "Ask and you will receive so that your joy will be complete" (John 16:24b).

Jesus invites us to embrace life fully. It's an invitation to the dance, a freeing of our spirits to get on the dance floor with courage, and trust where the music takes us. Sometimes the music is joy, sometimes sorrow. Either way, the leader can be trusted.

Chapter 10

Invest Wisely

One of the most interesting ways Jesus explains to his disciples how to live out their calling is to speak of investments, both of their lives and of their resources. Jesus has an amazing ability to let go of what is not ultimately important. He has an even more amazing ability to let go of what may be important or of value—because it stands in the way of his calling. This matter of deciding what we must release in order to follow Jesus is determined by how we decide to invest our lives. To invest in one thing is to decide not to invest in another. The issue we now seek Jesus' help with is where to say Yes and where to say No.

JESUS SPEAKS OF TWO kinds of investments we as his disciples must make. Both are essential to following him. One is the investment of our lives, the other the investment of what has been given to us personally.

With respect to our *lives*, Jesus calls us to a complete conversion, an all-or-nothing where we give up everything we are and have for the kingdom of God (Matt 13:44–46). Jesus' parable of finding the treasure and the pearl and selling everything else to gain them advocates a radical flip-flop. Such behavior looks to be rash and risky. Is the treasure or the pearl really worth that much? How can we be sure? Can the value of the discovered treasure or pearl be known so quickly? And by what standards would their value be determined?

These are good questions without neat answers. And yet the discoverer risks everything on the conversion. He takes a huge leap of faith. It's all or nothing. The kingdom of God changes everything for those who risk entering it.

This radical investment of our lives in Jesus and his kingdom is transformational for us personally. We are no longer our own, and our life's calling is no longer our own. We lose our lives for the sake of Jesus and his mission (Mark 8:35; Matt 16:25; Luke 9:24). Discipleship and the mission of Jesus require the total giving of our lives. They are not a hobby we engage in only when we are active in the life of our church. They are not spare-time voluntary engagements. They are a complete life calling for which we place everything else on the line. When we do this we are a compelling witness to Jesus' claim on our lives. Furthermore, in living this new life we also model life in the kingdom of God. We are letting our life shine in the world to give witness to the life of Jesus in us (Matt 5:12). We are authenticating the life to which Jesus calls us. We are actually investing our lives in Jesus. And in doing so, we are gaining our lives (Mark 8:36; Matt 16:26; Luke 9:25).

This is not a work ethic, it is a stewardship of compassion. Jesus calls us to a mission of radical compassion, to love others in the way he does. Mother Teresa is a model of this stewardship. Surrendering her life to Jesus and investing totally in the kingdom of God, she gave her life over to serving and saving "the least of these." Her life investment was in the marginalized rather than the market. In following Jesus we give our lives not to our own success, nor even to the advancement of the institutional church, but to the mission of his compassion (Matt 25:31–46).

The second kind of investment Jesus asks of us is our *individual resources*. These are the gifts, talents, resources, and opportunities that are uniquely ours. Jesus most often uses the metaphor of investing money to illustrate how his disciples are to use all the assets they have been given for the kingdom of God (For example, Matt 25:14–30; Luke 19: 11–27). He asks us to take all our gifts and figure out how, under the guidance of the Spirit, they can best be invested in his compassionate mission.

Every disciple of Jesus has been given a unique set of gifts to enrich and strengthen God's kingdom. *Every* disciple. Let's consider them:

- *Natural endowments or abilities* that can be developed and deployed by the Holy Spirit in Jesus' mission. The challenge of every Christian community is to value and utilize every member's natural endowments and abilities, including the less public (and often less appreciated) ones. The apostle Paul gives very helpful guidance about this (I Cor 12, and Rom 12).

- *Tangible resources* a disciple has that can, under the guidance of the Spirit, be wisely invested in advancing Jesus' mission. This includes such assets as money, property, gifts in kind, etc. Jesus relied on money that was donated to his ministry (Luke 8:1–3), and he required one of his disciples to manage it. John Wesley once warned that prosperity is a "sweet poison" (*Notes*, 6:20), sweet when shared with others and poison when hoarded. The idea that our spirituality has nothing to do with our material resources, leaving us free to use them as we wish, reveals a false spirituality. It misses the insights of Jesus, who says far more about our relationship to and our responsibility with money than he says about prayer! How we use *all* our resources is a discipleship matter.

- *Opportunities* arising that open doors to building the kingdom of God in new or unanticipated ways. The opportunity will likely require some level of risk and the possibility of failure, but unless we take the risk and brave failure, we will confine ourselves to actions lacking the courage of a new thing God is doing. We will be safe disciples who become stale. One of the persistent themes of the investment parables of Jesus is God's great displeasure in the steward who plays safe with the talents entrusted to him (Matt 25:24–30; Luke 19:20–27).

Jesus calls us, his disciples, to invest what he has entrusted to us. *Woman of Bethany, what will you do with your precious alabaster jar full of sweet perfume?* She breaks the jar and anoints Jesus' head (Mark 14:3). *Simon the leper, what will you do with your nice house?* He opens it for the comfort and entertainment of his Lord (14:3a). *Zaccheus, what will you do with your horded money?* He gives half his possessions to the poor and repays those he has cheated four times as much (Luke 19:8–9). *Widow, what will you do with those two copper coins, the sum of your meager wealth?* She gives them both to her temple (Mark 12:41–44).

Disciple of Rabbi Jesus, what will you invest in Jesus and his mission to save and serve the world? The answer the Gospel seeks is clear: your lives and your resources. These form the one piece of a calling, each contributing to the other. Investing in the spiritual depth of our lives without investing our gifts and our resources in mission will lead to a spiritual self-indulgence that will suffocate us. Investing our gifts and resources in serving without investing our lives in our spiritual journey will lead to spiritual starvation and burnout. What the call of Jesus does not divide, his disciples should not put asunder.

Chapter 11

Live Simply

A few years ago Keitha and I joined our friends Chick and Margaret on a pilgrimage. It was the last 75 miles of the Camino de Compostela in Spain. For the past one thousand years Christian pilgrims have made this spiritual journey, many if not most of them starting at the very beginning in France. The destination of the pilgrimage is the Cathedral of St. James in Santiago. Over these centuries pilgrims have undertaken the journey as a discipline to address a key spiritual issue, need, or challenge in their lives. For some their specific purpose was clear from the beginning, for others it became clear over the course of the pilgrimage. Today the motivations of the thousands who walk the Camino vary considerably, ranging from a deeper spirituality to physical health to simply mastering another life challenge.

My own motivations were mixed. Keitha and I looked forward to spending a week walking in the beautiful countryside of Spain as part of celebrating our fifty years of life together as husband and wife. We also knew we would enjoy that time with our friends Chick and Margaret. Each of the foursome also wanted it to be a deepening of the spirit toward a closer conformity to Christ. I had decided that the Lord's Prayer would be my spiritual guide for the week and that I would focus on a different petition of the prayer each day.

As it turned out, the petition that stayed with me most was "Give us this day our daily bread." Why was that? All the other petitions deal with important spiritual realities—like "your kingdom," "your will," "heaven," "trespasses," "temptation," "evil," "the power and the glory"—and one other mentions a very large chunk of physical matter called "earth." The one that claimed me that week was the one about a very small chunk of physical matter called "bread." What was the meaning of the imposition of this insignificance onto my spiritual ambition for this pilgrimage? I'm to come away from this spiritual journey with a one-sentence grace before daily meals?

Most of the Camino pilgrims of earlier centuries, especially the poor ones, did have to worry about where the next meal was coming from, not to mention lodging. There were a few pilgrim hostels along the way, but they filled up quickly. As for our group of four, we actually had guaranteed reservations at modest hotels spaced an average of fifteen miles apart. We at least wanted the assurance of a place to sleep. It was during the course of the daily fifteen-mile treks that we felt some uncertainty, wondering when we would come to the next eating place or bathroom (and would it even be open?). Two of the four of us developed foot problems, and we wondered if we'd be able to continue. The most difficult day was the longest (nineteen miles), and that was the day of incessant rain and we thought we'd never find our lodging.

There was a coarse bread aptly named "pilgrim bread" served in many of the small cafes. The crust was the toughest I've ever eaten. I became fond of that bread, however, even though when I bit into it I sometimes wondered if my teeth would remain intact. There's hardly anything more basic as a symbol of life sustenance than bread. There's no image more evocative of an uncluttered life of simplicity. There's no more powerful metaphor of sharing fellowship with one another than saying "Let us break bread together." Bread calls us to the most basic and important things in life. It represents a life of simplicity, a day uncluttered by the things we don't really need.

Forced to experience life reduced to a comparative simplicity on the Camino, I had to own how much I take the small gifts of life for granted. The Shaker hymn is right: "'Tis the gift to be simple, 'tis the gift to be free." Simplicity is a key to freedom. The pilgrimage has served as a living reminder to me of how the elaborateness and extraneousness of my life can so easily hinder my discipleship, my ability to follow Jesus.

JESUS WAS A MASTER of living simply. He was a homeless man without material wealth, an itinerate rabbi who traveled light. He said of himself, "The Human One [Son of Man] has no place to lay his head" (Matt 8:20; Luke 9:58b). Is Jesus saying to us that if we want to be his disciples we, too, must live in material poverty? I doubt it. He does say, however, that we cannot serve God *and* Mammon, two different masters (Luke 16:13). *Mammon* is an interesting word in the New Testament. It can be translated "money," but

Jesus usually uses it in a way that suggests it is a god vying for our worship. When we consider money to be our most precious treasure, it has become Mammon, our God.

It could be that some of us are so in thrall to what wealth we do have, however great or small, the only way we can follow Jesus is to give it up. That is the case with the rich young ruler, a good, devout Jew who obeys all the commandments, but evidently Jesus sees that his personal identity, the whole meaning of his life, is inseparable from his wealth and the security and status it brings him. So Jesus says to this man who undoubtedly already gives generously to the poor, "Go sell what you own, and give the money to the poor. . . . And come, follow me" (Mark 10:17–21; Matt 19:16–21; Luke 18:18–22).

Chief tax collector Zaccheus, on the other hand, doesn't need to be told. "Look, Lord, I give half my possessions to the poor. And if I have cheated anyone, I repay them four times as much" (Luke 19:8b). *If?* Tax collectors in those days *were* skimming and overcharging, and chief tax collectors also skimmed off the skimmers. Zaccheus knows his wealth has so corrupted him, he must give most of it to the poor and cheated if he is to enter the kingdom of God. Jesus is so struck by this quick divestiture and new compassion he blurts out, "Today, salvation has come to this household" (v. 9a).

Jesus, however, saves the greater commendation for a poor widow who literally puts every last penny she has into the temple treasury (Mark 12:41–44; Luke 21:1–4). Admittedly, this is an absurd act. What will she now live on? What relative or kind neighbor will now take care of her? Of course we don't know all the details of her life, but immediately before this occurs, Jesus condemns the teachers of the law who find insidious ways to cheat widows out of their homes while hiding their own sin behind impressive, long prayers in public (Mark 12:38–40; Luke 20:45–47). Jesus commends the widow for faithfully living and giving out of her poverty, but not without judging those who exploit or profit from the poverty of others. He therefore refuses to make her into some kind of martyr whom we can admire at a distance, an exception to the norm by which *we* must live—in short, someone before whom we need not be judged ourselves. We all participate in a social system which enables extreme poverty to be forced on others, and there's no use our denying it. The beautiful extremity of the widow's gift should not isolate her from the rest of us, says Jesus. Her gift of "more than everyone" gets to the issue of what it means for each of us to give all of what we don't need. To give in that way is to release that part of our possessions which has become a diversion from a life of Christian simplicity and from the extreme generosity of Jesus. The kingdom of God is run by a strange economics:

Those who lose their lives for Jesus and the gospel will save their lives (Mark 8:34–35; Matt 16:24–25; Luke 9:23–24).

Our discipleship has a lot to do with how we relate to material things and to money. We have already pointed out that Jesus said far more about money than he did about prayer. The god of Mammon is very powerful. He was in Jesus' day, and still is—probably more so. He seems to pursue two strategies. First, he tries to convince us we're nobody in this world without money. Second, he plants fear of our running out of things we need or want. It seems he pursued the rich young ruler with the first strategy: his wealth made him a somebody, a person to be admired and certainly envied. The twelve disciples of Jesus, those who gave up a decent livelihood to follow their Rabbi, now living hand to mouth, seemed to be targets for the second strategy. When Jesus asks them to find food for a crowd of 5,000 men plus their wives and children, they hear him asking the impossible. After all, they're not sure from day to day that they can feed themselves (Mark 6:35–37; Matt 14:16–17; Luke 9:12–13; John 6:5–7).

Materialism plants in us the suspicion of scarcity. We think, *We don't have enough, we're deprived, we may not make it.* Why do we get so worried about our well-being—even in this day when life for those who live in the Western world is nowhere near as fragile as it was in Jesus' day? Why do we allow ourselves to be driven to acquire, over-buy, over-eat, over-indulge, when the truth is that materially the great majority of us in the West have enough and more? Why do we fear poverty when Jesus embraced it?

Scarcity, of course, is relative to our view of sufficiency. If sufficiency is seen as no less than a large mass of wealth, then fear of scarcity can hardly be satisfied. There's never enough wealth to make us feel secure. There are always plenty of people scheming to relieve us of it, and the market can collapse at any time, or we could make a foolish investment. Studies show that the more wealth we acquire, the more we want because we are still as insecure as ever. So if our eyes are focused on wealth, if our heart is motivated by acquisition, if our treasure lies in matters material and worldly, then we cannot enter the kingdom of God to which Jesus invites us. It's as simple as that; it really is. We can qualify what Jesus says about wealth all we want, romanticize (and therefore soften) the direct relevance of the widow's mite for us all we want, laugh at the ridiculous hyperbole of a camel trying to go through the eye of a needle all we want, and pay no attention to Jesus' admonition to his disciples to be like the ravens in the trees or the lilies in the fields who do not worry about sustenance or sufficiency all we want. If we choose to do so, we dismiss the call of Jesus and the reality of the kingdom of God. Jesus calls us to exchange our obsession with material prosperity for a new and liberating obsession called the kingdom of God. As our eyes cannot focus on two things at the same time, so our souls cannot have it both ways. It's God or Mammon.

Jesus calls us all to live simply. He wants us all to be *fully willing* to "give up all our possessions" (Luke 14:33). How that calling plays out is different from one person to another. For some it means a divestiture, as it had to be for that rich young ruler. For others it means the management of their wealth in a way that simplifies their lifestyle, enabling them to serve the good and the greater prosperity of the poor, the marginalized, and the abused. For others with lesser resources, it means abandoning their drivenness toward personal material success and signing on for success measured by kingdom-of-God values. For all of us it means learning from ravens and lilies, letting *God* take care of us, and living our lives and doing our work as a delightful service rather than a desperate grasping for more and more so-called security.

Someone has compared the kingdom of God to a huge family dinner table. It's so huge the whole world is seated at it because God wants no one excluded from his generosity. Sharing is the order of the day, and taking more than we need is both gluttony and bad manners. How much do we then take? Are we brave enough to pass the plate of God's generosity?

If we can pray "Give us the bread we need for today" and mean it, we have sat ourselves at that kingdom table, content with the sufficiency of God and with the irreplaceable joy of enough.

Chapter 12

Forget Greatness

JESUS WAS A LOUSY self-promoter. He could never have been a rock star. John's Gospel tells us that just when the energized crowds are about to make him king and get this new kingdom of his going, he slips off, embarrassed. The people must have wondered why he disappeared just when they were anxious to launch a political campaign to make him the reigning monarch (John 6:14–15).

When Jesus is sharing his last meal with his disciples, he says, "I confer royal power on you just as my Father granted royal power to me. Thus you will eat and drink at my table in my kingdom, and you will sit on thrones overseeing the twelve tribes of Israel" (Luke 22:29–30). Wow! The disciples are thrilled. They're in high cotton now!

How can they sit on thrones and act like servants at the same time? What kind of "thrones" is he talking about anyway? Good question.

Go back earlier in Jesus' ministry. The disciples are talking among themselves on the subject of who (presumably one of *them*) is the greatest of Jesus' followers. It heats up to a loud argument, so loud that Jesus overhears them, which they didn't intend. He sits them down with him and says, "Whoever wants to be first must be least of all and the servant of all" (Mark 9:33–35; Luke 9:46–47). On still another occasion they come directly to Jesus with the question, "Who is the greatest in the kingdom of heaven?" (Matt 18:1). And then—can you believe this?—at their very last supper together with Jesus, the *same* argument breaks out and Jesus gives them the same counterintuitive teaching: Be last to be first, be servant to be master (Luke 22:24–27).

There's more. Just before Jesus' triumphal entry into Jerusalem, only a week before his crucifixion, James and John come to him and ask for a personal favor. Now perhaps the two of them have given up on that childish debate about who is the greatest, but it's still there, implied in the favor they're now asking. "Allow one of us to sit on your right and the other on your left when you enter your glory" (Mark 10:37), as if they really deserve to be there. Poor Jesus doesn't believe what he's hearing. They obviously don't know what they're asking. He has just told the disciples that when they get to Jerusalem he is going to be ridiculed, spit on, tortured, and killed. Do they want to be by his side for that, share that honor? And then he tags on a comment that the decision about where disciples sit at the table in the coming kingdom lies elsewhere. He seems strangely uninterested in the kind of seating arrangements we concern ourselves with. Mark reports that the other disciples are indignant when they hear about James and John's request—as if they didn't want the same for themselves! The pot calling the kettle black.

Matthew, Mark, and Luke all report different and similar accounts of this drive for status and position on the part of Jesus' inner circle, the ones who know him best and love him most. Hmmm. . . . If we are anything like those disciples—and we probably are—we might do well to take notice and look at ourselves. Jesus announces, teaches, and demonstrates a kingdom *the least* of whose members are greater than John the Baptist (Matt 11:11; Luke 7:28), and still the disciples don't get it. Do we? It's easy to condemn those clueless disciples, to be quick to fault their self-serving motive. As if we now know better. As if now that we can point our finger at them, we are somehow absolved ourselves. As if we ourselves have solved the lusting-after-greatness problem in our own hearts. Have we? Honestly?

Does Jesus really expect us to have no interest in power, recognition, status, and public acclaim? But what if these accrue to us because we live really good and respectable lives? If we do good, we may or may not be recognized or elevated because of it. Make no mistake: Doing good does not necessarily pay off for the person who does it. Evil and exploitation of others can bring material prosperity to many and masquerade in respectable, even morally acceptable, presentations. Courageous opposition to such can then be demonized as working against the common good. Think of those who opposed slavery in the mid-nineteenth-century South, or those who crusaded against factory owners who took advantage of overcrowded labor markets, hired at disgracefully low wages, and exposed their workers to dangerous factory conditions. Those who fought such inhumanities were often impugned and violently attacked. Public acclaim and recognition is no proof of a pure goodness. It is certainly no verification of authentic Christian discipleship.

Perhaps that is why Jesus is sometimes suspicious of acclaim. He knows that many of the false prophets were spoken well of (Luke 6:26). He has no problem with the public affirmation per se; he is attentive, however, to the motivation behind what is being acclaimed. He invites us to confront the recognition-grasping, status-searching temptations that still come to us in one form or another. He sees the danger of our thinking we've moved past it. The holiest people are not those who convince themselves they have. They are the ones who recognize and confess the temptation to claim some kind of distinction, some superiority over others, in whatever way it comes to them. They know they need to repent.

The interesting thing about Mark's account of the disciples' jockeying for position is that it is set near the end of Jesus' final journey to Jerusalem, where he will enter the great city of David in a victory procession . . . on a donkey, no less! The beast of humility and derision. Don't you get it yet? Jesus seems to be saying. "I did not come to be served but to serve." What would it be like at the kingdom-of-God banquet feast to have the privilege of sitting next to a Servant? Who wants the dubious honor of being the disciple of a Servant? Answer: those who want to be *like* this Servant Lord. Those who want the servanthood rather than the status to rub off on them.

John's Gospel helps us here. He carries the story further, to Jesus' last supper with his disciples and the last opportunity to teach them something that is his obsession. He does it by wedding action and words. Action: He kneels before his disciples and washes their feet, the job of a household servant. Words: "If I, your Lord and teacher, have washed your feet, you too must wash each other's feet. I have given you an example: just as I have done, you also must do" (John 13:2–15). "Come down to earth," Jesus might say today. Earth—the Latin word is *humus*, the soil, the ground. *Humus*, from which we get the word humility. Being the lowest.

The meal will live on in the church's memory by replaying the drama of the broken bread and the shared wine. Perhaps the drama of the foot-washing, the sacrament of servanthood, needs now to find equal place in the memory and practice of the church. In our world most cultures do not practice foot-washing before meals, but there is a desperate need in the church of our day to learn how to be a servant church rather than a self-serving church. There are plenty of churches, it seems, who engage frequently in internal power struggles as members jockey for position, and some congregations pursue empires and fight for market share, so anxious are they for their numbers to go up.

Remember when Jesus is invited for Sabbath dinner in the home of a prominent Pharisee (Luke 14:1–24)? As soon as he arrives, he causes a stir by doing something you are not supposed to do on the Sabbath. A man has crashed the party because he wants Jesus to free him of a disease that causes bloating. Jesus heals him, fully aware the prominent lawyers and Pharisees present think he has transgressed the law. Well, now that *that* is over, it's time for everyone to find their places.

It looks, however, as if Jesus is about to cause another stir. He has noticed the scramble for the most honored seats near the host. He decides to make an announcement. Listen up everyone! In my kingdom we take the *lowest* seats, he says. The place becomes quiet. Then the murmurs start. And Jesus continues by saying what he has probably said many times before: Here's the thing. You see, everyone who exalts him- or herself will be humbled, and everyone who humbles him- or herself will be exalted. This starts the guests wondering how in the world that is supposed to work.

He's not finished yet. He turns directly to the host, the prominent religious leader, and gives him some advice not found in the etiquette book: When you host a lunch or dinner, don't invite your friends, your brothers or sisters, your relatives, or rich neighbors. If you do, they will invite you in return and that will be your reward. (And you know what *that* starts: an endless cycle of reciprocal invitations back and forth, back and forth.) Try this, says Jesus. The next time you give a banquet, invite the poor, the crippled, the lame, the blind—anyone who is marginalized—and you will be so blessed, you may just make it a habit. The beauty of it is, they can't repay you, but when you leave this mortal coil and enter eternity, you'll be so much more at home at that incredibly diverse banquet Jesus is hosting.

A few years ago the Salvation Army church we attend had a banquet to raise money for missions. Keitha and I bought four tickets and invited two of our neighbors, J. D. and Deanna, who are faithful Christians and good Lutherans. The dinner was open to anyone who bought a ticket. What I didn't know till that evening was that the homeless people our congregation serves were also invited, free of charge.

And of course, two of the scruffiest, dirtiest, and smelliest guests from the street came over and sat at our table. I had a mild panic attack. How will our respectable Lutheran neighbors handle this? Well, J. D. and Deanna introduced themselves to the unexpected guests, found out their names, and engaged them in conversation. No problem, no discomfort. When the meal and the program were over, and we were on the way home, I asked J. D. and Deanna about the homeless people who had joined us for the meal. It was wonderful, they said, to be with a church community that invites the homeless, the marginalized, to their banquets. They were deeply moved, while I had been worried. These good Lutherans taught me I needed to repent.

That wasn't the only time I've had to repent over my failure, or my unwillingness, fully to embrace, and openly refuse to apologize for, the open-armed inclusiveness of the church of our Lord. It wasn't the only time I've had to be reminded of what it means to be a member of the everybody-welcome, come-as-you-are, whoever-you-are, body of Christ. It wasn't the only time I've had to be reminded that my place *is* the lowest place.

When Jesus invites us to lower ourselves, he is not inviting us to cower in fear by being "your humble servant." Genuine humility is a huge step of courage, because when you lower yourself you begin to shed all those layers of protection and those masks of self-importance and the sweet comforts of a good position and its benefits. It's just you without the facades, just *you*. No better than the next guy or gal. You can't even hide behind your claim to humility, because then it wouldn't be humility, just another pretense.

So what's the good of it all? What's the good of coming down to earth? Well, for starters, that's where Jesus is and where we must go to meet him. And once we've begun to shed those ambitions for greatness and those cravings for even a little status and recognition, Jesus can get a start on showing us who we *really* are: his friends, his brothers and sisters, his disciples, his church. That's who we are. And everything else is bogus Christianity.

Jesus was a very impressive person when he walked this earth—but he refused to impress. Remember his temptations in the wilderness? (Matt 4:1–11; Luke 4:1–13). Turn all these stones to bread! (That would be impressive.) Successfully claim to be head of all the kingdoms of the world! (Impressive again.) Throw yourself off the pinnacle of the temple, and at the last minute get a legion of angels to swoop down for a dramatic rescue! (That would be spectacularly impressive.) Well, Jesus?

Nothing doing. John's Gospel tells us there were many people who believed in Jesus because they saw all the marvelous miracles. But Jesus wouldn't entrust himself to them (John 2:23–25). Jesus was powerful, but he only used his power to empower us. Jesus had authority, but he never hid behind it or used it just to show he had it. Jesus was Son of God, but, says the apostle Paul, he emptied himself.

Why don't we get it? Perhaps we do get it, but we also *forget* it all too often. So we ask the Lord's forgiveness. We ask him to show us the next step to servanthood, the next step to lowering ourselves. The next step to *becoming* ourselves.

Chapter 13

See Truth, Judge Humbly

I recently re-read Harper Lee's classic *To Kill a Mockingbird* and was struck again by how she was able to use events and people in a small town in mid-twentieth century southern Alabama as the backdrop and cast of a story of universal appeal. The story presents the population of Maycomb at its worst and its best. The main characters are Atticus Finch, a widowed lawyer, and his two children, daughter Scout and son Jem. Scout, the younger sibling, is only six at the beginning of the story and is forever asking Atticus for explanations about this or that.

One afternoon Scout tries to talk Atticus into not making her go to school. She's had a tough time with the new teacher, and the new teacher has had a tough time with her. Scout doesn't understand why Miss Caroline is the way she is. She's sure she won't be able to get along with her. Atticus encourages Scout to try hard to see Miss Caroline's point of view. You can't understand and appreciate the way someone is "until you climb into his skin and walk around in it," he says.

This chestnut becomes a kind of theme that holds the whole story together. We see the refusal of people to climb into the skin of the African-American people of Maycomb, Alabama, resulting in a horrible willingness to assume Tom Robinson's culpability and wreak deadly violence on him. We see the stereotyping and isolation of the "other," the strange, traumatized person on the margins, whom no one at first wants to connect with or expose themselves to: the tragic loner, Boo Radley. And then there is the Ewell family, descendants of generations of ignorance, irresponsibility, and abuse, and even though Bob Ewell is the main villain of the story, the reader is given enough background to understand, if not excuse, him.

Atticus's suggestion about climbing into someone's skin and walking around in it before making judgments is akin to

Jesus' invitation to humble ourselves, step out of our prejudiced skin, confess our own sin, and only then take the risk of making judgments about a person. This, says Jesus, is how we free ourselves to see the truth about ourselves and others and to make judgments with humility. We shall now see how he helps us to see truth and judge humbly.

IN ONE WAY OR another, all four Gospel writers describe Jesus as the source, even the embodiment of truth. Let's consider how John, in particular, introduces Jesus to the reader.

John is especially unique in how he opens his Gospel. Like the Evangelist Mark he includes no birth stories, but unlike Mark he takes the reader back to before Creation, when there was only God and the Word of God. This Word of God is God speaking, expressing himself, making himself known. This Word of God, says John, is not separate from God, but actually *is* God. When this living Word becomes flesh (a human being), it is God himself who is taking on the form and life of a human. The person in whom this enfleshment becomes reality is the man Jesus of Nazareth. This appearing of God, says John, is like the radiance of an inextinguishable light giving life to those who receive it. The Word who becomes flesh carries the glory of the Father's own Son. It reveals, says John, a new and glorious fullness of "grace and truth" (John 1:1–18).

These opening verses of John's Gospel carry grist for the mills of many theological discussions and debates. Our particular interest here is the connection between God, Jesus, and *truth*. If Jesus is, in fact, the Word of God in human flesh, then he is the embodiment for us of what we can possibly need to know of God. Because we humans are specifically made in the image of God, Jesus is also the embodiment of what we need to know about ourselves. In one of his final discourses with his disciples, Jesus describes himself as "the way, the truth, and the life." He shows us the way to live, he teaches us the truth that makes us free, and he gives us abundant life. Philip begs Jesus to "show us the Father; [then] that will be enough for us." Perhaps a little perturbed that Philip hasn't yet gotten the point of what he came to earth to reveal, he reminds him: "Whoever has seen me has seen the Father. . . . I am in the Father and the Father is in me. . . . I don't speak on my own." In other words, what Jesus says is what he hears the Father saying, what he does is what he sees the Father doing. Jesus is claiming that he speaks and interprets the very truth of God (John 14:1–10, 5:19–20).

In the Jewish world of Jesus, this raises a very big question. Jews believe that the Torah or Law (the first five books of the Old Testament) is the repository of the central truth of God. As practicing Jews, Jesus and his disciples also agree. Jesus, in fact, goes out of his way to emphasize the Law's endurance "until everything there becomes a reality [is accomplished, NIV]." Further, he criticizes those who knowingly transgress the Law and teach others to do the same, describing them as "the lowest in the kingdom of heaven." As he upholds the Law in this way, however, he makes an interesting claim with respect to his own relationship with it: "I haven't come to do away with [the Law and the Prophets]. . . . but to *fulfill* them" (Matt 5:17–19, italics added).

What does Jesus mean by the Law being *fulfilled* through him? He clearly doesn't mean he is replacing the Law with some private personality cult of his own. He doesn't see himself as superseding his own Jewishness; in fact, he remains a practicing Jew his entire life. He and his disciples seek to live in obedience to the Law. On the other hand, there are some practices of his fellow Jews he considers himself to be under no obligation follow. In most instances these practices are not actually enjoined in the Old Testament Law but are elaborations of it, often into detailed and demanding observances. Jesus seems to believe that one can lose the actual purpose of a law or the essential truth it contains by creating complexity out of simplicity and diversionary minutiae out of straightforward obedience. Furthermore, there are times when human need overrides strict observance of the Law, as for example when Jesus considers the need of his disciples for food not otherwise available as more important than following the law of not working on the Sabbath by picking grain (Mark 2:23–28; Matt 12:1–8; Luke 6:1–5).

For Jesus, the Law is compassionate. ("The Sabbath was created for humans; humans weren't created for the Sabbath.") It exists to facilitate our relationship with God and each other; it is not an end in itself. In that sense it is very personal. It is designed to help us know the Person of God. The four Evangelists see Jesus as the fulfillment of the Law because he reveals God *in Person*. We discover the truth in the actual Person Jesus. The truth that sets us free *is* a Person—God Incarnate teaching us, modeling for us, *being* for us the whole truth and nothing but the truth.

If Jesus is the truth, how do we get on to that truth? Obviously, God has given us minds to understand and articulate at one level. Our minds enable us to stand back and frame an objective, understandable view or concept of the truth Jesus reveals and embodies. There is, however—and more to the point—a different way of seeing and grasping truth. It is a knowing of the heart, which can hold deeper truth than the mind can comprehend. "The mind cannot show what the heart longs to know" is a line from the pen of a poet from my own faith tradition. Head knowledge comes in varied ways— books, lectures, conversations, the internet, TV, etc. And, in fact, Jesus gives us plenty to get our minds around. Heart knowledge, however, comes through a relationship. Jesus invades the heart, becomes an intimate companion, and out pours the truth which only the heart can speak and grasp. When the truth is a person more than a doctrine, pat or easy answers lose most or all of their validity. A person is not a pat answer, and pat answers cannot bring us closer to a person's heart. "Are you the Messiah of God we're looking for?" asks a desperate John the Baptist from his prison cell. John is eager for a clear answer: yes or no. Jesus doesn't give it. Perhaps because John does not yet have a full understanding of the kind of messiah Jesus is. John may be seeking confirmation because some, perhaps most, of what his mind expects Jesus to do or accomplish hasn't, in fact, happened. So instead of answering John's question directly, Jesus asks John's messengers to describe for him "what you hear and see" (Matt 11:2–6: Luke 7:18–23).

Seeing the truth in Jesus and understanding what he is really about is a matter of listening to what he is saying and seeing what he is doing. It's in what he says and what he does that he reveals himself, and *that's* the Truth. We learn more and more of it—or better, see deeper and deeper into it—the more we hang around Jesus. This isn't a Jesus who shields and coddles us with sweet talk, though there are times when, like the sheltering hen with her endangered chicks, he does console and protect. But he's also the confronting Jesus who pushes us to see truth about ourselves we want to ignore because it means we would have either to change or become hardened. He pushes us to see the truth of the other person's need or pain, forcing us to choose either compassion or indifference. He pushes us to see the truth about a world beset by grasping empires, personal corruption, and inordinate self-absorption, forcing us either to engage the larger forces of evil or to hide out in our protected lairs. Getting to know Jesus up close will unsettle us, stretch us, and broaden us with the truth.

How can we face such overwhelming truth? Only with the grace of our Lord Jesus, the rabbi who sees us as we so deficiently are, and accepts us. Only with the truth of our Lord Jesus, the rabbi who sees us as we so blindingly are, and empowers us to begin opening our eyes to the truth he reveals. And what does this require of us? *Humility.* While it is true that what our minds acquire is worthy of a certain respect, it is not true that this knowledge necessarily leads to insight. Only humility does.

The humble are not proud of what they know, nor do they force their views and conclusions on others. They have an uncanny ability to listen to life and see into the heart of another. They make themselves available to God, who enables them by grace to make themselves available to others. With no imposing agenda, no pre-drawn conclusions, they see a truth that emerges on its own, from the heart. This gift is why they are truly helpful people.

Deep truth is not to be confused with the explanations we devise or the rationalizations we contrive to impose some convenient understanding about a person or situation. It's natural that we want to figure things out in a way that makes sense to our own worldview. It may be, however, that our worldview is too designed to prevent us from being honest about ourselves while being searingly judgmental about others. We may come to quick explanations or conclusions about another person in order not to look into our own heart. Personal insecurity and fear are often the root cause of judgmentalism. The truth about someone else is so much easier to see than the truth about ourselves.

In his Sermon on the Mount Jesus mounts a full-scale attack on judging others. It's not that we his disciples are not supposed to make judgments about actions that are sinful, inhumane, degrading, or abusive. It's that we're to do so in humility. What exactly does that mean? According to Jesus it means bringing ourselves down a few pegs, stripping away some of our self-delusion so that we can look into our own hearts truthfully. The heart softened by honesty encourages us to see ourselves as we really are. Without such clear inner vision, we see no truth that ultimately matters, and we certainly will be in no position to make helpful judgments about others. The greatest clarifying step is to confess and repent of our own sins. From that position of true humility, we are in a position to begin to see the sin of another in a way that is less judgmental, more perceptive, and potentially helpful. Jesus makes all this clear and vivid when he speaks of not presuming to take a splinter out of someone else's eye without removing the log in our own (Matt 7:1–5; Luke 6:41–42).

Some people take the position that none of us can see the heart of another person clearly and therefore the best way forward is to make no judgments about each other whatsoever. They might take Matt 7:1 precisely in that sense: "Don't judge, so that you won't be judged." For them, non-judgment is an absolute: Jesus intended for us not to judge anyone under any circumstances. This, of course, is unrealistic since any community of people—disciples of Jesus included—must be able to discriminate when community values and standards are being violated or not, and to administer helpful remedies. Refusal to do so eventuates in the dissolution or even destruction of the community, as utopian community experiments prove. We then ask: Why would some refuse to take this responsibility? Perhaps their refusal to make judgments about others is a way to excuse or hide their own sin as well. Or perhaps they are of a mind to avoid unpleasantness and conflict at all costs. Their way is avoidance, especially when they pursue it and appear to be non-judgmental.

How, then, do we make judgments about each other responsibly and fairly, especially in light of our own imperfections? We can begin in a spirit of genuine humility, confessing that none of us can see into another person's heart and judge his actions with absolute clarity. We all make errors of judgment, we miss the real truth. We pray for insight, and God's Spirit sends it, but we may not hear or see it right, perhaps because we're not ready to receive it. We may be taking the wrong posture: an elevated seat rather than a standing alongside. It may be helpful to describe what we're doing as making judgments rather than judging, as judging has come to carry the connotation of something that is sealed and permanent, even as a kind of dismissal of the other person's character. The straightforward words of Jesus stand as a searing critique of such attitudes: "Happy are people who show mercy, for they will receive mercy" (Matt 5:7). In the Gospels, whenever someone approaches Jesus asking for mercy, Jesus gives mercy. The same goes for forgiveness. When Zechariah announces the coming of the Messiah, he interprets it as the fulfillment of the promised mercy and the forgiveness of sins (Luke 1:72, 77). As citizens of this merciful kingdom, we disciples of Jesus are called to make judgments about each other with the humility of grace and with an awareness of our own sin.

Jesus, who is grace and truth, invites us to trust our pretenses no longer and find our true selves in him. He invites us, in his presence, to face the truth of both our sin and our salvation, our failures and our progress in grace. As we humble ourselves before the truth about ourselves, we humble ourselves before each other. This is what our rootedness in the love of God makes possible. The heart takes over the mind, and, says the apostle Paul, in this way we shall "have the power to grasp love's width and length, height and depth, together with all believers." We shall "know the love of Christ . . . beyond knowledge" and "be filled entirely with the fullness of God" (Eph 3:18–19). It is from this place of humility that we are given eyes to see the truth that sets us free and keeps us on our knees.

Chapter 14

Practice Solitude

Solitude is not highly valued in the culture of distraction that is preempting and defining our world. It is a world that interrupts and informs us every minute. Our omnipresent, ever-active iPhones are icons of this distraction. They send out incessant signals we can hear, or silently transfer messages we are fully aware are already waiting there for us to access. We wonder what our iPhones want to reveal. Should we answer now? Ever-new news is the persistent tempter. Its ubiquity overwhelms us. Is it luring us from a focused life, from a calling of consequence? The incessant invasion of new information, most of it trivial, seems to define and form the day for us. It can keep us very busy just trying to take it all in. In such a distracted world is there any room for solitude?

The internet, for all the value it otherwise has, can so consume people that they become addicted to information-as-information-itself because there is insufficient time to see any real meaning in the ever-changing cyber landscape. It comes and leaves too rapidly. It is a world that sabotages solitude and undermines reflection. It is perhaps an even more pernicious version of materialism, not only because internet shopping makes acquisition far easier and therefore more irresistible, but also because information itself is the material we compulsively consume, and we can't get enough of it. Information is the new irresistible temptation. I would love to claim it doesn't tempt me—and I can't.

My iPhone is usually near and my computer not far away. My mind sometimes drifts toward it, and I wonder what it presently has to offer to fill the current space of my day. Should I go on line?

Interruptions were a part of Jesus' life—in fact, they were the stuff of many of his most significant and helpful encounters with people. We see examples of unexpected intrusions from people seeking his help, and when the desire for help is sincere and the trust is present, Jesus responds. Interruptions of this kind are, in fact, integral to Jesus' ministry, as they are to the ministry of we who are his disciples.

A different kind of interruption also occurs in Jesus' life. He does not have to contend with the distractive power of hi-tech internet devices, but his life is also inundated by interruptions that vie to pull him off course and lure him from his mission. His three-year ministry is crammed with diversions from preemptors who want to use him for their own ends and admirers who misunderstand what he is really about. When some of these admirers want to make him their earthly king, for example, he says nothing and slips away unnoticed the first chance he gets. It's worth pointing out that he removes himself to a mountain. Does he feel the need for solitude? Was the offer of kingship a real temptation for him (John 6:14–15)?

Why is solitude so important in Jesus' life? Again and again in the Gospels we see him removing himself to some deserted place, often on a mountain, to converse with his Father, or plead for help, or perhaps to say little or nothing, only listen for his Father's assuring voice. The sheer quantity of these retreats referenced in the Gospels, both brief and extended, require that we, his disciples, consider their importance for our own calling and living.

It's important to notice, first, that there is no indication that these times of solitude were occupied with sustained spoken prayer. If Jesus' prayer in Gethsemane is any indication, the words spoken were usually brief and to the point, a plea of utter dependence and need, a surrender to the Father's will and to the power of love (Mark 14:35–36; Matt 26:39; Luke 22:42–44). The capacity for silence, it seems, is a requirement for solitude. Perhaps Jesus was familiar with the words of Ecclesiastes: "The more the words, the less the meaning, and how does that profit anyone?" (Ecc 6:11, NIV). The more we speak, the less we listen. Solitude is about quieting ourselves with a few words, a request, a cry, a plea, a stillness . . . and then listening to God. The gift comes with what we hear, not what we say or how we control the conversation.

Consider the examples of Jesus' solitude in the Gospels. There's the time when Jesus is struck with sadness over the news of John the Baptist's murder and he withdraws "to a deserted place by himself" to grieve before God and perhaps to wonder in his Father's presence what this now means for him. His solitude is interrupted by a crowd of thousands who have followed him. He ministers to them, feeds them, and sends them and his own disciples on their way. He then goes to a mountain nearby to pray, perhaps to complete the needed time of solitude for his grief (Matt 14:13, 23; Mark 6:46). Solitude also precedes important decisions. The night before Jesus chooses twelve of his disciples to be apostles, he goes yet again to the mountain to pray all night (Luke 6:12). Sometimes Jesus and his disciples need a retreat. Upon returning from their demanding but successful mission, he says to them, "Come by yourselves to a secluded place and rest a while" (Mark 6:31b). The side trip to Tyre and Sidon seems to have been undertaken as a needed retreat. Otherwise, why does he want his whereabouts kept secret, and why does he seem uncharacteristically annoyed by the woman's request for a compassionate healing of her demon-possessed daughter (Mark 7:24–30)?

Jesus' own mission begins and ends with solitude. He spends forty days in the wilderness fasting and praying before he launches the mission. He is tempted by Satan, who presents him with three spectacular ways to fulfill a messianic role. The text only records three sentences spoken by Jesus during those forty days, each of the three in rejection of one of Satan's temptations. (Mark 1:12–13; Matt 4:1–11; Luke 4:1–13). What words does he pray to his Father? My guess is, not many. He is listening past the winds, earthquakes, and fires of his own vulnerabilities, and, like Elijah, hearing the still small voice of a God who is loving and yet demanding. From there he returns "in the power of the Spirit," ready for his saving mission (Luke 4:14a). His last night of solitude in the Garden of Gethsemane the night before his crucifixion is also a time of prayer with few words. Once again the question of his mission and how it is to be accomplished looms before him. By now he seems fully aware it means crucifixion. His spoken prayer is brief. A last request: Is it at all possible for me to be Messiah without a horrible suffering? And a final surrender: Father, I give in to your will over my own fears. And in between, the still small voice of God whose love Jesus is now being called fully to embody (Mark 14:32–42; Matt 26:36–42; Luke 22:39–46).

Jesus' own example and words teach us that solitude is a closeness to God that prepares us to live his life and carry out his mission in the world. Consider what we his disciples are called to, and then ask yourself if it is possible without times and places of spiritual sanctuary. Can our ministry with people happen without the solitude of prayer (Mark 9:29; 14:38)? Can our public prayer be authentic without the deep spirituality shaped in solitude (Luke 20:47)? Can we have the presence of mind to be able to discern what is happening in this confusing world without solitude (Luke 12:54–56), or be able to see the invisible by faith (John 20:29)? Without solitude can we wait expectantly so as not to miss God's appearing (Mark 13:32–37; Matt 24:44–51; Luke 12:35–48)? It hardly seems possible that without a strengthening solitude in the presence of a providential God we can shed our materialistic cravings, our grasping ways, and our deep insecurities (Luke 12:22–34). Surely it is in the secure and accepting refuge of solitude that we can strip away the fears that paralyze us and the diversions that distract us so that we can lose what is worth losing and save our lives (Mark 8:35; Matt 10:39; 16:25–26; Luke 9:24–25; 17:33; John 12:25). And alone in the presence of God are we not loved into seeing and accepting ourselves in our failure and faithlessness, opening the door to restoration (John 21:15–19)?

If solitude is so essential to the full and focused life to which Jesus calls us, how do we practice it? We must begin by refusing to consider ourselves helpless victims of all the tempting sources of distraction and commitments that press upon us today—overwhelming job demands, enticing television, the complexity of social expectations and obligations, for example—and, of course, the excessively demanding world of cyberspace. Our susceptibility to the control of these forces and influences has primarily to do with *us*, not *them*. They capture us because of our own boredom, our failure to find meaning and focus, leading us to pursue something else to fill up the spaces of our lives. We are all too aware of these ready-made fillers, waiting to give us something else to occupy our attention, our minutes, our lives.

The question is: Why? What is it we're escaping? Why does our life seem so empty, so inadequate, so boring? The answer to that question may well come to us as we engage the practice of solitude, where we come in all honesty, confess our helplessness and failure, and open ourselves to the still, small voice of God. There, by his grace and mercy, we begin to see the Jesus-led way before us. We begin to understand the fear that has held us back and seduced us into distractions that deliver only diversions without substance.

It's worth remembering that the most revered, iconic disciples of Jesus have experienced days of distraction, boredom, and uncertainty. Thomas à Kempis said that he had

> never found man so religious and devout that he had not sometimes a withdrawing of grace, or felt not some decrease of zeal. There was never a saint so high caught up (II Cor 12:2) and illuminated, who first or last was not tempted. For he is not worthy of the high contemplation of God, who has not been exercised with some tribulation for God's sake. (*Of the Imitation of Christ*, 80)

These same sometimes-disturbed saints have found restoration through solitude, where they listened to God, confessed their sin and their needs, and discovered or rediscovered the purpose of their lives and the joy of living.

Solitude may take time to cultivate. It probably will. In fact, waiting is often an essential for gaining clarity—hence, the line in one of George Croly's hymns: "Teach me the patience of unanswered prayer." Patience, indeed. Jesus certainly needed it. He waited thirty years before he knew to set out on his life's mission. And he needed plenty of it during those last three years when he chose solitude so frequently and regularly.

Those who choose to follow Jesus must choose to live fully engaged in the world, as he did. They must also choose to spend time alone with God—confessing, listening, getting their eyes opened and their hearts purified. Failure to do so in this distracted age is courting spiritual decline.

Chapter 15

End Well

We were finally told the day before my father died. He had been diagnosed with lymphoma about seven months before that day. The oncologist had suggested a plan of chemotherapy treatments. My father, a very upbeat person, was hopeful this might kill all the cancer. He got the rest he needed but continued his job as the head of our denomination's national office. He would not let this cancer stand in the way.

Five or six days before Pop died, Mother called me from New Jersey and asked that I come. He had become extremely weak and was back in the hospital. I was at a retreat. I caught the first plane I could after arriving home. Mother was clearly unsettled. I think she sensed the end could be very near. A couple of days later the oncologist called us to meet him. He had the hospital social worker present. (Why not a chaplain?) His first words were: "Mrs. Needham, your husband is dying." He said it not so much with sadness as with resignation. This was a failure. He, the hospital, the medical profession, or medical science had failed to keep my father alive, as if preparing him for death was not on the table at all. I asked the doctor why he had only just now discovered that my father, a patient whose cancer he had been treating for six months, was now fast approaching the end of his life. His answer seemed to deflect personal responsibility: "The chemotherapy treatment killed many cancer cells, but new, more aggressive cancer cells took their place. Your father wanted so much to believe that this cancer could be licked that I thought it wouldn't be right for me to tell him what my medical expertise and experience told me. He wanted to hold out hope, and I believed his positive attitude would actually help your father survive a little longer." There was an element of kindness here, but also, I sensed, a deflection of personal responsibility in helping a dying patient deal with what was likely to happen. This all happened over thirty years ago, when, I dare say, many if not most doctors hesitated to speak of death as an inevitability best dealt with when sufficient time is available for preparation to be made. We quickly called in all the family. Pop died the next day.

How prepared was my father to die? He was a strong believer in the resurrection to eternal life. That was not in question. What I found during those last few days was that he didn't seem to know how to let go. He would say again and again, "We must have faith." I don't think he was talking about the reality of eternal life, nor about the sufficiency of God's grace to bring him there. He was hoping his life was not to be so soon over. Why not, since his oncologist was not being forthright about what his medical expertise told him? On the very day he died, Pop said it again, "We must have faith," as they wheeled him off for a procedure (draining accumulating fluid in his body cavity) which I'm sure the oncologist knew was useless at this point. My father died as he was being prepared for the procedure.

Much has been written about our death-denying culture. Our faith in science makes it tenable for us to believe we will find ways to extend our years well beyond current average life spans, if not indefinitely. Death is merely another problem to be solved. For the present it is an unpleasantness to be shielded from. Hence, it is largely outsourced. People tend to die in hospitals where extraordinary procedures are often used to prolong life artificially, leaving loved ones as observers rather than participants. The bodies of our loved ones are handled by professionals (funeral home personnel), and we usually see our deceased loved ones only after they've been "prepared."

The appearance of hospice facilities, which are admissions that approaching death is a reality to be dealt with as such, has been a positive step for the benefit of both the dying person and the loved ones. Even better, in my view, is home hospice care. I am deeply grateful for the physician's assistant who gave my very elderly and failing mother a choice between either being put in the hospital where they could, by various and sundry means, prolong her life, or being comfortable at home with nursing care for her final days. For Mother and us, there was really no choice to be made. Mother had always wanted to die at home, the place where she graced so many with her overwhelming hospitality. For her last days she was well cared for and we were able to visit her in her own place of grace. One day we brought Peter and Suzanne to meet her, relatives from Australia she had no knowledge of. Peter was the grandson of an uncle she had never met and had long lost track of. They themselves were visiting America to meet relatives they also had only recently discovered existed. Mother had had a tough week, but she rallied for the visit. Peter gave her a beautiful letter from his mother, also in her 90s. When Mother read the letter from her newly-discovered cousin, she came to life in a way we hadn't seen in recent days and smiled one of the most contented smiles I had ever seen. It was as if the circle of her family had been completed, in her home, on the last day of her life. She died late that evening. She ended well.

How does Jesus, our Rabbi, invite us to face the last days of our life? When we study the Gospels we realize that much of what he says and models illumines a life of giving away, a divestiture, if you like, preparing and leading us to the surrender of our mortal lives. The new way to live we've been discovering in the Gospels actually readies us to accept, even welcome, our death. The willingness to change by being changed will always involve divesting ourselves of something worth not keeping. Embracing life fully includes accepting death courageously rather than living in denial of it. By living simply we have less to lose in the face of death and more enduring treasure to take with us. Cleansing ourselves of dreams of greatness and acclaim, we weaken death's threat to rob us of treasured presumptions. By seeing truth through the eyes of humility, we more readily accept the failure of our mortality and the reality of our earthly demise. By practicing solitude, we withdraw from the threat of our mortality and deepen our relationship with God which that mortality cannot destroy. The rich life to which Jesus calls us empowers us to face the demise of our earthly life with the courage of eternity.

Jesus invites us to be confident treasure hunters of incorruptible heavenly endowment rather than nervous collectors of the flashy, corruptible, steal-able earthly treasures (Matt 6:19–21). Death robs the latter of life; it cannot rob the former. Earthly treasure chests have no eternal value. If that is where your heart is, death wins. If your treasure chest is your relationship with God and the graces that are birthed in that relationship, eternal life wins. The earthly treasures we grasp will eventually crumble in our hands; the heavenly treasures endure. Jesus says, " . . . none of you who are unwilling to give up all your possessions can be my disciple" (Luke 14:33). Discipleship, Jesus is saying, is a journey of earthly divestment, which prepares us for the final earthly goodbye and the gift of eternal life.

The Jesus we meet in the Gospels lives in full sight of his death. As we have seen, from early on he prepares his disciples for his death and the way it will come about. Death does not figure into their own understanding as an integral part of Jesus' *life*. They never like it when he mentions his destiny of suffering and death. They are too caught up in the idea of a new and enduring reality now present in Jesus. Death is not on their radar screen. It took three years of Jesus' teaching, the trauma of the last days of his life, the post-crucifixion encounters with the resurrected Jesus, and the Spirit-led prayer and reflection that immediately followed, for them to embrace his death—and then their own.

Jesus lived close to death. Every day of his ministry, death was a possibility. And so it is with us. Thomas à Kempis said we disciples should order every day of our lives as if preparing to die (*Imitation of* Christ, 51). Frederick Buechner reminds us: "You are seeing everything for the last time, and everything you see is gilded with goodbyes" (*Listening to Your Life,* 88). William Law recommended that the Christian go to bed each night as if for the last time, laying himself in his coffin, ready to face death. Living every day fully is also dying to that day, knowing that the day will be gone. It is there to be received, lived, and left, preserved only in our memories. What happens that day is for the last time. In acknowledging this, we free ourselves to be attentive to today in a way we might not otherwise be. We see the day more clearly and live it more fully.

Living the day more fully means neither grabbing for all the gusto we can get nor acquiring all the assets we can obtain. Quite the contrary, it means, in Jesus' metaphor, investing in the heavenly treasures, not earthly. The investment strategy focuses on what has eternal value—works of grace, compassion, mercy; attitudes of understanding, support, trust; practical ministries of witness, help, advocacy. Whatever specific responsibilities we carry in any day, which may be our last, what is eternally important is that we glimpse the opportunities of eternal value in the complexity of our tasks and responsibilities, receive them, and pursue them. Living the day fully means treating it as eternally important, as if it could be our last day on earth.

This way of living requires accepting and preparing for our death. Not long ago PBS ran a series on the history of cancer treatment. For many years treatment focused on attacking the cancer itself through such means as surgery, radiation, and chemotherapy. More recently, there has been greater focus on treatments that assist the patients themselves to build up natural resistance. Along with this development there seems to be a move on the part of oncologists and their staff to be more revealing of the facts and the prognosis with their patients in a pastoral way, enabling them to prepare better for the real possibility of death. I was quite moved during the feature of a young oncologist at a hospital in Charleston, West Virginia. She shared with her patients what was realistically possible in terms of both success and failure in stopping the spread of the cancer. She took her time and responded patiently and thoroughly to her patients' questions and concerns. When patients were shattered by discovery of a significantly metastasized cancer or the failure of treatment to stop the spread of the cancer, she would stay with them, compassionately hear them, and help them begin to plan. In the context of her medical practice, this oncologist was teaching the church one of its most important tasks: helping disciples prepare for death so that they can live fully the remaining days they have.

There is much for us to learn about preparing for death by following the life of Jesus. As we've seen, Jesus again and again made his disciples aware of the death he would be facing. Let's look in particular at the last evening of his earthly life. He arranges for a final meal together. Remember that Jesus often compares the kingdom of God to a banquet feast. In this last supper he merges his crucifixion and his resurrection, earthly death with eternal life, the end with the beginning. We see this in all the Gospel accounts, but especially in the last-supper discourses and prayers of Jesus in John's Gospel, chapters 13–17.

As the twelve disciples sit at this last meal with Jesus, they are becoming worried about their incredible three years with Jesus. Will all that come to nothing? Will history record those three years as a cause that never really materialized? Why is Jesus leaving us now? Where is he going?

Jesus senses their uncertainty and fear. So what does he do? He knows they presently cannot possibly understand what is about to happen. He knows one of them will betray him, another deny him, and the rest of them run like cowards into hiding. He knows it won't be till later that they will understand what these hours mean. Should he go over it again?

No. He'll serve supper. He breaks bread. He lifts the cup. He gives thanks, perhaps in the words of a prayer often used before meals in Jewish families: "Blessed art thou, O Lord our God, king of the world, who dost bring forth bread from the earth."

As they partake he talks about the future. "I tell you," he says, "I won't drink of the fruit of the vine from now on until that day when I drink it anew with you in my Father's kingdom."

His disciples say: But Jesus, you're leaving us! Jesus responds: I'm giving you the bread and wine of my life. Remember when I told you about bread from heaven, and you pleaded with me to give you this bread. I said it then, and I say it now: I am the bread of life. He who comes to me will never go hungry, and he who believes in me will never be thirsty. I go away as one man on earth, and I will come again to be present with you anywhere and everywhere. Remember these words when you sit around the table as we're doing now. I am there with you, and I won't leave you or forsake you.

Jesus continues: I'm calling you to a new kingdom, a new way of life. And when you sit around the table with those you love, as well as those you are trying to love, as well as those you feel distant from, I'm there. I'm there once again, breaking the bread of my love and inviting you to leave your worry behind and fully embrace this very different kingdom of mine. I'm letting it loose in the world, I'm letting it loose in your lives.

He goes from there to die a death too cruel, chosen though totally undeserved. For him and for us, it's a liberating death. It releases the very compassion of God that brought him there, releases it in us his followers so powerfully that we find ourselves unaccountably loving those we're not socialized to love, even enemies. He lives and dies to make us all inclusive lovers. The treasures he calls us now to store up in heaven are acts of boundless compassion and mercy.

In the end love remains, embraced by faith and hope (I Cor 13:13). The treasure that never fails (v. 8). The end that is a beginning, an eternity—in the company of God and all creation redeemed by the Son and given life by the Spirit (Eph 1:9–10).

Section Two

Jesus on Loving

*Finding Our Center
in the Great Commandment*

THE GOD OF THE Old Testament is a lover. This revelation strengthens as we keep reading. God loves his people. They've strayed and he longs to have them back. They've sinned and he forgives them. His love is a covenant love, a faithful love. He calls Israel, his covenant people, to love him back and to reflect his love in their relationships with each other.

The Old Testament prophets often speak of this covenant relationship in a very personal, intimate way. None more so than Hosea: Israel's unfaithfulness to God is like his wife's unfaithfulness to him, and God's relentless pursuit of his profligate Israel is like his own search to reclaim his promiscuous beloved. God is the deserted lover who is hurt by our infidelity, but never stops loving, never stops pursuing us. The covenant is not a contract; it's a lover's pledge never to stop loving.

This characterization of God, revolutionary in its day, persists in the New Testament. John, in his first letter, tells us that it is essential to understanding who God is: "The person who doesn't love does not know God, because God is love" (I John 4:8). In his Gospel John says the love of God becomes incarnate in (literally, "takes flesh in") Jesus of Nazareth (John 1:14a; 3:16). And as the New Testament progresses, we begin to understand how God, alone before Creation, could be a lover. What emerges is the understanding that the one God is Three—Father, Son, and Holy Spirit . . . a Holy Community . . . the Holy Trinity.

Why, of course! How else could God be a lover, or how could he, in the words of John the Evangelist, *be* love, if he has not always had someone else to love. It obviously takes at least two for there to be love. Father, Son, and Holy Spirit have always loved each other. Loving has always been a part of God's God-ness. Furthermore, his creation of us in his image is an extension of his loving. During the Christmas season you may have sung a very old carol with these two lines (speaking of Mary): "To show God's love aright, she bore to us a Savior" ("Lo, how a Rose e'er blooming"). To *show* us. For us, created in his image—an image of our God who lives and loves community—loving God and loving each other is essential to who we are, and essential to learning how to find and live our lives. Jesus shows us.

So God has not only created us, he's let us into his family of love. Jesus says, "As the Father has loved me, I too have loved you. Remain in my love" (John 15:9). Jesus then moves from this participation we have in trinitarian love to the transference of that love to our relationships with each other: "This is my commandment: love each other just as I have loved you" (v. 12). As we draw together in this community of love, even if we are only two or three, Jesus is there with us (Matt 18:20), sharing the love of the Trinity.

Jesus further says this community of shared love has the character of *eternity*. We tend to think of eternal life as unending time or everlasting life. It actually means far more. It is a *quality* of life, a life with God and his family. Near the end of his earthly life Jesus tells his disciples that eternal life is "to know . . . the only true God, and Jesus Christ whom [he] sent" (John 17:3). It begins when we enter into relationship with the family of God. It's real life, heavenly life, kingdom-of-God life, and it is forever.

An expert in the Jewish law stands up to test Jesus: "What must I do to inherit eternal life?" Jesus asks him, "What is written in the Law? How do you interpret it?" The man answers, " . . . love the Lord your God with all your heart, with all your being, with all your strength, and with all your mind, and love your neighbor as yourself." Jesus gives him an A+! "You have answered correctly. Do this and you will live"—that is, have life in all its never-ending fullness (Luke 10:25–28).

Being a disciple of Jesus means learning to love as he loved. This love has the aroma, taste, and texture of eternity. Love is the very atmosphere of eternity. Love never ends, never fails, never loses (I Cor 13).

This is the furthest thing from sentimentality. Jesus teaches us that love is proven by its works, by the risks it takes, by the threat of embarrassment it accepts. Love for him is not a harbored emotion that can be preserved and treasured privately like a ship that never tests itself in the riskier waters of

84

the open sea. We cannot finally keep our love without giving it. The heart is proven by what it reveals and does, as a tree by its fruit.

It is also true that we may pretend love and do loving things for effect, but the scam cannot be sustained. In time, the true motivation of our heart will show itself. Without an uncompromised heart, loving action grows sour. We cannot truly love someone when our hearts are set on our self-advancement. A self-absorbed person with vast resources can afford to be generous at times in order to please and to enhance his public profile and further his hold on power, but this is not love. A self-absorbed person with meager resources can exercise strategic kindness and attentiveness for the purpose of advancing himself, but neither is this love. For Jesus, the motivation is central. Love given with the expectation of a benefit in return beyond the genuine joy of the act itself is not love.

This is why Jesus focuses on the heart and points out that the Father knows our hearts. He says that love requires a purifying of motives, a heart-cleansing. He invites us to deal with our mixed motives, our cross purposes, our subtle deceptions. He invites us to have the courage to ask what is really in our hearts, to identify and confess so that we can deal with the impediments to love.

The study of Jesus which will now engage us is the study of what has been called his Great Commandment: to love God and love our neighbor. It is absolutely central to being Jesus' disciple. We'll look first at who it is Jesus calls us to love—we'll call them "our beloveds." Then we'll learn the art of loving, or how to love, according to Jesus.

Our Beloveds

Chapter 16

God

H. A. Williams speaks of a longing deep within all of us. It is a dissatisfaction that pushes for resolution, an emptiness that cries out for a fullness. It resides in the heart, the soul, the center of who we are as human beings. It drives us to seek out this or that other source of satisfaction, none of which can satisfy the longing or fill the emptiness. It is the longing for God, or what Augustine called a persistent restlessness which can find its peace and satisfaction only in God. Williams, using a phrase of poet Thomas Blackburn, calls it "The end of love's immensities" (Williams, *The Joy of God*).

THE LOVE STORY THAT is the gospel is framed by two claims. The first is that God loves us more than we can imagine, and the second is that we are endowed, not only with the capacity to love him in return, but also with an innate desire for God that can only be fulfilled by God himself, "the end of love's immensities." Within this frame is painted the story of Jesus, who invites us to love the God who loves us beyond comprehension, love him with everything we are and have, and to embrace our neighbors within the huge matrix of this overflowing, uncontainable love.

Love begins with God, who first loved us. Who is this God? He is not some Unmoved Mover, not some distant, uninvolved deity. Some, however, do see him that way.

Jesus tells a parable near the end of his earthly life (Matt 25:14–30). It is to become one of his most remembered stories. It is the most often quoted story to encourage us to take the talents and resources God has given us and invest them in God and his mission. We, however, are looking for something different, something that holds an important key to understanding the parable. Let's summarize the story:

A man is leaving for a long trip. He calls together three of his servants and entrusts them with money in varying amounts. When he returns after a long absence, he finds the first two have invested the money entrusted to them wisely, bringing good returns for their master. The third man, however, took no risks and hid his money in the ground till his master returned. He is punished.

The important aspect of the parable we should not miss is the *fear* of the third servant, the unfaithful one. He cannot get beyond seeing his master as someone who has the power to do him great harm: "Master, I knew that you are a hard man. . . . So I was afraid. And I hid my valuable coins in the ground. Here, you have what's yours" (vv. 24b-25). You can almost see him cower.

He doesn't know the heart of his master. To him, the master is distant and cruel.

I think there are many people who cannot seem to get beyond the power of almighty God and their fear of what he might do to them. They live their lives in a cringe. Every bad thing that happens to them is God inflicting punishment. They can't bring themselves to love God because they don't believe that God loves *them*. They can't imagine that God longs for their love. They don't know God's heart.

One of the greatest gifts of Jesus to us is to show us a God who longs for our love. If Jesus is God-in-the-flesh, as Scripture clearly attests, then we should be able to see that longing of God for us in Jesus. As we study the Gospels, we see clearly that Jesus himself longs for his disciples' love, desires them to be in his presence, and for all the ways they disappoint him, fail him, and in the end even abandon him, they are always more than his followers. He says to them in John 15:15: "I don't call you servants any longer. . . . Instead, I call you friends." And so, just before that final arrest, he prays, "Father, I want those you gave me to be with me where I am. . . . " (John 17:24).

Obviously, Father, Son, and Holy Spirit long for our love. I think it's not an accident that in John's Gospel Jesus' long, final prayer with his disciples right before his arrest, trial, and crucifixion, concludes with these moving words: "[Father,] I've made your name known to them and will continue to make it known so that your love for me will be in them, and I myself will be in them" (John 17:26).

Now, what can we learn from Jesus about loving God? As we've seen, the first and most important commandment, Jesus says, is this: "Love the Lord your God with all your heart, with all your being, with all your mind, and with all your strength" (Mark 12:30). There's so much we could say here about how Jesus modeled this. Let's focus on one key aspect of how Jesus expressed his love for the Father.

You may remember the film "Chariots of Fire" which told the story of the great Scottish runner Eric Liddell, known as the Flying Scotsman, who, when asked why he ran, replied, "God made me fast, so I run to give Him pleasure." When you love someone you want to please them, you want to give them pleasure. Jesus lives life and does what he does, to give God pleasure. During his ministry he says more than once, "I always do what makes [my Father] happy" (John 8:29). And near the end of his earthly life, it gives *him* great pleasure to pray to the Father: "I have glorified you on earth by finishing the work you gave me to do" (John 17:4).

You and I live to give God pleasure. It's not that we're nobodies who have no purpose in life other than to wait hand and foot on some God who exploits us. The real truth is this: We're *somebodies* because we are the beloved of God, whose love frees us to love him and to be our true selves by living in his love—and that gives him immense pleasure.

We can't help ourselves. We're pleasure givers. We're like Mary, transformed by the love of God she's received through Jesus, taking that very expensive jar of perfume worth a year's wages, perhaps for a moment wondering if she should spare it in one rash act of love, and then dismissing from her mind any guilt about waste, as she says, *Yes, yes, a thousand yeses, I shall pour my love at his feet and spread it over his feet with my hair, and the house will be filled with the fragrance of my love for Jesus.*

How excessive! How out of control! How beautiful.

Jesus says to his disciples (including us), "As the Father has loved me, I too have loved you. Remain in my love" (John 15:9). How wonderful to live in the environment of God's love and to have the privilege of loving God in return, to be able to give him pleasure, to love him excessively—and yes, even foolishly—so that the fragrance can spread around to our neighbor.

Whatever else discipleship is, it is certainly a life lived for God's pleasure—which, as we always discover over time, is what gives *us* pleasure, a pleasure that lasts.

If you love someone, *tell* them. If you love someone, *show* them. Tell God regularly how much you love him: think it, feel it, say it. And show God you love him by giving him pleasure, by doing what pleases him.

One more important thing needs to be said about loving God. As we've said, Jesus makes clear that God is a lover who loves us passionately and also wants us, his beloveds, to love him. Now it's difficult to love someone who is not in the flesh, someone we don't know in person. I may "love" J. S. Bach for the soul-stirring music he gave us, even though I've obviously not met him in person. I do know, however, some of the music into which he poured his soul and genius, and I know something of the kind of life he lived. But I can't love *him* fully.

The problem with God is that no one has seen him. That's what John 1:18 and I Timothy 6:16b say. He is not a physical presence.

Or *is* he? Jesus, as John the Evangelist tells us, is the Word of God enfleshed in the person of one particular man (John 1:14a). In John 12:45 Jesus says, during the last week if his earthly life, "Whoever sees me sees the one who sent me." Even today Jesus is God in our world, even in our community, our neighborhood, even in this person or that. (Was it Luther who said Christians are all "little Christs"?) Jesus is God breaking the barrier between divinity and humanity, between inaccessible distance and palpable intimacy. God *is* a physical presence in Jesus, a real person who lived 2,000 years ago—we have the records, we know the story. And the Holy Spirit makes him a real presence today. As Jesus said to his disciples in John, chapter 14, and says to us today, "I will ask the Father, and he will send another Companion, who will be with you forever. This Companion is the Spirit of Truth. . . . I won't leave you as orphans. I will come to you" (vv. 16–17a, 18).

The Holy Spirit re-presents Jesus to us. He gives us Jesus to love, and in loving Jesus we love God. He gives us Jesus as Scripture comes alive for us today, as we see him in each other, in our communities, and especially in the unlikeliest persons and places. We see him in other flesh, other bodies, other events, calling us to love him in all of these appearances.

Does our love for Jesus sometimes falter? Of course it does, and Jesus himself knows it. Listen to him speaking to his disciples just before he's arrested: "Tonight," he says, "you will fall away because of me" (Matt 26:31a). They all protest his prediction, but Jesus is right. What's so important and telling in this story is that as soon as Jesus says their love will falter over the next few days, he adds that he'll be going on ahead of them to Galilee, where he'll meet up with them again. He'll give their love another chance, and another, until their love for him becomes so deep and so contagious it spreads all over the world, gathering a church so in love with him, he makes her his bride.

Jesus, God in the flesh. Jesus, the God we find in one another. Jesus, open door to God himself, "the end of love's immensities." Jesus, whom to love is loving God.

Chapter 17

Our Neighbors

"If we are to love our neighbors, before doing anything else we must *see* our neighbors. With our imagination as well as our eyes, that is to say like artists, we must see not just their faces but the life behind and within their faces. Here it is love that is the frame we see them in." (Frederick Buechner, *Listening to Your Life: Daily Meditations*)

As we read the Gospels, we are struck again and again by the fact that Jesus has an extraordinary ability to see into a person. A Samaritan woman at a well, a rich young ruler, a respectable scribe, a Roman procurator, and many others present themselves to Jesus in one light and Jesus surprises them with a deeper truth about who they are. These insights of Jesus include few external details; the substance of what he reveals is what is in their hearts.

Are we, his followers, to see our neighbor in like manner, in a deeper way? As one could say a great painter wants us to see more than what is there on the surface, Jesus wants us to see beyond the dismissive labels and stereotypes: the bums, the lazy poor, the filthy rich, the disgusting addicts, the unbearably righteous, the stand-offs, and a host of other stereotypes by which we conveniently classify anyone who threatens to be our neighbor. It is far easier to deal with and ignore them under one of those kinds of labels. With each label comes a built-in strategy by which to dismiss the person as easily as possible, sometimes even under the guise of neighborliness— kindly but quickly giving the beggar a buck, avoiding the unpleasantness of the person who always seems angry, ignoring the racist statements of a co-worker, and so on. For Jesus, a neighbor is someone framed not by our convenience but by his or her inconvenience, someone we actually trouble ourselves to see. In the seeing and in what we allow the seeing to call from us, we become neighbors.

How, then, do we become those who see their neighbors in this way, or who genuinely want to *be* neighbors?

Let's look at the Jews of Jesus' day. They know full well that God commands them to love their neighbor. It goes all the way back to the Ten Commandments (Deuteronomy 5:7–21). The last five of the Ten Commandments relate to not abusing our neighbors or robbing them of their rights as fellow human beings. Is this high regard for our neighbor not a way of loving them, valuing them as God's child? But what does that look like?

Consider the "expert in the law" who approaches Jesus and asks him how to inherit eternal life. "What is written in the law?" asks Jesus. The man's answer is right on target: "Love the Lord your God with all your heart, and with all your being, with all your strength, and with all your mind, and your neighbor as yourself."

But the lawyer isn't finished. Some lawyers never are. He pushes Jesus for a better definition of a neighbor. He's so confidently proud of how he measures up to *everything* in the Law, but he doesn't know what his question is letting him in for. I imagine in his own mind he's already building up a case for how completely, how perfectly, he is kind and caring to everyone in his neighborhood. "So Jesus, *who is* my neighbor," he asks, while he's probably saying to himself, *Boy, wait till he hears the long list of people I've helped!* However many definitions of a neighbor Jesus is going to give, this guy is sure he'll have examples—"Oh yes, I've done that, too!"

On the other hand, maybe I'm too hard on the lawyer. Maybe, along with all his good deeds toward God and others, there's honest self-awareness, a nagging suspicion he's lacking something. Maybe there's even some guilt—maybe, and hopefully, some readiness for honesty.

In reply to the man's question, Jesus tells a parable about "a man [who] went down from Jerusalem to Jericho" (Luke 10:30–37). Jesus' story does three things with that question:

> First, it *obliterates the convenient definition of the day* that says your neighbor is the person in your neighborhood or social group who is a lot like you—not that we don't sometimes have trouble treating *that* person with understanding and love. But here the story is saying there *are* no such boundaries in defining who our neighbor is: he or she is the person God puts before us or allows us to stumble across. However we define "our neighbor," it's too narrow because God will probably confront us with a neighbor that doesn't fit the profile, someone we never thought of or didn't choose.
>
> Second, the story *actually fails to give a definition of a neighbor*. It avoids abstractions and dogmatic conclusions. Who

is my neighbor, Jesus? Tell me! Well, sorry, anything goes here. A definition can't contain what can't be contained. It's the wrong question anyway. Oh? Yes. Notice the third thing the story does:

It *turns the man's question completely upside down.* "Who is my neighbor?" is taken by the story and turned over into another question: "Who was *being* a neighbor to the man in the ditch?" I think Jesus is using the story to say, "You're asking the wrong question. You're a very responsible and religious person, and you want to live up to God's command to love your neighbor. But I won't tell you who your neighbor is. I will teach you and show you how to *be* a neighbor." If that's the question, then the answer is always, "The one who shows mercy." It's not about picking the right person to be your neighbor; it's about letting someone else—anyone else!—claim *your* mercy. The question is not whether that particular person is my neighbor; it's whether *I* am a neighbor to him, willing to give him mercy.

The problem with Jesus is that just when we think we've got something he asks of us figured out, he shows us we've hemmed it in—made it too conveniently and legalistically narrow, something easier to feel holy about. Now let me be clear about what I'm saying when I say this. I'm not saying we can't ever, possibly, meet Jesus expectations. I *am* saying this: Jesus knows who we are capable of becoming, and I'll guarantee it's more than we are now, no matter how far we have or haven't come on this journey called discipleship. He invites us to open our minds, sensitize our hearts, and enlarge our vision of who we are and how we can live as His people.

That is no more true than in understanding who we are called by Jesus to *be* a neighbor to, to love in very specific, concrete ways. Your world and my world—our immediate world—is very rapidly becoming a wide diversity of races, ethnicities, needs, and ideologies. In *this* world in which we live and move and have our being, to whom am I called to be a neighbor? Who is the one in whose face and heart I see Jesus beckoning me to give mercy?

We're not finished with that question and we'll come back to it later because there are some other things Jesus taught and modeled that shed further light on the matter.

Before we move on, we do need to note this: Jesus tied together loving God and loving our neighbor as the two great commandments (Mark 12:29–31). They always go together; they're inseparable. Here's how the Evangelist John, in his first letter, carries Jesus' words to an unavoidable conclusion: We cannot love God and not love our neighbor (I John 4:7–21).

It has been said that some Christians find it easier to love God than to love their neighbor, and other Christians find it easier to love their neighbor than to love God. Is this true? Really true?

The reality may be quite different. Perhaps a person's difficulty in loving his neighbor betrays a shallowness in his love for God. And perhaps a person's difficulty in loving God betrays a shallowness in his love for his neighbor. Perhaps Jesus' invitation for us to see him (Jesus) in "the least of these" is a helpful way into understanding the connection (Matt 25:31–46). Seeing Jesus in our neighbor frees us to love our neighbor. How can we not love the one in whom Jesus cries out for our compassion? The love of God frees us to look into the human heart, which is where God, our Lover, is waiting for us. We see God in *others*, not in distant, cold space, and we see others through the vision Jesus bequeaths to us again and again, as we meet our neighbors, and especially "the least of these."

Chapter 18

All Manner of Outsiders

At the entrance to New York Harbor stands a gigantic statue. Poet Emma Lazarus called it "The New Colossus" in the title to her famous poem graven on a tablet within the pedestal of the Statue of Liberty. The poem mythically contrasts the statuesque celebrations of the cruel conquests of European empires with this warm, hospitable figure, the "Mother of Exiles," from whose "beacon-hand glows world-wide welcome." "'Keep ancient lands, your storied pomp!' cries she/With silent lips. 'Give me your tired, your poor,/Your huddled masses yearning to breathe free,/The wretched refuse of your teeming shore./Send these, the homeless, tempest-tossed to me,/I lift my lamp beside the golden door!'"

Come they have—entrepreneurs looking for new opportunities, non-conformists fleeing religious persecution, imprisoned debtors given a second chance, and many others, mostly from England, Scotland, and Wales. Later, other waves of immigrants came, a more diverse mix of nationalities and ethnic groupings, one wave after another; and as an honest history of this country reveals, the "beacon-hand glow" was not so happily extended, as the descendants of the earlier immigrants, now American blue-bloods, were alarmed and threatened by the different habits and ways of the new arrivals and the inevitable social upheavals caused by their intrusions. Frankly, some of these new arrivals were treated with scorn and even cruelty.

As these waves of immigrants became assimilated over time, however, they themselves became blue bloods of a sort—unless they were of African, Asian, or more recently Latino, extraction. The misfortune of these three groups was that they looked too different, and they either were brought to this country as slaves (Africans) or, for the most part, came as exploited workers (Asians and Latinos). They were "welcomed," not by the beacon glow of full participation in the American Dream, but by the appetites of the hungry engine of economic prosperity. They were allowed in to be exploited. The nation did not want them but needed them. And the callousness with which they were persistently treated was almost as persistently ignored.

The statue still stands in the harbor, and the ideal has in many ways been honored, but it has also been violated. Ideals run up against the reality of fallen humanity and are easily compromised or sometimes transgressed. Human societies tend to tighten their borders, protect them, and hide behind them in fear. Even a nation like America, founded as a refuge for freedom, can occasionally experience a xenophobic outpouring of racial and ethnic hatred.

Against this reality, we hear the message of Jesus. The kingdom of God is an open invitation. Come one, come all, says Jesus, and I will give you rest. No one is excluded who wants to join my family. When you become a family member, you must leave your racism, your ethnic exclusions, and even your xenophobia behind. My church is comprised of people who welcome anyone.

Really? The fact of the matter is that the church's record isn't that clean either.

LET'S REMIND OURSELVES WHERE Jesus grows up and where he ministers. Born in Bethlehem in Judea, raised a proper Jew, he goes to the synagogue (if there is one) wherever he travels. He spends almost 90 percent of his life in Nazareth of Galilee, a very small town. For a while, he settles in Capernaum of Galilee. Matthew calls the province "Galilee of the Gentiles" (Matt 4:13–17)! Originally a part of the Northern Kingdom of Israel, Galilee has been conquered, ruled, and sometimes resettled by a number of Gentile nations. In the time of Jesus Galilee has a substantial Jewish population, but Judean Jews consider them lax and less than diligent in the practice of their Jewish faith. It is worth noting that Jesus spends the lion's share of his three-year ministry outside the heart of Judaism. It is *here*, in Galilee, that he launches his ministry, not Judea, the land of the Jews.

So Jesus is preaching and teaching in Galilee, and the crowds come from everywhere to hear him. They come from the margins, places like Decapolis, the region across the Jordan, and probably Syria, and they also come from Judea of the Jews, including Jerusalem. And where do they go to hear Jesus? To "Galilee of the Gentiles."

In Luke's Gospel a seemingly failed hometown visit to Nazareth follows on Jesus' forty days of temptation in the wilderness. It almost seems a first test of his mission. For a while everything seems to be going well with the visit. On the first Sabbath he is afforded the respect of serving as a reader of a text from Isaiah and of offering comments. When he's finished he sits down and calmly but firmly announces that the prophecy "has been fulfilled just as you heard it." Everyone's amazed at what he says, and they start raving about him. Others are skeptical: Isn't this Jesus, son of Joseph—our local carpenter! Is our small-town boy now presuming to be the Messiah? Who died and passed the royal mantle on to him? And who said the coming Messiah would be giving preferential attention to the poor, the prisoners, the blind, and the so-called oppressed (Luke 4:14–30)? Mark's Gospel especially emphasizes the opposition and scorn of the hometown crowd (Mark 6:1–3).

Things are starting to get ugly, but the situation isn't yet dangerous. However, when Jesus talks more specifically about *Syrians*, like the widow of Zarephath near Sidon, the *only* widow to whom the prophet Elijah was sent, or the Syrian Naaman whose healing by Elisha was the *only* one recorded in Scripture though this particular skin disease was a widespread plague in Israel, things *really* heat up. Imagine the gall of Jesus to put *outsiders* front and center!

Not only do they run Jesus out of town, they try to throw him off a cliff to his death. What is it about the outsiders, those who are not like us, that brings out the worst in us? Why do we see their inclusion as such a threat?

We followers of Jesus would do well to consider our relationship with the outsiders, the "others," those who are unlike us. There's no question we must take them seriously. *Jesus* did. It's interesting, and disturbing, however, that over the course of the church's history, time and time again so many Christians have had a problem realizing that Jesus also came for people who are "*not* like us." George G. Hunter III has given us numerous examples of this surprising Christian paranoia about outsiders in his book *Radical Outreach: Recovering Apostolic Ministry and Evangelism*—surprising because Christians claim to be followers of Jesus, who commissioned his disciples to "go and make disciples of *all nations [ethnicities]*" (Matt 28:19a, italics added). Hunter gives a thorough analysis of how and why this abandonment of the church's mission takes place. Perhaps we could summarize simply by saying that in every instance of abandonment, a self-preserving, self-protecting, selfish spirit infiltrates the church. Fear of other cultures, other lifestyles, other ethnicities, and other races replaces gospel inclusiveness, and fear of adaptive changes that would upset church complacency and open church doors wider paralyzes congregations. Further, a view of the church primarily as a refuge from the world rather than a launching pad for mission immobilizes outreach.

Here are a few of Hunter's historic examples of the church excluding those who were considered outsiders and those who stepped forward to help the church see what they were doing and to lead the way toward inclusiveness:

- Jewish Christians excluding Gentiles in the New Testament church. A response: the apostle Paul and the first-century Gentile mission.

- Urban Christians (most Christians of the second- and third-centuries lived in cities and towns) excluding the less sophisticated rural farm people whom they considered too crude and uncivilized for Christianity. A response: Martin, Bishop of Tours in Gaul in the fourth-century initiating a successful mission to rural populations.

- People of means excluding the working-class poor in eighteenth-century England. A response: the Wesley's revival movement aimed primarily at reaching these people through such measures as preaching in the out-of-doors (a scandal to many Anglicans!).

- The established churches and denominations largely ignoring the great majority of poor who were unchurched and in desperate economic straits in latter nineteenth-century England and other industrial countries. A response: William and Catherine Booth launching a mission in urban slums and creating a Christian movement permanently identified with the poor.

- In the church culture of the latter nineteenth- and early twentieth-century, white Americans and African Americans worshiped separately and almost everyone thought this was the way it was supposed to be. A response: William Joseph Seymour and the Azusa Street Revival in Los Angeles, a fully integrated mission enterprise.

How does this exclusion of certain groups happen in a Church founded by Jesus, who said, "Come to me, *all* who are struggling hard and carrying heavy loads, and I will give you rest" (Matt 11:28, italics added)? How can we exclude *anyone* when John the Evangelist says, "For God so loved the *world* that he gave his only Son" (John 3:16, italics added)? How can a follower of Jesus consider anyone an outsider as far as the church is concerned? The more we read the story of Jesus, the more we are sensitized to the radical inclusiveness of his heart, his action, and his mission. It begins right there with the birth of Jesus in a cow stall, visited by crude, low-class shepherds and strange foreigners we call magi. The child's arms are open in innocent love, the rabbi's arms are open in welcoming love, and the crucified's arms are open, now with redeeming love. Open arms: that's the good news the church too often forgets, sometimes even violates.

Jesus came to the Jews first, because God's mission to the world was to start with them. They were the original people of the Covenant and through them the kingdom of God was to be established in the world. But some of the Jews who were originally converted to the Christian faith forgot that last part. And ever since that time there have always been Christians who have forgotten the mission of Jesus, the mission that excludes *no one*, not even those who are very different from us Christian types.

Reggie McNeal (*The Present Future: Six Tough Questions for the Church*) has described many congregations as very much like private church clubs. Members of those congregations are happy for others to join—so long as they look like, think like, act like *them*—and of course, pay their club dues (otherwise known as tithes). Many congregations don't know what to do when a *real* outsider walks in.

Let us never forget Jesus' encounter with the Samaritan woman at the well, where Jesus crosses all kinds of barriers to connect with a despised half-breed Jewess, someone very unlike him, someone who actually gives him a hard time at first (John 4:1–30). There are many other examples of Jesus' radical inclusiveness in the Gospels.

Consider another kind of person that makes us uneasy: the person whose moral decisions offend us, and we think they are therefore deserving of our exclusion and sometimes our retribution. The story in John's Gospel about the woman caught in adultery is the one that comes to mind (John 8:1–11). This is an amazing story from a number of angles, but I want us to think about what Jesus made the woman's accusers realize: that they are sinners too, and have no right to punish this woman for *her* particular sin (and I presume she *was* guilty).

And after the accusers have all departed, leaving only Jesus and the woman, he says to her, "Woman, where are they? Has no one condemned you?" He then gives her the most powerful blessing she can possibly receive in her disgraced state: "Neither do I condemn you." And he releases her to go and sin no more.

Jesus once said that he passes judgment on no one, leaving it to the Father (John 8:15, 16). We could do the same, if we want to be like our Rabbi Jesus.

Yes, Jesus gives us a very specific guideline for deciding who we are to love: *everyone*—and *especially* those least like us! Loving with boundary-breaking breadth makes us look surprisingly and dangerously like a disciple of Jesus.

Chapter 19

The Shut-Outs

I'm liable to remember Alexander sometimes when the weather has gotten cold. He was a tall, lanky man who used to come to our adult Sunday school class at the church where we were members when we lived in Charlotte. Alexander often wore a bathrobe over his clothes for extra warmth and sometimes carried a small briefcase which we assumed contained his "valuables," perhaps remembrances of family and better times. Some of his nights were spent and meals taken in our emergency lodge, and I'm sure other charitable groups provided him with lodging and food, as well. Who knows where he spent the other nights.

Alexander didn't say much in our SS class. I guess he came because of the warmth and the free coffee and donut. But I'm convinced there was a deeper reason. His eyes were drenched in sadness. His face told us he was lonely. I think he wanted some companionship and a measure of love, to be with people who acknowledged and accepted him as he was. I sensed he wanted to be a part of us, but for reasons lodged in a past I suspect damaged him severely, he didn't know how or was afraid to try. And to be honest, I'm not sure we were sufficiently equipped or willing enough to risk attempting to cross the boundary of his strangeness. At least he kept coming back, searching for something in his own quiet way.

Alexander was a stranger in a world of strangers. The street people of our world are a manifestation of a fact far more pervasive than we may want to admit: strangers are everywhere, they live next door, and some are even members of our own families. It may be even more pervasive than that. It may be all of us are strangers in one way or another.

I grieve over Alexander for a number of reasons: he was poor, emotionally unwell, marginalized. I grieve over our inability to do more than we did to address his deep and largely hidden pain. I also grieve because Alexander points me to a host of other street people, a heart-rending reminder to us that the world in which we live is a haunted woods of the lost. Perhaps we're uncomfortable around street people because their disturbing aloneness shouts at us, and loneliness is not what we want to face because it may push us to feel our own. Street people may remind us of what we have become because we're wandering half-conscious through life, performing our daily routines, but beginning to wonder how well we know each other and how well anyone knows us. Or how well we know ourselves. When's the last time we looked someone right in the eye—really looked that person in the eye—and saw his heart? Or for that matter, when's the last time we took the time to get to know ourselves?

Perhaps I remember Alexander on a winter day because he all too well personifies my own experiences of wintery loneliness. The stranger he puts me in touch with is the stranger in me.

THE GOSPEL PUSHES THIS even further. It says Alexander and his company put us in touch with Jesus. Jesus tells a story about sheep and goats. (It's not really about sheep and goats.) It's about those who find Jesus in the poor, the sick, and the marginalized, and those who don't. Jesus in the shut-outs, those we might otherwise be closer to were it not for their unfortunate economic circumstances, their poor health or disability, or some other condition that makes us uneasy around them. The sheep are the people who share compassion with all sorts of shut-outs. The goats are those who *don't*. What neither the sheep nor the goats yet realize is that they are also showing compassion, or not showing compassion, to *Jesus*. Jesus has to tell them. He has to tell them that he actually resides in the shut-outs, the strangers nearby, the people who suffer the isolation of their poverty, their bad health, or an outcast status. The strangers like Alexander (Matt 25:31–46).

Why is Jesus found especially in the shut-outs? The Old Testament, of course, teaches us that God has a special place in his heart for strangers (Exod 23:9). His covenant people were to remember that they were once strangers in Egypt, and this memory was to be a continuing reminder for them to reach out to the stranger in their midst (Deuteronomy 24:17–18). The Gospels, and especially Luke, are quite explicit is describing Jesus' special affinity to the poor and the outcasts (Luke 4:18; 6:20; 14:13, 21; 18:22; 21:3). Matthew likes to point out Jesus' predilection for spending time with publicans and sinners (Matt 9:10–13; 11:18–19). Jesus shared his heavenly Father's special concern for those considered "extraneous" (from

Latin *extraneus*, meaning something or someone "external," like a stranger, someone who doesn't belong to us, someone to be excluded from our company even though they live in our community). The stranger is therefore someone we think we can and should ignore. "Don't talk to strangers," our parents drummed into our heads when we were small—wise caution for children.

When it comes to adults, however, Jesus takes the opposite view. Befriend strangers, he says. Is he instructing us to do this because he's intent on being the obedient emissary of the Father, who loves the shut-outs? Or is there also something else going on? I suspect there is. I suspect Jesus sees *himself* in the shut-outs he comes across. He knows what it's like to be the stranger in our midst, someone who doesn't fit, makes people feel uncomfortable when they're around him, and often feels almost totally abandoned, especially near the end of his life. "Stranger of Galilee" indeed.

The Word of God doesn't just become flesh in Jesus. The Incarnation is more extreme than that. Jesus risks the strangeness of the most marginalized humans, and he tells us, his disciples, to get in their skin, as he did all his life and especially on the cross.

How can we do that?

Maybe the place to begin is to get acquainted with the strangeness of Jesus. He was acutely aware of his own strangeness, that part of him which others couldn't understand or connect with. We sense his extreme frustration and sadness when even his closest companions are at a loss to grasp what he is saying, sense what his heart is feeling, or know where his journey is leading. Even in the close company of his disciples, he is part stranger. This is not to say they don't have their moments of shared intimacy and joyful fellowship together. It is to say the strangeness of Jesus never disappears. We can never fully understand him, and he is forever finding ways to throw us off or radicalize our all-too-typical behavior. There continues to be something about him that puts us ill at ease. It's the stranger in him, and it calls us to the stranger in us.

What are we ill at ease with about ourselves? What is the part of us that we don't know or don't want to know? Who is the hidden stranger in us? There's a good chance that this stranger, this shut-out part of us, resists the stranger in the other person. What we hide from ourselves hides the other person. I cannot receive the stranger before me if I cannot receive the stranger within me. I cannot enter her pain if I cannot enter my own. Jesus teaches this by the way he receives strangers and shares their pain. The healing he does comes not through a condescension but rather an identification. Stranger meets stranger, shut-out meets shut-out. Suffering is shared. This is compassion. Jesus dispenses no magical healing; he heals through the transformative power of shared love and suffering.

Jesus calls us to share mercy, not pity. Be merciful, he says (Matt 5:7; Luke 10.37). Enter the suffering of the shut-outs. Mercy is not help to get someone off our hands for the time being. It is not help to encourage dependency. And it is not help to make us feel better about ourselves. We show mercy when we actually enter the world of the shut-outs with hearts open and mouths shut, ready to listen and learn, enter their stories, and maybe provide some good help. One of the things that amazed Malcolm Muggeridge about Mother Theresa was how she looked upon the suffering people with whom she worked. Rather than seeing them as "the unfortunate," she saw them as friends of long standing, even as brothers and sisters.

Something changed after World War I, says Philip Slater (*Pursuit of Loneliness*, 20). Before then, the wealthy and middle classes in this country encountered the poor, the sick, and the marginalized on a regular basis. After World War I the better-off began to live in separate areas of the cities, leaving the remainder to areas which soon became poor working-class neighborhoods and slums. This separation became the norm, and it persists to this day. The better-off usually see the poor only occasionally and through a car window. The disabled elderly are in nursing homes, the mentally ill are housed in group homes and out of our sight, and the sick often find themselves in hospitals where the medical professionals take over care. It is certainly far more unusual to encounter them in our world than in Jesus' day. We have to be more willing and more intentional because our society has allowed and legislated them to be shut out.

What can the disciple of Rabbi Jesus do? Maybe start owning the stranger in themself so that they can be brother or sister to the stranger they meet. Maybe choose to cross social boundaries, enter a less secure world, and meet someone they're not entirely comfortable with. Maybe start simply by waiting for an Alexander to show up at church for Sunday school, befriend him when he comes, and try to enter his world in a compassionate way. Learn to be like Jesus with the shut-outs.

Francis of Assisi is also a good model. The young son of a wealthy twelfth-century Italian merchant, Francis is riding his gaily caparisoned horse one day along a road in the Umbrian Plain. As the story goes, he suddenly notices that up ahead of him is a leper, a dreaded sight as leprosy was believed to be highly contagious. Something that isn't fear seizes Francis. He dismounts and walks toward the leper, who is surprised actually to be approached by someone. He is even more surprised when Francis embraces him and kisses the rotted stumps of his arms. Unable to resist the fire of Francis's compassion, he embraces him also. Francis then gives the man alms and gets back on his horse. After he's ridden a few paces, he looks back. He sees no one, and he realizes it was the Lord.

Chapter 20

The Privileged

Chimamanda Ngosi Adichie recently spoke at the Wellesley College commencement. She did not tell the graduating class the kind of things we expect on these occasions: that they must make the best use of their privileges—social, economic, educational—to contribute to the betterment of the world. Instead she told them: "Privilege blinds, because it's in its nature to blind. Don't let it blind you too often. Sometimes you will need to push it aside in order to see clearly" (Quoted in Parul Sehgal, "Power Play").

Adiche may be on to something. We know that in recent years the income gap has been widening. The privileged are becoming more and more privileged, and the underprivileged are becoming more and more underprivileged. One would expect this fact to move a host of the privileged to become concerned about the poor, but a growing body of research reveals the opposite: With a few outstanding exceptions, people with the most social and economic power pay scant attention to those with little such power and have less compassion toward their hardships. (Daniel Goleman, "Rich People Just Care Less," *The New York Times Sunday Review* [October 6, 2013] 12). Nicholas D. Kristof describes "a compassion gap." Many of the privileged, when they see images of poverty, are likely only to reproach. A professor at Princeton found that our brains—presumably the brains of more privileged people—sometimes process images of people who are poor as if they were not humans but things. The poor also tend to be seen as lazy and irresponsible—as if there were not plenty of wealthy people who also fit that description! Evidently, it's inexcusable in the poor. In one psychological experiment, when research subjects were asked to imagine great wealth, or just look at a computer screensaver picturing money, they became less inclined to share or help others. Wealth and

privilege seem prone to attack our feelings of empathy and generosity, which may explain the odd fact that the poorest 20 per
cent of the population give a larger percentage of their income
to charities and churches than do the richest 20 percent. Those
with the largest resources to share with the less fortunate give
a smaller piece of their income. What does that tell us? Does
wealth and power tend to blind people to compassion and dull
their hearts?

A RICH YOUNG MAN wants to inherit eternal life. He tells Jesus he keeps all
the commandments. Jesus knows he has. Mark's Gospel says, "Jesus looked
at him carefully and loved him" (Mark 10:21a). Let's not fall into the trap of
thinking that because Jesus deeply loves the poor and spends most of his
time with them, he cares little for the privileged. His love is not portioned
out inversely according to economic status. He is, however, quite willing,
though sadly, to judge the wealthy harshly when they find the significance of
their lives in the wealth and the status they inherit or attain in this life (Luke
12:15–21; 22:25–27). The reason Jesus tells this rich young man to give away
his wealth is *because he loves him*. When a person's wealth, modest or great,
so consumes his heart and his attention so as to become a ruling Mammon
and therefore his God, Jesus' love for him becomes a love song wooing him
to leave his deceiving lover.

We have seen how Jesus teaches us to guard against allowing wealth
to become Mammon, a false god by which we reckon our human worth or
claim divine favor. The rich young man is told to sell what he has and give
the money to the poor, so thoroughly has he fallen into Mammon's trap.
Only divestiture will now save his soul. (It is a curious fact and should also
be noted, that a certain divestiture of wealth is needed from some who are
underprivileged. Their hearts are corrupted by wealth because they envy
the privileged and lust after their wealth. They are enslaved by this desire,
and it can destroy their soul. Mammon can claim the heart of those with
meager resources, and we should consider no one holy simply because he
lives on little.)

It was the responsibility of every Old Testament Jew to share his resources with those in need. Deuteronomy, chapter 12 describes three essential actions the Israelite must take in order fully to express his gratitude
to God for his providential care. Two are to bring an offering of gratitude
to the Lord (vv. 1–11) and to live as a people in obedience to the Lord and
in holiness before him (vv. 16–19). The third is to share from their blessing
and bounty with "the Levites, the immigrants, the orphans, and the widows

so they can eat in your cities until they are full" (vv. 12–13). The Israelite is to see the underprivileged in the land clearly, keep them ever in mind, and share generously with them. This is a frontal assault on the strategy of Mammon to blind the human soul to the suffering of the economically excluded.

Wealth and status do not automatically corrupt the soul. In Luke, chapter 16 Jesus gives good advice about how to handle our financial resources. He says to use them wisely (v. 8). (The Greek word is *phronimus*, which can mean shrewdly, wisely, sensibly, or thoughtfully.) He says to use them in a trustworthy way (vv. 10–12). He also says, in a curious expression, to use them generously "so that when it is gone, you will be welcomed into the eternal homes" (v. 9). This may refer to giving alms to the poor. As the privileged can help the poor with alms in this age, so the poor can help the rich in the age to come by vouching for their righteous generosity. In Jesus' story of the rich man and Lazarus, Lazarus can provide no help for the rich man in the age to come because of his chosen blindness to the needs of poor Lazarus and his failure to practice practical compassion in the present age (vv. 19–31).

The question the privileged must answer honestly in the presence of Jesus is: For what purpose are you using your money and influence? Whom does your privilege benefit? All of us must answer that question, but in a time like the present of expanding wealth disparity, the answer given by the privileged has larger implications. "Much will be demanded from everyone who has been given much, and from the one who has been entrusted with much, even more will be asked" (Luke 12:48b). Jesus loves the privileged as much as he does the poor. His love, however, is not blind. He knows that amassing wealth and power without acknowledging greater obligation to share it with the underprivileged has two disastrous consequences: the underprivileged suffer more and the reward of the privileged is an eternity of terrible suffering. Jesus loves the privileged by inviting them to love the underprivileged. God calls them—all of them—to compassionate generosity. He knows their temptation to worship their Mammon is particularly acute. He knows that privilege tends to blind. And he knows the combination of the two is spiritually lethal. How, then, can he not call them to see clearly the need before them and share from an enormously generous heart?

Please don't feel sorry for the privileged because God is asking more of them. He is not. He asks the same from everyone. He asks for *everything*. As our lives belong to him, so our resources. As we live to love, honor, and serve him, so we use our resources in ways that express his love for all humankind, honor the values of his kingdom, and invest in what ultimately matters. This is the privileged calling of all disciples of Jesus, whether economically privileged or underprivileged.

How, then, is the disciple of Jesus to love the wealthy and the powerful? As genuinely and as fully as he loves anyone else. Wanting each of them to discover their true humanity in Christ, which in their case cannot happen until they stop defining themselves by their wealth and power and begin using it for holy purposes and acts of compassion.

Chapter 21

Our Enemies

On the day the planes crashed into the Twin Towers, we quickly called a prayer meeting for professional staff and employees in the large foyer of our denomination's regional headquarters. We invited any who wished to offer prayers. One employee prayed a beautiful, moving prayer for the victims, their families, and the rescue workers. She then prayed for the perpetrators of this horrible act. After she finished praying, someone nearby, referring to the prayer for the perpetrators, whispered, "Wasn't that amazing?" A person next to me said, "Yeah, what was *that* about?"

WHAT THAT WAS ABOUT is probably the greatest test—and proof—of our compassion. Our enemies are the outsiders we are most sorely tempted to feel we are justified in excluding from Jesus' command to love one another. We may think, "Lord, we must fight our enemies. But how can we do that if we love them? Jesus, you've got to let us hate them. Surely you grant an exception for people like those Islamic terrorists." And Jesus doesn't back down, doesn't give us an excuse slip.

Consider the words of Jesus in Luke 6:27–29a: "But I say to you who are willing to hear: Love your enemies. Do good to those who hate you. Bless those who curse you. Pray for those who mistreat you. If someone slaps you on the cheek, offer the other one as well."

Jesus could not have said it with greater clarity, and he could not have lived it more fully and courageously than he did. The Gospels give us no example of Jesus using violence, save once or twice when he drives the money-changers out of the temple for abusing and desecrating the court of the Gentiles with their exploitation. His actions have nothing to do with responding to a personal attack on himself; it is not retaliation. And there are no injuries reported. He is defending the victims of this unfairness by interfering with a despicable business, and he is delivering a living parable of honoring the sacred places of our lives. It's one thing to resort to more extreme public action to resist the exploitation of people, as Jesus seems willing to do; it's quite another to take such action or resort to a form of violence on one's *own* behalf, as Jesus has many opportunities to do, but never does.

Recall him on the cross, having every possible justification for hating those who are inflicting on him more pain than we could ever imagine and are enjoying every minute of it. And his only response is, "Father, forgive them. They don't realize what they're doing" (Luke 23:34a). These words, among his very last, were too much for some of the later copyists of the parchment of Luke's Gospel. Unable to let themselves copy down such radical forgiveness, they left those words out of their version! We dare not leave them out of our lives, as so many have.

Forgiving our enemies is a kind of last step toward wholeness. It releases "the love of God that has been poured out in our hearts through the Holy Spirit," to use a phrase of the apostle Paul (Rom 5:5b). It brings love full circle, as refusing to forgive our enemies is commonly seen as the one acceptable hatred on the part of otherwise caring and generous people. If acts of love are love's greatest proof, forgiving our enemies is its greatest test.

Discipleship, as taught and modeled by our Rabbi Jesus, is clearly not for those who allow their fears to control them and turn them into haters. One of the great myths that seduces us is the myth that problems can be solved and our fears relieved through violence. To be sure, sometimes violence is the only way to stop violence that is out of control or that threatens the innocent. Using violence in this way, however, does not solve the underlying problem; it only staunches the flow of animosity for the time being. The solution lies elsewhere, in the place where the grace of God gives us the courage to love our enemy and to let love take us where it chooses. Violence is often the easier way out when we are unwilling to deal with our fear of our enemies, whether that fear is rational or irrational. There are many ways to use violence without much risk for ourselves, whether the way is high-tec drones and missiles used against an enemy nation, or lethal rumors spread about a personal enemy. In the ethics of Jesus and of us his disciples, striking back, getting even, cutting people off is for cowards. The real test for a disciple of Jesus when it comes to dealing with our enemies is to reach out to them, refuse to give or return hate, seek to understand them, love them as precious children of God—in other words, do the direct opposite of what much of our upbringing and socialization has probably taught us!

When the southern states and the northern states of this American Union went to war against each other, it was brother against brother. Citizens of one Union took up arms against other citizens of the same Union.

It was America's greatest family tragedy, resulting in massive carnage. How does one nation family, earlier bound together by a common creed and shared aspirations, now become not only a divided family but sworn enemies? The causes are multi-faceted, but the disputed specifics are not our concern here. We simple want to point out that the American Civil War is just one example of how time and time again over the course of human history, God's created human family has become divided by fear and hatred, brought on by any number of unfortunate circumstances. Brothers become enemies and therefore "legitimate" targets of hatred. Years after the hatred has spent itself in war of one kind or another, the once-divided brothers sometimes wonder how it ever happened, how they or their country could have been caught up in such a cruel tide of retribution, why the violence could not have been prevented. Looking back, they may wonder at the sheer stupidity of it, as if they had allowed themselves to be drafted into a fiction as mad as it is sad.

In Ken Burns's television series on the American Civil War, the narrator describes a remarkable scene which takes place in 1913 on the fiftieth anniversary of the battle of Gettysburg when what is left of the two armies decide to stage a re-enactment of Pickett's charge. The old Union veterans take their positions on the hill, behind the rocks. All the old Confederate veterans start marching toward them across the field below, and then the extraordinary thing happens. As the old men among the rocks begin to rush down at the old men coming across the field, a great cry goes up, only instead of doing battle as they did half a century earlier, this time they throw their arms down, embrace, and openly weep (Frederick Buechner describes this in *Christian Century* [July, 1996] 721).

What has happened here? The war, now a distant memory, was driven by a madness that possessed a nation, the tears of its survivors on that fiftieth-anniversary day the huge flow of a nation's regret. The hatred of war aside, the veterans now see clear, recognizing each other as the brothers they are.

We are like them. We, too, have regrets, and probably many of those regrets go back to when we disinherited another person or group and allowed them to be our enemies. We have no control over who chooses to be our enemy; we only have control over whether *we* decide to have enemies. If we choose Jesus' way of radical love and surrender our enemies to him, there is no telling where it can lead. It may become increasingly difficult for our enemies to hate us if we don't hate or even dismiss them in return. Keeping hatred strong requires that the hatred be returned, or the hatred has lost the vile reciprocity that sustains it. Only inclusive love, which is God's gift, is able to stop the reciprocity. When that happens, having and hating enemies becomes more and more ridiculous, and love begins to look like the only thing that makes sense.

Jesus is our model, pure and simple. Jesus our Rabbi wants us and commands us to love as *he* does—no exceptions, and *especially* no exceptions when it comes to our enemies.

Chapter 22

The World

Look to my right and there she is, staring at me defiantly. The day has only just begun to dawn with enough tree-spotted light to see her clearly. She is an early feeding doe preceding a herd below our cabin. I cannot be seen from below, but she is now to the side of me where the ground passes the large window by my basement-level desk. I am engaged in morning prayers, trying to converse with God, when I'm startled by this very earthly, living presence no more than six feet away. The ground outside is a few feet above the level of my floor, making the large doe appear even more imposing. She stares at me, then snorts, then stomps her right front foot in an aggressive way, and repeats that sequence a few times, never taking her angry eyes off me. She probably has no idea the window glass between us is actually a barrier. Had she known that she would come across me at such a close distance, I'm sure she would have chosen a different route. Too late for that. She must stand her ground and stare, stomp, and snort me down. I hardly move for two or three minutes. Deciding I'm no threat after all, she moves on.

Throughout that encounter I sense this beautiful and magnificent doe is saying to me that this forest is her world, and she's not at all sure I fit into it that well. She's checking me out to see if I can be trusted. I don't think she resents my living here; after all, she quite enjoys eating some of the plants and flowers I grow. Maybe she's observed enough humans in her life to wonder how well we do fit into this world.

Wendell Berry and others who spend time looking at our relationship to the world we inhabit make a distinction between seeing our planet primarily as a place to appropriate for our own ambitions and seeing it primarily as a place to call home. They wonder if those who see our planet as an environment to be exploited and despoiled are winning out over those who see it as a world to be treasured and cared for. If you follow the money, the weather, and the pollution, the answer by far would be the first group. A growing body of scientific study suggests that short of major changes in lifestyle and intervention in practices that do serious harm to the planet, we are headed toward one environmental crisis after another.

Christians seem divided on the question. Some talk and act as if they have no doctrine of Creation. They think this world is going to be trashed anyway, so they let it be raped while they sit around waiting for the Rapture. I remember occasionally hearing disparaging remarks about liberal, tree-hugging Christians. Fortunately the tide appears to be changing, as more and more churches are re-discovering that this planet is God's miracle that he asks us to cherish and a rich resource he expects us to manage responsibly.

THE GENESIS ACCOUNT OF Creation describes God creating everything else, and then us. This world is the natural setting for our human story. He places us here as our suitable, tailor-made home and calls it the Garden of Eden. Banishment from the Garden comes with our denial of the God-given humanity (holiness) with which God has endowed us. Perhaps the banishment is a sign of our now incongruous relationship with this place which was to be our home. Homeless in our earth-home, we often do not treat it as the gift it is. God surely grieves when we become disconnected from our home, when we treat the world as alien, something to be trashed.

Jesus speaks of the created world around him in the most easy, natural way. He spends enormous amounts of time out-of-doors. He speaks, for example, of springs of water, gardens, lilies, grass, mountains, fields, deserts, seeds, streams, harvests, and animals of all kinds. We, on the other hand, live in increasingly artificial environments. The life rhythms of earth mean less to us. The further removed from these rhythms we are, it seems the less our respect and reverence for God's Creation. We enjoy the beauty of mountains and seashore on a three-week vacation or a weekend getaway, only to return to a way of life that is made possible by more extensive exploitation of our planet than we realize. How, then, can we connect with Jesus over this important matter of our relationship to this planet into which God has placed us? How, in our overwhelmingly industrialized civilization, can we love our God-given earthly home caringly rather than abusively?

No doubt Jesus was familiar with Psalm 148, an amazing invitation for all Creation to join together in praising God. The psalmist has the whole universe sounding out, interacting around praise, singing to their Creator.

In our day, where the quest to understand nature is relegated to science, the Psalm seems strange, foreign, even primitive. But is it?

The truth is, scientists are increasingly realizing they are over their heads. There is so much going on out there they do not yet know or are prepared to understand. Theories abound. Many are short-lived or are constantly under revision. One certainty that does seem to be emerging and enduring is that this world is far more alive than we thought, and at levels and in dimensions we never imagined. The previous scientific distinction between animate and inanimate objects, clear as it was, now seems inadequate. There is a lot going on inside that solid rock. When we look at the world around us on a quiet, sedate day and think nature is calm, we are very mistaken. The world is ever awash in interactivity beyond what we can see or hear or feel. Psalm 148 may not now seem so foreign to us. Maybe God is up to something just about everywhere. Maybe Creation does sing to its Creator. Maybe the psalmist knows what he or she is saying.

Jesus looks out on the world around him and sees the aliveness. None of it is outside God's care; all of it he watches over. The lilies and tall grasses of the fields, the birds of the air, all are under his providential care (Matt 6:26-30; Luke 12:24-28). All are loved by their Creator. All are praising him.

God is in love with this world. The psalmist David says that "God's compassion extends to all his handiwork" (Psalm 145:9b). The Gospel of John says God is so in love with it that he gives his Son to it as his gift-in-the-flesh (John 1:14; 3:16), not to condemn the world but to save it (v. 17). In his book of Revelation, John sees in his vision "a new heaven and a new earth" (Revelation 21:1). The earth, it seems, will be re-birthed. All things will be made new. God will then be fully present with humankind. This is the end that is a beginning. The apostle Paul says that Creation's anticipation is so intense it is groaning like a woman about to give birth as it eagerly awaits this salvation on a grand scale (Rom 8:19-22).

We participate in this rebirthing of earth as we love our God-given planet-home and put our love to work by doing our part to restore and renew it. It makes no sense for us to be trashing what God is working to renew. It even makes no sense for us to be leaving it all in the Creator's hands, when he commissioned us to take responsibility for this his earthly creation (Genesis 1:28-31). This earth-care is a stewardship, not a blank check. We are called to love the world as God does.

The old gospel song says, "This world is not my home, I'm only passing through." The lines are both true and not true. It all depends on what we mean by "this world." To some extent our confusion stems from the fact that there are at least three Greek words which the English New Testament translates as "world," and sometimes the same Greek word is used in different ways. The result is that in one passage the English word "world" in our New Testament means God's Creation, and in another passage it means the fallen world, the world under sin's domination. Sometimes "world" has a positive and sometimes a negative connotation. The interpreter needs to be very aware of the intended meaning in each case. The situation is further complicated by the biases of those Christians who see the world as totally and hopelessly under the dominion of Satan, as well as those who see the world naively as a place of innocence. One group, ignoring the doctrine of Creation and our God-given responsibility for the world, sees the earth as a lost cause. The other group, blinding itself to embedded, pervasive, and institutionalized sin, lives in an idealized world of unreality. We should not allow negatively-intended uses of "world" or "worldly" in the New Testament to weaken our doctrine of Creation and God's loving plan to redeem the world. Nor should we allow our naiveté about the world to blind us to its need for redemption. To love God is to love the world, to believe in its ultimate salvation, and to live and work consistently toward that end.

As lovers of God we are called to a worldly discipleship, a discipleship that affirms God's love for the world and participates in his work to redeem it. Jesus invites us to enter the kingdom of God—not a far-off ethereal world of the spirit, but a kingdom set and lived out on earth, our home. According to Jesus, we have to become like children to enter it. It's the child in us that's able to look beyond the messy and messed up, corrupted and exploiting world we see or make as adults, the world we allow to immobilize our souls and freeze our hearts. If we're willing to become like children, however, we see a world transformed by beauty and grace. A world we can truly love. A world we're at home in.

Chapter 23

Our Families

Families birth us, love us, nurture us, form us, teach us, prepare us for life. Some families do it well; others, not so well. Whatever the case may be, we find our first identity in our family. That identity can be so strong that even a family we judge to be highly dysfunctional will usually band together when threatened from the outside or when one family member is attacked. There seems to be a love for our family embedded in us, even though we may not get along. We may even love the parent we never had. I remember hearing a grown woman who had just met her father for the first time being interviewed on the radio. Of all the things I heard, what struck me most was her saying with calm simplicity, "I have always loved him." Always loved her father, having never seen him. No resentment in her voice.

Loving our families seems so built into our DNA that the love is strangely felt even when the parent is absent or abusive. Some family environments, however, are so damaging to children that surrogate parents have to be found. All of us, in fact, find new families as we mature, families that challenge us in new ways—social groups, friendship bonds, church congregations. Leaving home, we find other homes, we begin to work out our connection with the larger human family. If we fail to leave home, even a happy home, we may shrivel under grasping love and suffocating protection, or oppression.

I well remember the beginnings of my independence as a young teenager. My parents were wonderful people who gave me more love and guidance than any child has the right to expect. I had been a dutiful child. I imagine this was especially why they found my growing independence and different ideas difficult to process. It sometimes angered my father, and there were verbal fights. (When I became a father, I began to understand why it was so difficult for him.) My mother handled it all quietly. I can only guess what was going on inside her calm exterior. What I do know is that I needed to find new fathers and mothers, brothers and sisters—people who would accept me and my questions, befriend me, and mentor me. I needed to expand my family. I needed to leave home. Over the years that followed, my parents wisely and lovingly gave me their blessing, knowing I had left home with the very strength, conviction, and faith they had nurtured in me.

God, Christians believe, is a Family of Three—Father, Son, and Holy Spirit, perfectly united in love. Of course, none of them leaves home in order to grow up. The Son leaves home in order to bring us back into the family. The Spirit leaves home in order to help us become and act like one family united in love. Created in God's image we are a family, the family of God, but all too often we don't act like it. The story of our human race is the story of our failures and successes to be a family in God's image. It culminates in the mission of Jesus to bring us back into the family of God and to teach us how to live in the beloved families of which we are a part.

THE GOSPELS ARE STRANGELY quiet about Jesus' childhood and family life. Matthew tells us there was a traumatic period during his infancy when his parents had to flee with him to Egypt where they became undocumented immigrants. When things became more stable back home in Nazareth, they returned (Matt 2:13–23). Luke summarizes Jesus' first twelve years in Nazareth: "The child grew up and became strong. He was filled with wisdom, and God's favor was on him" (Luke 2:40). This would suggest a good family life. Luke then goes on to describe one incident that took place when Jesus was twelve, which in that day and culture was the age when a child entered adulthood. As if to mark this significant life transition, Jesus is in the temple following the Passover festival, questioning the elders and amazing the people with his own answers to difficult questions. He has decided to do this without informing his parents, who are already a day's journey on the way back to Nazareth and assuming Jesus is in the caravan. It took them three days to go back and find him. His mother begins to scold him for his lack of consideration for them. Jesus' answer is a classic version of the teenager beginning to separate from the family: "Why were you looking for me? [I can handle being on my own.] Didn't you know that it was necessary for me to be in my Father's house? [I know what I'm doing.]" Mom and Dad have no idea what he is saying. He's not ready, however, to leave home. He still needs to mature in wisdom, years, and favor with God. He continues to live in obedience to his parents, and his mother, realizing she has a son with personal insight and authority, starts cherishing his every word in her heart (Luke 2:41–52).

Somewhere around the age of thirty he does leave home, a single man. He walks from place to place preaching the kingdom of God. This calling requires that he leave home, family, and the occupation of carpentry for which the son of a carpenter would normally be destined. Does he carry his love for his parents and siblings on his heart to the end? Of course he does. One of the most poignantly tender moments of his last hours on the cross is of a grief-stricken mother looking up into the face of her tormented son, and the son, moved by her mother-love, proudly claiming his lineage through her: "Woman, here is your son." And then commending her over into the care of one of his trusted disciples (John 19:26–27).

Although not himself married, Jesus does emphasize the importance of marriage and family life. He speaks quite strongly of the sanctity and commitment of marriage (Matt 19:3–9; Mark 10:2–12). He emphasizes the importance of honoring one's parents (Mark 7:9–13; Luke 18:20). He also speaks forthrightly about not allowing our allegiance to our family to out-weigh or replace our allegiance to him and to the kingdom of God. On one occasion he expresses this in enigmatically strong terms. After a wonderful parable narrating the inclusiveness of the kingdom of God, he turns to the large crowd and issues a seemingly impossible demand: "Whoever comes to me and doesn't hate father and mother, spouse and children, and brothers and sisters—yes, even one's own life—cannot be my disciple" (Luke 14:26). This does not sound like a rabbi who wants his disciples to love their fami-lies! The truth, however, lies elsewhere. Jesus is using a classical rabbinical form of hyperbole to make an extremely important point. He is not suggest-ing we should actually hate our families, no more than he is suggesting we hate ourselves. He is teaching us to love our families in a way that values, honors, and respects them for themselves, rather than for some illusion we have about them. We give our families the best gift when we give ourselves to Jesus first. Putting our families first dishonors them by treating them as if they were God, which they are not. It causes us to give our ultimate al-legiance to them, which amounts to idolatry. They become our object of worship. They become crippled by the weight of such misguided love. We cannot truly love our families unless we are willing to let go of them when a higher allegiance calls us, or them.

Jesus goes on to say that "whoever doesn't carry their own cross and follow me cannot be my disciple" (v. 27). The "cross" means the ultimate sacrifice of allegiance to the one who is truly our God. Recall the three men Jesus calls to follow him (Luke 9:57–62). Two of the three decline because of family obligations, and Jesus then speaks of hands on the plow and eyes focused on the goal of his kingdom. When we truly love our families, we do not diminish them by making them a distraction to the life to which Jesus calls us. Parents love their children by mentoring them toward discipleship, modeling for them the joy of following Jesus, and caring more than anything for them to discover the love of God. To this end, Jesus is willing, by the use of hyperbole, to startle us into taking a hard look at our priorities. We love our families best when we love God first.

What about all the other families of our lives, our expanded family, the human family? On one occasion Jesus is not far from his home town, so his mother and brothers seize the opportunity to come and see him. Jesus, says someone, your mother and brothers are standing outside, wanting to see you. Your family. "My mother and brothers," he answers, "are those who listen to God's word and do it." (Luke 8:19–21) We aren't told, but my guess is that Jesus does go out to see them. I can't imagine him not doing that. But he decided a year or two before that he couldn't stay at home. His true family was to be a larger family of kingdom-of-God people.

Jesus invites us into a bigger family of "those who listen to God's word and do it." This whole family calls for our love and allegiance. Together as a family we try out living in the kingdom of God. We practice it in our local congregation. It is true that sometimes a congregation does not look like a loving family. It is also true that the best of families have fights. Their love for one another, however, is proven by their resolving the conflict in ways that bring family members closer together rather than further apart. On the other hand, congregations that fight the same battles over and over have fallen out of love, or they have forgotten how to love. Jesus calls his disciples to love one another through good and bad times, and in so doing to model his love for the world.

In becoming members of the body of Christ, we move beyond the narrower world of our natural families and into a larger arena of relationships with other disciples of Jesus. In this arena life becomes more complex, love is stretched by greater diversity, issues become more political. If the church of Jesus has the beauty and fragrance of a rose garden, she is not without her thorny issues as well. Jesus is fully aware of it all. And still he looks over these gathered people, flawed as they are, and says: You are the family I have chosen. You are those who also choose to journey with me and be my disciples. I will be with you the entire way as you help one another become more like me and come to look and act more like my church.

Sometimes becoming a part of Jesus' family divides the families we come from. Jesus is fully aware of this (Matt 10:21, 34–36; Luke 12:52–53). A decision to follow Jesus may put a person in conflict with his family of origin.

One's closest relatives may reject a gospel that reaches beyond their family, ethnic, racial, or religious boundaries. Their insecurity and fear, turned to hatred, may then turn them against another family member who has come to embrace the inclusive love of Jesus. The peace of Christ may stir the fear of reconciliation with perceived enemies. The call of Jesus to a greater love can divide a family. For some, joining the family of Jesus can mean a painful separation. Perhaps, like Jesus, the disciple's truest family is the church.

At their last meal together Jesus says to his disciples, "I give you a new commandment: Love each other. Just as I have loved you, so you must love each other." And then he throws in the real kicker: "This is how everyone will know that you are my disciples, when you love each other" (John 13:34–35). The quality of our family love as a church is central to our *witness*. We, the church, are Jesus' demonstration before the world of the love Jesus makes possible in his new kingdom. The church family is the proof of the power of the kingdom of God to make lovers of us all. "See how those Christians love one another" is recorded in early pagan documents.

It doesn't end there. That same evening, around the table, Jesus starts praying for his disciples, his family, his church. What's he praying about now? He's praying for them when they are out in the world, a scattered family. He's praying for their lives and for their mission. And he asks the Father to sanctify them for that mission (John 17:13–19).

The church is called to reflect that same passion for inclusiveness, that same prayed-for mission, that same openness to the world. There are congregations that do it well. Members love the Lord and one another, and that love flows like refreshing, life-giving streams into the world.

Some congregations don't do it well. Life in the church family can be self-indulgent. Members enjoy each other's company and have wonderful fellowship. They forget, however, that they are in mission to *expand* the family, to go beyond the church walls and invite people who may not be "like us" to join the family. There are congregations who appear to be healthy, loving families and really don't want themselves to be disturbed by anyone else, their claims to the contrary. Truth be told, they want to continue just as they are, or perhaps to return to some idyllic past—which probably never was as good as they imagine! They want a cozy, self-contained family with borders. They have forgotten, or choose not to know, that no such family is part of the family of Jesus.

When we love the church as Jesus loves his Bride, we do not love her as a closed society with cozy fellowship; we love her as a loving family supporting one another and following Jesus into the world in mission. The church is the disciple's ultimate family of identity because, like Jesus, she opens her arms to the world. Such a church is the one true family.

Chapter 24

Ourselves

It's the Saturday before Memorial Day, and I'm shopping at Lowe's to find the replacement part for the storm door at our cabin nearby. Carl, the customer service guy, tries hard to help me find what I'm looking for. When it becomes clear Lowe's doesn't have it, Carl, a Vietnam veteran, decides he can do something else for me. "Have you seen the full-size model of the portable Vietnam War Memorial on display in the park nearby?" "Yes, my wife and I have," I say, "just yesterday." "My best friend's name is on it," he says, the break in his voice giving away a story to be told. And he forgets he's serving a customer, and instead serves me a story about something that changed his life.

When he and his best friend had graduated from high school in Ellijay, they had signed up in the U.S. Army—a decision that brought them eventually to Vietnam. It was their great fortune that they had served together in the same platoon, friends in battle, side by side.

One day they were walking through a village. Everything seemed calm. Suddenly a cute little Vietnamese boy ran over and dropped a grenade right in front of them. Carl's friend was closest to the grenade and threw himself on it. The explosion tore him from limb to limb. Carl received only minor injuries. His friend was killed immediately.

When he finishes the story, Carl is quiet. The air around us is heavy with sadness. Then I sense something else. I see it in Carl's face: gratitude. What is our life worth and how much are we loved when someone is willing to suffer and die for us?

Carl's story reminds me of another story. In the Gospels Jesus also throws himself onto a place of death, lets his flesh be torn open for the love and life of his friends. Those of us who claim this friendship of Jesus have now become his beloveds. Such a privilege, it seems to me, robs us of the right to self-loath.

JESUS SAYS, CONSIDER THE ravens. They don't have to grow or store their food. Yet God makes sure they have it. Just think of how much more he values you! Same with the lilies of the field. God makes sure they are clothed. How much more does he value you! Don't be anxious about yourself, says Jesus. You are loved more than your mind can grasp. You can rest in that love. In fact, God loves you so much, he "delights in giving you the kingdom"! That means: everything worth having (Luke 12:22–32).

We live in a world, a culture that seems to be saying almost the same thing. We hear the message over and over: You're *special*, so you deserve to have everything—or as someone in a recent TV commercial says it, "I have the right to be unlimited!" I'm special because all the marketers tell me I am, and they have all these products I can (and deserve) to buy to prove it. They're telling me to take a break and indulge myself. I need to get away, take a trip—a cruise! It'll make me feel even more deserving and special. I need to get serious about loving myself.

If you were a person of means a few years ago, one of the ways you loved yourself was to have your own personal (and expensive) therapist. You could dump your own low self-esteem and angst on him, and he would help you feel better about yourself. A few years later, the personal coach came along. She helped you improve so you could feel better about yourself. And now it's the personal trainer (You do have one, don't you?). He will help you with your physical, emotional, and professional well-being—and you will like, even love, yourself more. This will build up your self-esteem. You will literally fall in love with yourself. (Oh, you have already?)

The apostle Paul seems to hit the target when he tells Timothy that in the last days "people will be lovers of themselves" (II Tim 3:2a, NIV). I don't deny that good can come out of giving attention to ourselves, giving ourselves a break, improving our self-esteem in some of these ways. I also know there are some real self-improvement, personal image-building scams out there. And I strongly suspect there is much, probably most of this, that doesn't touch the core of who we are as the beloved children of God. It's teaching us ways to love ourselves without giving us much insight into *who* it actually is we are loving. Most people don't see themselves as God sees them. Then who are they loving?

What it means to love ourselves depends on how we see ourselves. If we see ourselves as the center of the universe, then I suppose loving ourselves means giving ourselves everything—because "we deserve to be unlimited." If we see ourselves as having no value whatsoever, then I guess loving ourselves means—well, how *does* such a person love himself? Maybe by trying to please everyone so they'll say nice things about him that he doesn't otherwise have the courage to believe and love about himself.

Why is it so many followers of Jesus, who believe we are incredibly valuable to the heavenly Father, don't seem to love themselves?

Jesus tells a story about a widow (Luke 18:1–8). She is being treated unjustly by an adversary. She goes to the judge, who is well known for his lack of compassion. Again and again he refuses to give her justice or defend her cause. In those days, widows were very easy to take advantage of. So what's she to do? Accept her situation? Just say, "Sorry, but that's just how things are for widows; there's really no way to stand up for yourself, low person on the totem pole of justice"?

She doesn't buy it. She's worth more. She's a beloved child of God. So what does she do? She makes an absolute nuisance of herself. Demands her rights. Again and again.

Finally the judge relents. Gives her justice, even respect. Treats her like a person. And Jesus follows up by saying, "Won't God [who unlike the judge in the story actually cares deeply for us] provide justice for his chosen people who cry out to him day and night? Will he be slow to help them?" Of course not.

Crazy as it may sound, every one of us is on the top of God's priority list. He loves us, and the important thing for us to realize is that we don't know how to let him love us, don't know how to receive his love, *unless we're ready to begin learning to love ourselves.* Unless we can start accepting that we have genuine worth. The Talmud says that when a human being walks down the street, a host of angels precede him saying, "Make way, make way for the image of God."

From time to time we may hear a false teaching that parades as truth about how Christians should treat themselves. It goes something like this: "Jesus is everything, I am nothing. I must ignore my own desires, my own wishes, my own needs, my own interests, my own *life*—for Jesus. In fact, I can't *have* a life. All my love goes to Jesus; there's nothing left for myself."

After all, we were taught in Sunday school that we find joy when Jesus is first in our lives, others are second, and we are last. So we work hard for Jesus, and for others, and sometimes (maybe often) there's not much love left for us. Myself last, last, last. . . . We may even think we'll please Jesus if we work ourselves to the bone, or to the point of a breakdown.

William Law said if we love God and are in his image, we will then love who and what he loves. And this includes ourselves. Self-love is a legitimate form of Christian love. It is, in fact, the standard for love of our neighbor: " . . . love your neighbor *as you love yourself*" (Matt 19:19b, italics added). John Wesley said proper self-love is not a sin but an indisputable duty of a follower of Jesus. It's sinful to hate who or what God loves. If God loves me, I love me. But doesn't that sound egotistical? I'm learning it's just the opposite.

People we label as egotistical don't really love themselves, or they wouldn't be so desperately bragging or self-promoting or trying every which way to impress you. They don't *really* love themselves, and God wishes they would.

What is even sadder are the people who have been beaten down and have a very low self-image, thinking more lowly of themselves than they ought to think. People like:

- The woman taken in adultery. Jesus defends her against her self-righteous, misogynist accusers, refuses to define her by her sins, and gives her a new beginning (John 8:3–11).

- Jesus looks past the put-down by blind Bartimaeus's detractors and, opening his eyes, releases him for a new life (Mark 10:46–52).

- Jesus sees a crippled man by the Pool of Bethsaida who is powerless to claim the waters when they are brimming with healing, and lifts him to full stature and respect (John 5:1–9).

Jesus' empathy for the lowly-regarded knows no bounds, freeing them to love and respect themselves.

Some of us have trouble loving ourselves, so we're always trying to make ourselves worthy in some way. We aren't comfortable letting someone express their love and appreciation to us because we have always to be proving ourselves to everyone. It's a very strong temptation to those of us who are workaholics. As if our work, our accomplishments are what make us likable.

John's Gospel records an unexpected event at Jesus' last supper with his disciples. He begins to wash his disciples' feet. That is not something the host is supposed to do; it's the house servant's job. Once again, Jesus is violating a social norm, so it must signal something worth taking notice of. Yes, Jesus is modeling servanthood, but that isn't all. He is expressing in a rather intimate way his love for his disciples. Always-trying-to-prove-himself Peter tries to resist. "No," he says, "you will never wash my feet." The voice of Jesus says, "Unless I wash you, you won't have a place with me." I think the eyes of Jesus say, "Peter, let me treat you as my beloved." And Peter does (John 13:1–9).

Keitha and I had a foot-washing with the teaching staff of our college for training Salvation Army officers. Afterward we asked each person to share with the group what the experience was like, or what it may have revealed to them. What was intriguing was the number who were uncomfortable letting a Christian brother or sister wash their feet. Part of the discomfort, of course, was the strangeness in our social setting and culture of allowing someone to touch and clean what was not the most beautiful part of our bodies. But it was more than that, and some confessed it with insight about themselves: They were at home ministering to others; they were not comfortable with letting someone minister to them, especially in this very physical way—as if the tender touch of the minister's hand unleashed in them a discomfort with their lovable-ness.

Jesus invites us to learn to love ourselves. Why? Because we are those whose feet Jesus wants to wash, to show us how much he loves us. We are those he loves so much he walks this earth for us, and then he dies for us. We are those the risen Christ is present with, still loving us, through eternity.

Jesus wants us to love ourselves.

Luke records a parable of Jesus that is startling (Luke 12:35–37). When you start reading it, you think it's going to be one of those stories about being watchful and prepared—and it is, only there's more to come. The master of the house is evidently off at a wedding banquet, a late night affair. The servants are probably saying to themselves and each other: Don't fall asleep. Be ready to welcome him back and serve him. That's our job, our calling.

When the master does return, they're in good form, ready to serve him. So far, the story is going in the usual direction of showing preparedness for Jesus' return. Something strange happens, however. There's a departure from the expected script. The master changes into servant's clothing and asks *them* to recline at the table for a meal. Then he waits on them. The master waits on his servants!

Some of us may need to get ourselves prepared to let Jesus wait on us, serve us, care for us, love us. Allow ourselves to be treated as the deeply loved and valued persons Jesus says we are. All of us are those more-than-servants. We are the dearly beloved of God.

Jesus' love for us is so strong it frees us to love ourselves. Not by surrounding ourselves with the stuff we think makes us look more impressive, not by self-indulgence and over-indulgence, not by desperately doing things to makes us look more lovable. Jesus invites us to love ourselves because *he* does, because he claims us as his own, because he knows us far, far better than we know ourselves. Warts and all. He sees the image of God in us, even when we don't or it isn't showing so well at the time.

There's far more to us than we know. Jesus does know, and we can trust him with it all. If we try to understand ourselves we come face to face with mystery. Fact is, we're beyond definition. That's the way God made us.

While he was a prisoner at Flossenburg, awaiting death at the hands of the Nazis, Dietrich Bonhoeffer wrote a poem about his identity. In the poem, he admits he's a mystery to himself, but he expresses the most important thing about himself in the last two lines:

Who am I? They mock me, these lonely questions of mine.

Whoever I am, Thou knowest, O God, I am thine!

(*Letters and Papers from Prison*, 173)

In the care of the God who knows us and loves us for reasons only he fully understands, we can believe there's reason enough to love ourselves. In the company of Jesus, who lived and died for us, we see down-to-earth proof of it. Through his Spirit he draws us into the fellowship of his church where we live our lives among those who help us love ourselves and love each other. And we live our lives in the world in such a way as to give those we interact with the impression that they, too, are God's beloveds.

The Art of Loving

Chapter 25

Loving Extravagantly

Our grandson Will was about two years old when we took him Christmas caroling to a nursing home. A quartet sang the carols in the hallway while Will and I went in each room to greet the residents, wish them a merry Christmas, and give them a modest but practical Christmas gift and a Christmas publication.

As you would expect, the residents were usually most delighted by the presence of a two-year-old boy. Shy little Will got all the attention. There was a lady in one of the rooms who decided to tease Will a little. She complimented him on his beautiful bright red sweater, told him she liked it so much she wondered if he'd give it to her. Without hesitation he started taking it off. When the lady realized he was actually going to do it, she was embarrassed. I guess she thought she was teasing him into a state of childhood uncertainty about what to do with such a strange request. For Will there seemed to be no perplexity.

A couple of years later, Will learned that there were people so poor that they slept under bridges and overpasses. Every time we drove under one, he would scan each side of the road to see if there were any homeless people. With so many fascinations in his media-drenched world, why would Will be so drawn to this suffering? Was it because in a world of families and homes, there seemed to be something terribly wrong when some people had neither?

I wondered at what point in a person's life does he lose this sensitivity to the suffering of others? At what point does he refuse to give the sweater off his back when asked? When does our loving become particular and choosy? When does loving others lose its spontaneity and become measured and calculated? When does the suffering of others start to affect us less and less? When do we all start learning the dreadful habit of not giving away?

THE GOSPELS ARE SUFFUSED with the extravagant love of God. God loved the world *so much* he gave *his Son*! Jesus' life is an extravagance of compassion, climaxed at the end with his accepting unspeakable violence against his body and his personhood. And he does it, not as a helpless victim but, he says, "because I want to" (John 10:18). He allows love to kill him so that love can live. The extravagance of divine love.

The first miracle of Jesus recorded in John's Gospel is found only there, and yet it sets a theme we hear in many variations in all four Gospels. It is this theme of divine extravagance. Jesus, his mother Mary, and his disciples are attending a wedding in Cana, not far from Jesus' hometown of Nazareth. For such important occasions the host is expected to have plenty of wine in store. On this occasion the wine runs out. Either the host planned poorly or more people showed up than anticipated. Mary may sense her son can do something to solve the problem. She says to him, "They have no more wine." He takes it as a hint and expresses an understandable caution about his taking this particular miraculous action so early in his ministry. After all, this miracle, if he performs it, could be understood as the sign of a messiah totally focused on better physical conditions, a messiah of the world of power politics and economic prosperity. This is not his mission, though he clearly cares about physical suffering in the world and the abject poverty of so many. His mission is to transform the heart and restore authentic community. His response to his mother's urging is therefore very guarded: "Woman, what does that have to do with me? My time hasn't come yet."

Mary senses her son's reticence, but probably more than anyone she knows his heart. Quietly and without fanfare, she whispers to the servants, "Do whatever he tells you." They follow Jesus' instructions and fill six stone jars with water.

The real significance of what then happens is not just that Jesus turns the water into wine. The miracle is that it's the best wine yet. Typically, the host serves his best wine first, and if that runs out, he brings in the lesser wine for the now inebriated (and therefore less discriminating) guests. Jesus doesn't simply fulfill the need for wine—*any* wine—he exceeds the need with extravagance. (John 2:1–11) He sees what the Father does, and he does the same (John 5:19; 10:37). The Father who gives in abundance is imitated by Jesus, the Son, who follows the divine family pattern and gives extravagantly.

Jesus our Rabbi is teaching us to see God as an extravagant lover who gives us better than we ask or expect. This "better than" has more to do with quality than quantity, more to do with what is deeply fulfilling than what is temporarily satisfying. It's the forever thirst-quenching water Jesus offers to the Samaritan woman at the well, water that becomes for the drinker "a spring . . . that bubbles up into eternal life" (John 4:13–14). It's water made into the wine of extravagant love.

We pray to the Father to meet our needs, and sometimes our requests are either petty or self-serving, paltry or bloated. We want a little, or too much, wine—and Jesus wants to give us truly satisfying vintage. His storehouse is compassion, fleshed out on a cross. As disciples of Jesus, we enter this world of the incredible abundance of divine love. We open our hearts to amazing grace, shocking serendipities, and deep fulfillment. And we go a step further: We share this abundance with the world. We become extravagant lovers.

Jesus teaches us that extravagant love is not indulgent love. It is humble love. It is not manipulative love, forcing someone to love in return, like a self-sacrificing parent who weakens his or her child into dependency by making sacrifices to garner the child's guilt and exert an insidious control. Extravagant love reveals a heart of genuine giving without a demand or implied obligation on the part of the other. It stands on its own as God's way of loving, an act inviting imitation rather than compensation. Jesus allows the rich young ruler to depart unresponsive, though it grieves him deeply (Luke 18:23). God made us in his image, and when we experience the abundance of his love, a call is heard to become who *we* really are: extravagant lovers in his image.

Jesus calls his disciples to be these extravagant lovers. "I've given you an example," he says: Wash one another's feet; do those kinds of extravagant things to release the power of your love (John 15:12–17). Don't stop the lady with the alabaster jar of very expensive perfume; let her be extravagant with her love for Jesus (Mark 14:3–9; Matt 26:6–13; Luke 7:36–47). Don't criticize that father who welcomes his prodigal son back with the open arms of grace; don't you require this returned prodigal to earn back every bit of what he threw away (Luke 15:11–32). Oh, and let the Johnny-come-lately workers in your kingdom receive more than they earned (Matt 20:1–16). And don't try to stop Jesus from giving that no-good thief on the cross next to him—What? *Paradise!* (Luke 23:32–43). Extravagant love gives us more than we expect or think we deserve, shocking us with our own value in the eyes of God.

Sometimes Jesus allows compassion to make exceptions even to the rules. Remember the time he is in a synagogue teaching on the Sabbath—a very proper thing to do on the Sabbath. He spots a severely crippled woman standing nearby. She's so bent over she can hardly catch his eye. Jesus invites her to step forward, and without a thought he puts his hands on her and straightens her up, and she praises God. He has healed her, but this is not a very good thing to do on the Sabbath according to the synagogue leader.

Jesus, you've got six days in the week to do this sort of thing. Why must you heal on the Sabbath? This woman didn't even ask you to (Luke 13:10–17). Such unnecessary extravagance!

Do we sometimes let our rules stand in the way of love's extravagance? Jesus does not set out to break the Law, but when it is a contest between compassion and conformity, guess which one comes out on top. Sometimes we are so bound up by our rules and bound in by our limits, we smother the tremendous capacity God gives us to care and help. Sometimes we let our own cautious, planned, calculated goodness stifle our openness to love's extravagance. It's worth keeping before us Jesus' response to the "wasteful" anointing of him by the woman at Bethany: " . . . wherever in the world the good news is announced, what she's done will also be told in memory of her" (Mark 14:10).

Extravagant love is always costly. If it comes cheap, it is something else. "Costly" is defined in relation to the source from which the gift comes. If a wealthy person gives, say, 10 percent of his annual income to the poor, that is commendable generosity, but it does not necessarily flow from extravagant love. If, however, the wealthy person looks at all his resources as God's gifts to be used for the kingdom of God and the betterment of the poor and marginalized (rather than his own self-advancement, self-indulgence, or self-aggrandizement), he is dangerously near extravagant love, liable to the accusation he takes the command of Jesus too seriously.

Most of us would not consider ourselves to be wealthy persons, but we all have a measure of wealth, paltry as it may seem in comparison to the top 1 percent of the population. Jesus still calls us to be extravagant lovers and view our resources as gifts to be shared. Furthermore, we all have other kinds of wealth, other gifts God has blessed us with, other advantages that have come to us by way of our particular circumstances or our own determination. We fully understand what Jesus asks of the rich young ruler when we see *ourselves* as those who are addressed by Jesus in the story, as those who are being asked to give who we are and what we have to this kingdom of extravagant love. The story is not told for the wealthy only. It is told for us all, who also have everything to give. How can we otherwise be disciples of Rabbi Jesus, who models for us extravagant love at every turn and at the very end?

Will God bless us for our extravagant love? Certainly—but not in the expected way! Remember the time Jesus is at the home of one of the leaders of the Pharisees, and he notices how the guests, when they arrive, tend to seek out the best seats for themselves? He comments that those who want to taste kingdom-of-God life do the opposite: they seek the *lowest* seats. Then he turns to his host and says, "When you host a lunch or dinner, don't invite your friends, your brothers and sisters, your relatives, or rich neighbors. If you do, they will invite you in return and that will be your reward." I imagine one of the dinner guests responding: Well, then, who do I invite? "Invite the poor, crippled, lame, and blind," Jesus answers. Still trying to figure it out, they conclude that the blessing must be the good feeling doing such a kind thing stirs up in us. No, says Jesus, the blessing is that "they can't repay you."(Luke 14:1–14). Our extravagant generosity, our outpouring of love brings a strange blessing: The recipients of our good works give us nothing in return. They *can't*. Can't pay us back. And this is precisely how we begin to learn the art of loving extravagantly.

Chapter 26

Loving Intimately

The Church of St. Paul in Venice, Italy has an interesting painting of the Last Supper by Tintoretto. Jesus is characteristically seated in the center facing the viewer, and the disciples are around the table. When I first saw the work I was struck by the disciple in the foreground who was positioned to face Jesus directly. His attention, however, was directed elsewhere. He had turned halfway around, to a beggar seated on the floor. He was giving the beggar bread. I thought to myself: Tintoretto is making a connection between this sacred, shared meal with Jesus and our calling to share our resources with the poor and marginalized. He is teaching us that our communion with Christ is empty religion if it does not compel us to compassion.

Then I learned what the painter actually intended. I had missed the detail of the moneybag hanging from the disciple's belt. He was Judas, the disciple who saw the kingdom of God in economic terms. Judas was aligned with Jesus' concern for the poor, but his hope to improve their lot lay in a political revolution. Perhaps his betrayal of Jesus, to take place later that evening, was his attempt to force Jesus' hand. Or perhaps he had given up on Jesus, seen the danger coming, and decided on treachery. His giving the beggar bread, his charity toward the poor, was his best. His failure to connect with Jesus in an intimate way and allow Jesus to change him was his worst. Jesus' mission was not to gather and train a cadre of militant rebels to establish a better political kingdom; it was to gather a band of intimate, imitating disciples who would allow their hearts and their lives to be transformed.

Judas chose charity over intimacy. At this most significant meal with his Lord, he looks away from Jesus to administer bread. Charity can actually be an escape from intimacy. In Matthew's Gospel, Judas leaves to arrange his betrayal just after the anointing at Bethany when the disciples object to the woman's actions of using up expensive perfume that could have been sold for money to give to the poor (Matt 26:6–16). Was the anointing the last straw for Judas? Was his betrayal the sign of his unwillingness to allow Jesus to look into his own heart, the act of his resistance to intimacy with God and his neighbors—even the poor, whom he wanted to help but not know? We cannot be entirely sure, but Tintoretto is raising these questions.

Another interesting aspect of the painting is that to the right and more in the background is another disciple who is reaching out to give bread to a child. Perhaps Tintoretto did not wish to exclude compassion toward others from the sacred meal. Perhaps he wanted to make a connection between real intimacy and genuine acts of compassion.

THE WORD INTIMACY COMES from the Latin *intimus*, which means innermost. Intimacy therefore means touching someone at a deeper level, to the extent the person is willing to be accessible and we are willing to take the risk.

Loving intimately is loving up close. Sometimes we love people at a distance, as when we contribute money to help someone or we love someone we don't have a close relationship with because, for example, we have been helped by their teaching or writing. There are, of course, many situations and settings where intimacy would be offensively invasive. In this hi-tech age, unfortunately, there are fewer and fewer places for real intimacy. The world of the internet is fast-paced and impatient. There is less and less space and time for deep conversation. Most relationships are short-term, most interaction brief, information is the higher priority, and depth is rare. The result is a growing hunger for real intimacy. We do not know one another's heart.

Jesus says, "I know my own sheep and they know me, just as the Father knows me and I know the Father" (John 10:14, 15). These words have the flavor of intimacy. Jesus has the heart of the Father, and as we get to know Jesus we get to know the Father. At the Last Supper Philip asks, "Lord, show us the Father; that will be enough for us." Jesus is surprised he hasn't caught on yet: "Don't you know me, Philip?. . . . Whoever has seen me has seen the Father. . . . I am in the Father and the Father is in me" (John 14:8–10). Jesus invites us to love him for who he *is*: the man in whom the heavenly Father dwells in all his fullness. *See* me for who I am, he says. *Love* me for who I am: the one sent from God, in whom God fully dwells. In me you see the Father; in me you love the Father.

Truly to love Jesus is truly to love God, who is not some distant deity "up there," watching Jesus play out the gospel story. He is *in* Jesus, one with Jesus, and when we see Jesus—really see him—we see God up close. Jesus offers us intimacy with God. Because of Jesus we don't have to love God at a distance. We don't have to love a God we don't really know. Jesus invites us to love God up close and personal by loving *him*, Jesus.

The Song of Songs is a very unusual book in Scripture. It is very intimate love poetry written by lovers. Apart from the honesty and forthrightness of its description of sexual love, why has it found its way into our Bible? What did the guiding hand of the Spirit have in mind? Importantly, it's an affirmation of positive, healthy sexuality. And it's more. It seems to parallel our relationship with Christ at the deepest, most intimate level. It speaks of a true knowing of another person, a knowing that is loving and not controlling, a knowing of the heart that the mind cannot fully grasp. A true Intimacy.

Jesus spends much of his time with the twelve disciples so that they can know him more intimately and he them. Their love is deep. In the end this deep love will win out in their lives, save for Judas, who never, it seems, risks intimacy.

Jesus tells a parable of people trying to enter a house, which in the story is a metaphor for the kingdom of God. Some aren't allowed in. The owner says he doesn't *know* them. They protest to the owner: "We ate and drank in your presence, and you taught in our streets." Surely this association is a sufficient entry visa. The owner responds with a chilling fact: "I don't know you or where you are from" (Luke 13:22–30). Now wait just a minute! God knows us all, and he knows where we all come from. Look how the parable ends: with people from all over the place, even places unheard of—north, south, east, west—coming into the family of God's kingdom, joining the banquet feast. People God knows and who know him—but not with fact checks. Heart to heart.

God knows the facts about us, the good ones as well as the hidden ones, the embarrassing ones, the shameful ones. And we may know a ton of facts or doctrines about God. Maybe we got an A+ in Sunday school. We ate and drank with you, and, Lord, we came out to hear you preach and teach. We've been in church a ton! Doesn't that count for anything?

Intimacy, real intimacy, is what Jesus wants, and what our heavenly Father wants. He wants a love affair with us, from here to eternity. He wants to know us, heart to heart, forever. So he invites us to get to know and love him deeply. He invites us to intimacy.

How do we find this intimacy? Like Jesus, we find it in solitude. We separate ourselves, as Jesus did, in order to hear God speak and to learn to listen. We study Scripture and practice the spiritual disciplines. We open our hearts and expose our needs and confess our perplexities. And we keep listening. That is not all, however. We do not stay within the confines of our private world. We find the intimacy we seek with God through one another. God speaks to us through one another. We seek Christ in one another. We help each other find the Christ within, the Christ who frees us to be who we really are. As we discover the Father in Jesus, so we discover Jesus in each other. The time will come, says Jesus, when "you will know that I am in the Father, you are in me, and I am in you" (John 14:20). Our love is not blind; I see Christ in you and you see Christ in me. This is what happens in the church. The church is where we see Christ in one another. Then we can learn to find Christ in the world, and particularly in those who suffer (Matt 25:31–46).

This intimacy does not require psychological training. It is not a one-way search to find hidden motives or deep-seated problems in another person. It is a willingness to share honestly what we are comfortable or willing to share with each other in trust, and an acceptance of one's decision not to share. It is not invasive probing, it is respectful, patient listening. It is where reaching the heart is more important than learning the facts. The result is the gift of a lover's insight rather than a therapist's analysis.

Jesus invites us to intimacy with him and with one another. He invites us to love each other insightfully, to see each other as we truly are, persons in whom Christ is being born. And if we help each other find the Christ in us, we will help each other become carriers of Christ and spotters of his kingdom in the world and in the lives of other people. We will share bread and other kinds of help with those whose stories we listen to and to whose hearts we open ourselves.

Chapter 27

Loving Un-possessively

Poet W. H. Auden portrays Mary, the Mother of Jesus, holding her child in her arms. She is aware that what the child sees in her eyes is a mother's tenderness, a jealous protectiveness. She wants only the best for him. Like any good mother.

Mary senses something else, however, and it's enough to tear her heart. While she was pregnant she had heard the angel prophesy the future of her child-to-be with words that astounded her: "He will be great, and he will be called the Son of the Most High. The Lord God will give him the throne of David his father. He will rule over Jacob's house forever, and there will be no end to his kingdom" (Luke 1:32–33). Why would such news be torture for the proud mother? Well, she also remembers the final words of Simeon's prophecy, when she and Joseph took Jesus for his presentation in the temple. "And a sword will pierce your innermost being too" (2:35b). What terrible thing will bring such deep pain? What will happen to my precious son? Is it really necessary that his success come though suffering?

Mary senses her own resistance to such an ugly and cruel way to save a nation. She may have heard Isaiah's prophesies of a suffering servant, but no mother wants that for her child. And yet she must know in her soul there is truth here. Prophets usually suffer for their courage to speak truth and confront the Godlessness of both pagan compromise and religious hypocrisy. Not to mention kings who do the right thing. Is there no way other than suffering for righteousness to win?

Mary is honest and humble enough to confess the selfishness of her own maternal love for Jesus, her own protective resistance to the fulfillment of his God-given calling. Auden imagines Mary wondering to Jesus if her love for him will "but tempt you from [God's] will" (W. H. Auden, For the Time Being).

The painful challenge for Mary—and for every caring mother and father, and for anyone who loves, for that matter—is how to love un-possessively. We all have hopes for those we love. None of us wants to see those we love suffer. But love must be willing to give up the dreams and plans for a beloved, no matter how good and noble they are. Real love cannot possess, only give itself and surrender claims.

JESUS IS OUR MODEL of un-possessive love. We see it in his interaction with people. He heals the deranged demoniac of Gerasa, who then places himself totally at the disposal of Jesus to travel with him and serve him; Jesus, however, releases him to return home and freely give witness there. He releases the woman taken in adultery, freeing her to go and sin no more. He levels with the rich young ruler by telling him that his way into the kingdom of God is to sell what he has and give it to the poor, and then he lets him go on his own to wrestle with the choice. Jesus could become a competitor to John the Baptist, and though some of John's disciples come over to him on their own accord, he never engages in sheep-stealing from his cousin. Those who become Jesus' disciples are not coerced or manipulated into dropping everything and following him; they sense in him what their hearts desire, and choose to follow.

Religious leaders who lead by control are not followers of Jesus. They are manipulators who actually crave the adulation and blind obedience of others. They are addicted to spiritual power over others. Possessive love is no love. It is idolatry of the self.

Some Christians see God as someone who simply wants to take charge of their lives, as if God were some kind of control freak. Their favorite testimony is: God is in control of my life. That may provide a kind of personal security, though who's to say that the control is actually coming from God and not from some tape playing in one's mind, some voice from another source? Furthermore, when the person says he is making a decision or taking a specific action because God told him to do so, is he absolving himself of personal responsibility? Who can question what I'm doing if I'm doing what God told me to do? Or perhaps what my divinely directed spiritual leader told me to do?

The question is: Does God actually want to control us? We could say that if anyone has the right and the power to love possessively, it is God. But does he? Is God's love a possessive love? What his heart and his ways tell us is that it is not. He doesn't want to possess us, and we don't lose our freedom when we give ourselves to him. Jesus speaks of someone being possessed only when he speaks of possession by an evil spirit or a demon (for example, Mark 1:32; 5:16; Matt 4:24; 8:16; Luke 8:36). It is the nature of Satan to possess; it is the nature of Jesus to free. And when we speak of "possessions" to refer to the things we own, Jesus clearly warns about the danger of those possessions possessing us (for example, Mark 10:22; Matt 19:22). The early church in Jerusalem took this warning to heart by sharing their possessions and even considering no goods or lands as their own (Acts 2:44–45; 4:32–35).

If God doesn't want to be in control of us, why, then, does Jesus, and all of Scripture for that matter, speak of obeying him? God, it seems, does ask for an obedience, but it is a peculiar obedience. He calls us to surrender ourselves not to his control but to his love. He is not interested in oppressing us, as the demons are. He's interested in loving us, giving himself to us, calling us to who we really are—and leaving the rest to us. He's interested in the voluntary obedience of our love for him and for his whole human family. This, in fact, is the pattern he gives us. The power of Jesus' life is not God's control over him but God's love for him, and Jesus responds to the Father with a loving obedience of his own. He tells his disciples that his very sustenance is "doing the will of the one who sent me and completing his work" (John 4:34). Near the end, in Gethsemane, he is still true to this consuming motivation, surrendering not to blind obedience but to knowing love, showing us a pure humanity (holiness). If we, Jesus' disciples, want to take the measure of our own love for God, we can study and meditate on the love story of Jesus, and begin to shape our lives accordingly.

Un-possessive love works both ways in our relationship with God. As God doesn't want to control us, we don't—and can't—control God. It's not that he doesn't want us to ask for favors. He actually gives us an asking prayer, and he says the Father knows what we need before we ask him (Matt 6:8b-14; Luke 11:2-4). He doesn't, however, give us all the answers we want; even Jesus didn't claim to have all the answers (Matt 24:36). Nor does he keep us from suffering. In fact, Jesus affirms the blessedness of suffering for living righteously (Matt 5:10-12), and the apostle Paul makes clear that persecution for following Jesus is inevitable when he tells the Philippian church that God has generously granted them the "privilege not only of believing in Christ but also of suffering for Christ's sake" (Philippians 1:29). Nor does Jesus guarantee we will not have times of emptiness or pain when we don't feel his presence with us—as he himself experienced during the agony of the cross (Mark 15:34; Matt 27:46). We can't control God as we may like.

How, then, do we deal with the occasions when Jesus not only encourages us to make our requests to God but also assures us that we will receive what we ask (Matt 7:7-8; Luke 11:9-10)? We can begin to understand when we read further in those Matthew and Luke passages. Matthew has Jesus qualifying God's answers by calling them "good gifts" (Matt 7:9–11), and Luke has him qualifying God's answers by saying that the response, the gift, is "the Holy Spirit" (Luke 11:11–13). We have moved from receiving whatever we ask (with no conditions stipulated at first), to receiving what are qualified as "good gifts," to (and here's a huge leap) receiving the Holy Spirit. Whatever the answers to our prayers, they come with the Holy Spirit. John's Gospel gives help, as well. He records Jesus as saying, "I will do whatever you ask for in my name, so that the Father can be glorified in the Son. When you ask me for anything *in my name*, I will do it" (John 14:13–14, italics added). Here we learn that we receive what we ask when our request glorifies the Father (as opposed to, well, ourselves) and we ask for what fits well with the name of Jesus. The latter assumes, of course, we know all about Jesus. If we don't, ignorance is not bliss but a blindness that has us asking for things that have nothing to do with the kingdom of God, or worse, work against it. In the next chapter of John we hear Jesus making the point on a deeper level: "If you remain in me and my words remain in you, ask for whatever you want and it will be done for you" (John 15:7). There is an intimacy where we know more and more of the heart of God through our knowledge of Jesus, and in the times when what we're asking is what God actually wants for us, or fairly near. This is un-possessive prayer.

Un-possessive prayer flows from our un-possessive love for God, each other, and his world. How do we nurture such prayer? One way, says Jesus, is to pray with others, in a group as small as two or three. With the guidance of the Holy Spirit, the group prays to discover God's will in a particular matter and then petitions that it be done (Matt 18:19–20). When God's will has not yet been discerned, whether by God's choice or by our blindness, it is still God's will we pray for. The lack of discernment may be the result of an unconscious resistance to what we fear God may have in mind and what it may cost us. Or how we see what we're asking for and how God sees it may be miles apart. When James and John come to Jesus and ask Jesus to seat one of them directly on the right and the other directly on the left of him when he enters his glory, Jesus quickly replies, "You don't know what you're asking! Can you drink the cup I drink or receive the baptism I receive?" They quickly respond, "We can," so eager are they for the prize of high position in a fully realized kingdom. They obviously don't get it: the kingdom will cost them everything. Furthermore, Jesus can't hand out positions; there is no telling what the Father will do. We cannot pray with grasping hands, only giving hands. Ask, and we will receive another way to empty ourselves of our possessiveness, so that the love of God can flow in the world and in our lives.

Chapter 28

Loving on Ground Level

My nephew Chris was staying with my mother for a period of time. Mother was a widow, living alone in retirement, and Chris was just starting out following his graduation from college. Sometimes Chris would come home late at night, after Mother had gone to bed. (Mother's early bedtimes and morning risings were legendary in our family.) The very small lamp on the counter of the bathroom Chris used was always on. And breakfast was always ready in the morning.

Years later, when Mother died, we four siblings first claimed those of Mother's possessions that she had specifically designated for each of us because she knew we were fond of them. Then we asked the grandchildren if there was something they were interested in because it reminded them of Grandmother. By this time Chris lived miles away and had to give his answer over the phone. It was quick and firm. "I'd like the little lamp in the guest bathroom."

Chris was uninterested in the big stuff. Only a little light that spoke of a person who loved him, gave him a place to call home, and shared the beginning of the day around the breakfast table. The little lamp was all he needed. It said everything.

I've read that after major disasters—avalanches, mudslides, fires—when personal loss is huge, and especially when a loved one is killed, survivors usually search desperately for little things, memories of their lives or the family members they have lost. Something visible, palpable, touchable—a photo, a ring, a set of keys, a military uniform, a pair of glasses, a toy, a journal, a Bible—to evoke memories of a life and a love. These little things preserve the specifics, the ground levels of life, where love must live and prosper. Like a small lamp with memories of a grandmother's love.

THE GOSPELS REVEAL A Jesus at ground level. He gives attention to the immediate, lives in the moment, engages people. He sees significance in the seemingly insignificant. The very environment of his life and ministry is in the furthest reaches of the Roman Empire, far from the center of imperial power. His location is an area of civilization considered remote, unimportant. Very few outside Palestine know anything about him. In the bigger picture of his time, he is a fairly obscure person.

Jesus does not seem interested in larger geopolitical matters. His concern is his immediate environment. He is grounded in the smaller world of his here and now. Most of what he says addresses a situation or a person he encounters directly, or it is aimed at helping his followers address an important situation in the lives they are actually living. He isn't an abstract philosopher, he's a down-to-earth storyteller and an artist of life portraits. His terminology is mundane, his stories open doors for common people, his teaching evokes action.

Jesus likes one-on-one. He knows his immediate environment and the people in it. A tax collector named Matthew cannot escape his penetrating glance. A little man named Zaccheus hides in a tree to see and not be seen, but Jesus' eyes catch him and bring him down. A woman with a serious medical condition tries to snatch power for healing without being seen, but Jesus' voice claims her and brings her into his presence. No one, it seems, escapes his attention.

Jesus especially likes to engage the small people on a personal level. He honors the special small places in their lives. He savors the small moments that bring delight. And he reveals how God cares about matters in our lives that others might consider to be insignificant.

Our culture worships the big people, those who have far more than most of us do—more money, more influence, more fame, more whatever. Jesus invites us to surrender our obsession with "more" so that we may see the beauty and savor the blessings around us at ground level.

Consider *the common people*. Even before Jesus' birth, pregnant Mary sings of what her son will do for them: the humble will be "lifted up," the hungry will be "filled with good things." (Luke 1:52–53) Jesus tells John the Baptist's messengers that "the poor [having] the good news proclaimed to them" is a key sign of the authenticity of his messianic mission (Matt 11:5; Luke 7:22). In Jesus' day and place, the poor are exploited by the prosperous classes, who reap the lion's share of material reward for the poor's work. Jesus could be focusing his mission on the prosperous classes, adapting his gospel to support their lifestyle and values, and thereby standing to gain much—not to mention avoiding a terrible death. Instead, he focuses on the people who cannot do much for him in the larger scale of things—certainly not save his life. Jesus shares his love with the powerless people at ground level.

When Jesus critiques the "big people" of his day, he points to the great danger of defining and determining the value of their lives by their rank in the social order. Many of the Pharisees claim a greater righteousness measured by the accumulation of their acts of piety (see, for example, Mark 7:1–13). A particular rich man foolishly measures himself by the considerable size and value of his agricultural storehouse (Luke 12:16–21). Many rulers feel a shallow importance by amassing more power over their subjects (Mark 10:42–45). In all these examples the clear message of Jesus and the teaching of his own life is that the true value of our lives in the kingdom of God can only be found at ground level. The public stature one achieves as a result of religious, economic, or political status adds nothing to our significance in God's eyes, and to think otherwise is to live in illusion. We meet the real person at ground level, stripped of worldly power and influence. Here is where we see what is in the heart. Here, at ground level, is where genuine love can be measured. A person who thinks he is in a superior position cannot truly love the person he considers to be in an inferior position. Condescending love is not the love Jesus models for us. Love can thrive when we come out from behind our public personas and meet each other face to face on a level playing field. What we have in common is far more important than our place in the social order. Love thrives at ground level.

Ground level is also where *the small places* are, the places we love because of what happens there. Most of our memories of Jesus are made concrete by the specific places with which he was associated, even if only briefly. We remember what he did in these places. What if we couldn't do that?

- Take away a little town called Bethlehem, and Jesus' Incarnation is lost in abstraction.

- Take away another little town called Nazareth, and we lose his childhood, the shaping of his mind, his growing awareness of his life's mission. We also would not know the pain of his harsh rejection there when he returns later in his life to announce that Isaiah's messianic prophecy is being fulfilled in him (Luke 4:14–30).

- Take away a larger town called Capernaum, and we would not know the profound implications of Jesus intentionally using as his home base a place in the region of ancient Zebulun and Naphtali, which in the Old Testament was considered to be the darkest, the forgotten, the marginalized place (Isa 9:1–2).

- Take away a well at Sychar in Samaria, and we would not be able to know one of the most shockingly beautiful encounters Jesus has with a woman (John 4:4–41).

- Take away a little second-story room in Jerusalem, and we would not be able to see ourselves sitting around the Lord's table where we belong (Mark 14:12–26).

- Take away a garden called Gethsemane, and we would not know where Jesus prays his heart out before he gives himself over to horrible death for our salvation (Mark 14:32–42).

- Take away a small hill outside Jerusalem called Golgotha, and we would not know where Jesus is broken and we are healed (I Peter 2:24).

- Take away a small stone tomb outside Jerusalem, and we would not know where the miracle that gives us eternity occurred (I Cor 15:17).

As with the life of Jesus, our lives are also memorialized by small places that have taken on special significance because of the impact of what happened there on our journey. The concreteness of them gives power to our memories. We love those places because, as small as they are or as insignificant as they are to those who were not part of what happened to us there, for us they represent a breakthrough that came then or thereafter. To lose those memories is to lose our grounded-ness in this world God created for us and at the sites where we have met him. We don't worship those sites, but they evoke and mark turning-points in our lives.

The ground level of our lives is also populated by *small moments* when things of importance happen on our life journey. Time is fleeting, but God gives us the capacity to capture moments that are open windows to meaning and insight. The four Gospels are not a continuous record of the life of Jesus. Space is given to events surrounding Jesus' birth, and only one incident from Jesus' adolescent years is recorded. The bulk of the Gospels cover the three years of Jesus' ministry. Even there we do not have a record of every day. Not even every week. What we have is largely a collection of moments. They are moments of personal significance:

- In a moment a man possessed by an evil spirit encounters Jesus in the Capernaum synagogue and leaves free of his scourge (Mark 1:21–26; Luke 4:31–35).

- Jesus, hurrying to heal Jairus's dying daughter, stops suddenly to face the woman who has surreptitiously stolen a healing touch—a moment forever remembered by her, not only for the healing she received, but perhaps even more for the face that noticed and blessed her (Mark 5:21–34; Matt 9:18–22; Luke 8:41–48).

- A Syrophoenician woman, a non-Jew, abruptly invades the privacy of Jesus in the vicinity of Tyre. Her daughter desperately needs healing. A tense encounter ensues. Jesus allows himself to lose the argument, is overwhelmed by the woman's die-hard faith, heals her daughter. That woman never forgets that moment of her life when her rash request was honored. I doubt that Jesus does, as well!

- Jesus' disciples are acting like children, arguing over which one of them is the greatest in the kingdom of God. Jesus overhears. He sits down and addresses their child's play by calling a real child to him, and he says, "Those who humble themselves like this little child will be the greatest in the kingdom of heaven" (Mark 9:33–37; Matt 18:1–4; Luke 9:46–48). A moment for disciples to remember.

- There is a brief moment in the temple in Jerusalem when Jesus calls the attention of his disciples to the person, a poor widow, who is putting less than anyone else in the donation box, two copper coins. Jesus makes a statement that puts to shame all pride of giving: "I assure you that this poor widow has put in more than everyone. . . . " (Mark 12:41–44; Luke 21:1–4). Enough said, plenty to remember.

- Jesus has the world on his heart and mind as he hangs in excruciating pain on a cross. He catches a glimpse of his mother watching him suffer, and for a moment he becomes her son, acknowledges her hurt feelings and deep pain, and commends her into the care of his disciple John. The woman who bore him becomes the mother whose care he assures (John 19:26–27).

Jesus knows the significance of what can and does happen in a moment of our day. He invites us to get our heads out of the clouds and seize such moments, or perhaps be seized by them; to let them become windows to see into the heart of God, of another person, of ourselves. Moments that call us to something we have not known, or done, or been.

It all happens at ground level where Jesus calls us to engage the people nearby who can do nothing for us, to treasure what happened at places in the gospel story and at the places in our own story where our lives turned in some new and better direction, and to open ourselves to transforming moments that may catch us unawares. These events will often happen without fanfare, but spiritual significance is not measured by size, it is measured by what changes our hearts and what actually makes us more like our Rabbi Jesus.

Chapter 29

Loving with Forgiveness

David Briggs (the arda.com) reports that recent studies strongly suggest that feeling forgiven helps us forgive others. One study found that "individuals who believe that a loving God forgives them are far more likely to turn around and absolve others." Furthermore, "trust in God's forgiveness . . . also may make it more likely for individuals to forgive themselves, which in turn seems to make it easier for them to extend mercy to others." Specifically, it makes a difference in how they treat friends, co-workers, relatives, and neighbors.

It must be acknowledged, however, that forgiveness can be a tricky matter, depending on individual situations. Whereas forgiving someone may naturally lift a heavy burden of anger or hurt from one person's heart, for someone else who, for example, is a victim of domestic violence or sexual abuse, forgiveness given too easily or without dealing with the suffering can be empty. In fact, it can be potentially harmful. For most people, however, belief in a forgiving God tends to make them more genuinely forgiving toward others. In fact, they seem to be healthier psychically and psychologically than the general population.

Another important conclusion from the research is that the religiously affiliated (i.e., members of a faith community) are more likely to forgive than those who are not. Furthermore, church members who are more satisfied with the emotional support they receive from church members are more likely to forgive themselves than are those who are not satisfied with the support they receive. Belief in a forgiving God combined with involvement in a caring church community seems to open our hearts to forgiveness (*Christian Century*, May 1, 2013, 15).

LUKE'S GOSPEL PORTRAYS THE forgiving spirit of Jesus as excessive. Jesus refuses to set a limit on how many times his disciples are supposed to forgive a person (Luke 17:3–4). Luke records these brief, tit-for-tat statements of Jesus: "Don't judge, and you won't be judged. Don't condemn, and you won't be condemned. Forgive, and you will be forgiven." (Luke 6:37) The first two are matters of *not* doing something. The last is a matter of proactively taking action.

Forgiveness is something you *do*. It is not just ignoring a wrong that has been done to you; it is reaching out in love to someone, with all the pain of the hurt, and even the damage that he or she has brought to you, and saying, "As I have been forgiven much, so I forgive you." It's not as easy as simply saying the words, but the words are the invitation to a process, a journey, toward reconciliation.

In Mark's Gospel Jesus makes an interesting statement about the relationship between forgiveness and prayer. He is speaking about a faith that moves mountains. He says, "Whatever you pray and ask for, believe that you will receive it, and it will be so for you." This promise is obviously not a face-value statement, as some prosperity-gospel proponents would claim: "If you just have enough faith, *anything* is yours!" Rather, it is a promise given to a disciple of Jesus who prays from a pure, not a compromised heart. The question, then, is: Is my prayer, my petition, coming from a pure heart, or is there some impediment blocking the purity of my prayer, something in my heart that undermines my conversation with God? Jesus goes on to give a particular example of an impediment: "And whenever you stand up to pray, if you have something against anyone, forgive so that your Father in heaven may forgive you your wrongdoings." (Mark 11:22–25) Jesus is saying two things here which are integrally related: An unforgiving person is both closed to God's forgiveness and blocked in prayer.

Forgiveness is an act that clears the way for love. We cannot fully love the person we have not forgiven. Jesus looks down from his cross at the tormentors, then looks upward to heaven and prays, "Father, forgive them, for they don't know what they're doing" (Luke 23:34a). The power of love frees us to forgive, and forgiveness keeps and strengthens love.

Matthew records a parable of Jesus that thrusts forgiveness into the forefront of love. Jesus has just given his disciples some guidance about how we resolve a wrong done against us (Matt 18:15–20). In Peter's mind this raises the larger question of how far we go in forgiving someone. If a person keeps sinning against us, should we forgive him up to the seventh time? Peter sees this as generous. Jesus counters with seventy-seven times (Some manuscripts say seventy times seven.) Why does Jesus multiply

Peter's number to this extent? Obviously to refuse to set a limit. We never stop forgiving. Why?

Jesus tells a story because it helps us grasp what ethical principles and rules cannot. The story goes something like this. A king wants accounts settled with his servants. There is one particular man who owes the huge amount of 10,000 bags of gold. As he is unable to pay, the king tells him he'll have to sell him and his family into slavery, the usual means of resolving this kind of situation. The man falls on his knees and begs for mercy, asking for enough time to allow him to repay the whole debt. The king, moved with compassion, goes further than giving him some rope. He forgives him the entire debt!

Clearly, however, the servant doesn't fully realize what has just happened. He has *not* gotten off scot free. He is now forever bound to live in the reciprocity of the forgiveness he has just received. The forgiveness that freed him must now occupy his own heart, assaulting every temptation not to forgive, even if the wrong against him is great or repayment of the debt owed him is his right. *To accept forgiveness is to become a forgiver.*

The forgiven servant in the parable doesn't get it. No sooner is he forgiven than he goes to another servant, who owes him only a hundred coins, grabs him by the throat and insists on immediate repayment. The man begs for mercy and a little time. But the forgiven man shows no mercy and has him thrown in jail. When the king hears about it he is understandably incensed. He has the first man dragged before him and gives him a tongue-lashing: "I forgave you all that debt because you appealed to me. Shouldn't you also have mercy on your fellow servant, just as I had mercy on you?" He then has the man sent to jail where he is to endure punishment until he repays the original debt. Jesus concludes: "My heavenly Father will also do the same to you if you don't forgive your brother or sister from your heart." (Matt 18:21–35)

Let's not get distracted by the harsh judgment promised against those who seem to accept God's forgiveness of them but do not reciprocate it toward others who wrong or owe them. We would do well to remember that Jesus' parables are very rarely allegories where every detail represents some truth or a particular character in real life, or the action of the "God figure" *literally* represents how God will act. The point of the parable is not to tell us how God will actually treat those who accept forgiveness but cannot give it. The point is that some people are willing to accept the immediate but not the long-range benefit of forgiveness. God forgives to free us up to become forgivers like him. The person with a heart that harbors a harm or injustice done to him is a person who has not fully received God's forgiveness into his heart and is unable to forgive. His humanity, if you like, has a heart blockage. And until that blockage is cleared, until forgiveness has its way, he will not have allowed forgiveness to do its real work, and his life will be torture. Joy lives only where debts are no longer harbored.

True forgiveness is not indulgent foolishness. It is not our getting away with something, our taking advantage of God or allowing someone to take advantage of us. It is love willing to bear the burden of its rejection. It is forgiveness knowing the forgiven may receive the forgiveness as release without a further claim. The forgiven of God, however, accept God's new claim on them as forgivers. Not to accept this claim is to consign one's self to the misery of living without forgiving, which is a hell.

You've probably said and prayed the Lord's Prayer many times over. Have you ever noticed that the only petition in the prayer that comes with a condition is the prayer for God's forgiveness? "Forgive us for the ways we have wronged you, just as we also forgive those who have wronged us" (Matt 6:12). Jesus has redefined forgiveness for his disciples. The end game is to turn us, the forgiven, into the forgivers.

Chapter 30

Loving with Mercy

As we know, in most (if not all) cultures a meal shared with others is seen as one of the more intimate social events in human relationships. I remember the days of segregated restaurants in the South where I grew up. In the early days of the civil rights movement there was especially strong resistance to integrating restaurants. One restaurant owner stood in front of his establishment wielding an axe handle, daring an African-American to cross the line. That image alone may well have insured his election as Governor in a state that wasn't ready to abandon separation of the races.

Civil rights freedom fighters of the sixties put their lives on the line by integrating public spaces. There was no stronger resistance than at restaurants. Mixing races in this more intimate setting was seen as an unacceptable crossing of a time-honored, deeply embedded social divide between "insiders" and "outsiders," those who are "our kind" and "those who are not," those of us who are white and those who are black. For the more sophisticated this overt racism appeared in more delicate dress, a softer racism, a myth all the more insidious for its respectability. It claimed that the relationship between the races works out just fine if we retain the separation. Our seperation is only honoring God's order, and that insures mutual respect. Eating together, or even dining in the same social space, is a violation of that order and the beauty of our respective distinctiveness. It is too threatening to the divine arrangement of our places in the world—and the separation is actually what the Bible teaches.

At its foundation, racism—and all forms of social, economic, and political discrimination—is the lack of mercy. If we can draw a helpful distinction between forgiveness and mercy, it is that forgiveness seeks to cross a divide caused by wrong done to another person or group, while mercy seeks to cross a divide that exists because one person or group looks on the other as inferior. I show forgiveness by refusing to allow a wrong committed against me to stand in the way of my love for the person who has wronged me. I show mercy by refusing to treat another human as inferior, thereby making genuine love possible. God shows mercy by loving us all as his precious children; we show mercy by seeing and treating each other as brothers and sisters.

How, then, does Jesus help us to love with mercy?

ONE DAY JESUS IS in the town of Capernaum where he is already becoming well known. He catches the eye of a tax collector named Matthew who is occupied at his collection booth. He says to Matthew, "Follow me." Matthew, somehow knowing this is a crucial moment, a kind of tipping point in his life, leaves his booth and follows Jesus. His life will never be the same.

Soon afterwards he decides this decisive step is something to celebrate with his friends. As it turns out, most of them are unsavory types—tax collectors like Matthew himself, and sinners. Tax collectors of that time and place are actually of Jewish ancestry but are looked down upon by fellow Jews as collaborators with the oppressive Roman government. They are also despised because they often defraud fellow Jews by charging higher taxes than they should and pocketing the difference. Those described as "sinners" are those whose standard of piety falls far short of Pharisaical righteousness. The whole unholy lot of them cram into Matthew's house. The character of the crowd, however, doesn't stop Jesus from joining the party to celebrate Matthew's turn-around. In fact, it seems especially to draw him.

Some of the Pharisees are watching closely, waiting, it seems, for yet another opportunity to condemn Jesus' violation of the separatism expected of a pious rabbi. What they are seeing before them is a clear violation of that standard. They see Jesus contaminating himself by association with those of ill repute. They see a challenge to the rules by which they define their high standard of spirituality: stay out of contact with those who are living outside the law; stay away from sinners; don't contaminate yourself with lower life forms. Jesus, however, sees it all differently. He likes these people. He gladly joins their party.

Jesus is introducing a radically different way of defining holiness. He's taking out the religious, social, economic, and political borders of it. According to Jesus, refusing to associate with people on the other side of such borders is relational heresy. Such heresy is founded on the myth that spirituality can be lived outside compassion and that mercy can be expressed behind a wall of prejudice.

Jesus' answer to the perplexity of those Pharisees is not an attack but a different approach to the practice of faith. It is an invitation to open the closed doors. He quotes Hosea 6:6—"I want mercy and not sacrifice." And then he clarifies his rabbinic calling: "I didn't come to call righteous people, but sinners." Not that the "righteous people" were not themselves sinners. They just weren't aware (Matt 9:9–13).

We should not be too harsh on those particular Pharisees. They are practicing their faith as best they know. They want to live a godly life as they have been taught to do it. When they see Jesus acting in a way contrary to their own religious training, they are understandably shocked. Just as you and I would be. Just as you and I likely are, if we are honest. How quickly our Christianity of compassion becomes a Christianity of condemnation. How quickly the merciful Christ, who embraces us with his accepting love, becomes in our now pious hearts the boundaried Christ who we imagine wants us to make of our religion a barrier to "sinners," whose sins are only more obvious than ours because ours are hidden behind a rigid, excluding righteousness.

The church has never fully mastered the inclusive righteousness to which Jesus calls her. In every age of the church's history, certain groups have been virtually excluded from her concern and outreach. It's as if amnesia sets in, in two parts. First, we forget how radically inclusive Jesus was. And second, though we may become aware of our Lord's inclusiveness, we forget that our calling as his disciples is to *imitate* our Rabbi Jesus. James becomes painfully aware of how poor the imitation is going in the church to whom he's writing his letter. So he states the facts in strong language. He says all will be judged by "the law of freedom," and he reminds them of what that means: "There will be no mercy in judgment for anyone who hasn't shown mercy. Mercy overrules judgment" (James 2:12–13).

What would the world look like if the church everywhere became merciful, as Jesus both defined it and lived it?

Chapter 31

Loving Compassionately

There are many things we call love. There's the kind of love that is more a liking: I love that outfit. . . . I love my wife's chocolate cake. . . . I love the way he plays the piano. These "loves" satisfy the tastes of the person doing the loving.

Another kind of love has to do with another person: I love what she (or he) does for me. Here love is what happens in a relationship when it gives some personal satisfaction. Still another kind of love is where two people are committed to each other in a deep way, each caring for the other. This could be a friendship or a marriage.

And finally, there is a kind of love that is willing to suffer. It's called compassion, a word that literally means "to suffer with someone" by choice. It's the willingness to enter into the suffering of another person because you genuinely care for that person in a deep way. The model for it is the love of God lived out in Jesus.

THE COMPASSION OF JESUS shows up in many ways. For example, when he's been preaching for three days in some wilderness area, some of his listeners have traveled a long way to hear him, and just about everyone's food has now gone. Jesus looks out on this famished crowd who have stayed with him even though their stomachs are growling. Moved by their hunger, he interrupts his sermon to find food (Mark 8:1–11). On one occasion Jesus risks touching a leper to heal him at a time when the disease was considered highly contagious (Mark 1:40–42; Luke 5:12–13). On yet another occasion Jesus and his disciples are beyond the eastern border of Judea, safe from the threats of growing hostility in the area of and around Jerusalem. He receives word from Bethany, just outside Jerusalem, that Lazarus is near death and his sisters, Mary and Martha, are begging him to come and heal him. After two days he decides to go, even though his disciples have warned him of the danger of returning to Judea. He is willing to take the risk for someone he loves. When he arrives he is told Lazarus has already died. Standing before the tomb, he cannot stop the tears for the man he loved as much as to risk his life for him (John 11:1–35).

The compassion of Jesus is revealed in a final, decisive way, as well. He sets the stage with his description of the Good Shepherd who lays down his life for his sheep (John 10:1–18). And over time the disciples come to understand what he means when they reflect on their Lord lifted up on a cross, suffering with and for us all—compassion astoundingly embodied in the final, decisive action of his life.

This crucified Jesus, whom we call Lord (the one to whom we claim total obedience), sometimes asks us to risk a hurting love, to care till it hurts, to show compassion for someone, or some group, or some enemy. And when we do that, we truly are his disciples. The apostle Paul picks up on this by describing it as an essential habit of the body of Christ. He refers to carrying the burdens of our brothers and sisters in Christ as "fulfill[ing] the law of Christ" (Gal 6:2). Carrying someone's burden can be tough and even painful. It goes beyond easy, convenient help. Compassion, painful love, shared with one another builds and defines the body of Christ. Refined in the body, it prepares us to fulfill the law of Christ by loving our neighbor (Rom 13:10).

Love without pain is easy; compassion is not. I fell in love with Keitha; that was easy. I married her and together we set out on a lifelong journey. Now love is not easy all the time. Sometimes there is pain, and we have learned that a love relationship grows deeper and richer as pain is shared and hurt is healed. The same is true of other committed relationships, including enduring friendships.

If this is the case with our close relationships, it is true as well when we reach out to someone outside our circle who may be struggling with a very difficult personal problem, perhaps an addiction. Suppose he responds to our concern, and a relationship develops. Things begin to work out well, progress is being made, and you feel you are being helpful and supportive. He appreciates your concern and care and accepts your friendship and advocacy. Then a few weeks later his attitude seems to change overnight. He avoids you and returns to his former self-destructive lifestyle. His life, it seems, has relapsed, as if the investment you made in him and the compassion you shared with him finally amount to nothing. You fully realize you are not responsible for his decision, but you cannot deny the pain.

To love someone deeply and commit oneself to him or her is to risk pain. During Jesus' three-year ministry, his pain comes from many sources.

He is pained by those who attack his healing of a demon-possessed man as the work of Beelzebub (Satan), as if the power of evil could overcome evil (Matt 12:22–24). At the end of his earthly life, he experiences the betrayal of the once-supportive crowds (Mark 15:9–15; Matt 27:20–23; Luke 23:13–23; John 19:12–16) and the cowardly betrayal of his own inner circle (Mark 14:50, 66–72; Matt 26: 56b, 69–75; John 20:19). Later on, his disciples come to understand that misunderstandings, hatred, and betrayals are also their lot as his followers and imitators of his love. They remember his telling them that the same world he loves and came to save will hate them just as they hated him (John 15:18–25).

There is no escaping the pain of loving as Jesus loves, and anyone who wishes to experience the fulfillment and joy of being Jesus' disciple is guaranteed a measure of suffering, and sometimes a great measure. We do not choose this suffering as such. What we choose is deep, enduring love. What we discover is that pain will come with it. What we know is what Jesus teaches us and what the cross shows us: Embedded in such suffering is redemptive, life-giving power.

Chapter 32

Loving Courageously

On a summer day in 1968, I remember being bothered by a photograph in the paper. It captured three runners after they had been awarded Olympic medals for the 200-meter race. The gold and bronze medal winners were African-American, each one looking down to the ground, his arm raised with a fist in what we in America knew as the Black Power salute. Their names were Tommie Smith and John Carlos. The silver medalist was Australian Peter Norman, and white. He stood with his arms to the side, and he looked straight ahead.

I was bothered by the photograph, not because I didn't fully agree that African-American empowerment needed to be taken seriously and addressed in my country, but because I thought Smith and Carlos had chosen an inappropriate occasion to publicize the issue. They had no right, I thought, arbitrarily to co-opt this event for a purpose outside the purpose for which the Olympics were held. And I must confess I was also a little hurt to see my country embarrassed before the world.

It wasn't until recently that I learned the full story. I now wish that at the time I had looked at what was really going on in greater detail before jumping to conclusions. The three athletes had quickly become friends during that Olympics and together planned the demonstration. All three wore the Olympic Project for Human Rights badges (OPHR) for the occasion. Smith and Carlos were shoeless to represent the poor and marginalized. They wore black gloves, black socks and Carlos a black scarf around his neck, all to represent African-American poverty. Carlos also had his tracksuit unzipped to represent solidarity with all blue-collar workers in the US, and a necklace of beads to remember those who were lynched and tarred and those who were thrown off the side of boats in the middle passage, those for whom no one said a prayer. Norman, the Australian runner, was a critic of the then White Australia Policy, which, as the name implies, sought to keep his country white. He obviously felt the Black Power salute would be an empty symbol if given by a white Australian, but he fully supported his friends, and when Carlos forgot to bring his black glove, Norman gave him his and suggested he wear it on his left hand.

All three athletes were booed and maligned that day at the stadium and thereafter and around the world, especially in their own countries. From what I've learned about these three men, I'm convinced they were not grandstanding, nor were they violating the purpose of the Olympics to foster peace and goodwill around the world. They were reminding the world that the exploitation and disempowerment of classes and races of people needed to be acknowledged and addressed, and that the feel-good spirit of the Olympic events performed by privileged athletes could threaten to diminish awareness of the millions of underprivileged. What they did was inappropriate, but prophets are not known for being socially or politically appropriate when they make pronouncements. And they often pay a heavy price for their rude interruptions, as did Smith, Carlos, and Norman—for the rest of their lives.

FROM THE BEGINNING OF his life, it seems, Jesus is in danger. He has no one to blame but himself. Leviticus is clear: "Anyone [any human being] who blasphemes the Lord's name must be executed" (Leviticus 24:16a). As soon as Jesus, a human being, claims to be the Son of God, he can under Jewish law be executed. Every day of Jesus' mission is a risk. Early on, it seems, he knows how his earthly life will end: he will be put to death. His disciples contradict him and protest when he shares this with them. They have a different script from his. But Jesus sticks to his own script.

What gives Jesus the courage to keep on, to stay the course to Calvary? Is he some kind of masochist who welcomes suffering as a warped, egotistical indulgence? Hardly. The evidence suggests otherwise: he is a healthy human being who loves life.

Then what is it that motivates him to take such dangerous risks?

The testimony of Scripture is compelling: he does it for love; he does it for us and for every member of the human race. Like the sacrificial lamb of Old Testament atonement ritual, his life is laid down so that we can have life.

There's still another side to it. He is giving us an example so that *we* will love courageously. Without courageous love the first Christians would never have been able to overcome their fear, and the Christian church would never have survived, much less grown. We stand in their line when we trust, embrace, and live by the love of Christ so fully that we live beyond our fears. After all, as the apostle John says so simply and elegantly, "There is no fear in love, but perfect love drives out fear" (I John 4:18). In the end, love wins.

The satanic forces that oppose the mission of Jesus are the forces of fear. John's Gospel tells us about some of the Jewish leaders who "believed in [Jesus], but they wouldn't acknowledge their faith because they feared that the Pharisees would expel them from the synagogue" (John 12:42). Luke's Gospel suggests that certain chief priests and teachers of the law want to destroy Jesus because they fear the support he is getting from the populace—afraid that if Jesus succeeds, their own power and influence in the community will be severely diminished or even ruined. The moment is then ripe for Judas's betrayal: "Then Satan entered Judas" (Luke 22:1–3). Fear is contagious.

Courage seems nowhere to be found, save in the compassionate heart of Jesus. At the arrest of Jesus, all the disciples flee, and after his crucifixion they huddle in fear behind closed doors. They cower until the resurrected Jesus appears and shows them that the fear of death—and all disempowering fears, for that matter—have been overcome (John 20:19–20), as promised (John 16:33). Overcome by a life that death cannot kill, overcome by the courage of compassion.

Loving as Jesus loves is not keeping peace at all costs and certainly not failing to confront evil or injustice. The Jesus who says, "Don't be afraid," is not inviting us to deal with our fear by lying low or hiding out rather than facing difficult situations. The Jesus who says, "Be at peace," is not inviting us to renounce bold compassionate action. He's speaking to our hearts. He's inviting us to accept his peace (John 14:27) so that our lives can be lived with holy compassion and courage. At the center of a life courageously lived is a heart at peace and in love. Perfect love and inner peace drive out fear.

> There was much for those three star athletes to fear when they surrendered their place of much-deserved world prominence as athletes to the millions of people whose suffering they believed needed a witness before the world. With the audacity of conviction, they risked everything—their promising athletic careers, their reputations, their safety. Opportunities were closed to them by their homelands. None of them were allowed to participate in future Olympics. They were an embarrassment to their countries. Of course they were, having exposed the painful truth of oppressed people, thereby interrupting the staged nicety of Olympic magic. Their compassion had called for courage, and they took the leap. Perhaps even those of us who disagree with

the tactics and the choice of occasion can honor the cause and the courage—*maybe even confess that all too often the courage is missing in us.*

Think about it: here we are, disciples of Jesus, claimed by and immersed in his incredible love, and there just isn't any real room left over for fear! How else are those early disciples finally able to look death in the face without flinching? As their Rabbi Jesus so convincingly showed them, love doesn't flinch, doesn't run from conflict when important matters of life and death are at stake. Our resurrected Rabbi extends to us, his disciples, this invitation: Follow me by trusting the love I poured out on Calvary. Follow me with courage.

Christians sometimes get a reputation for timidity in threatening times. After all, they think, Jesus blesses "the meek." Clarence Jordan gives a surprising interpretation of what Jesus means when he blesses "the meek" (CEB translates "the humble") and says they are the ones who "will inherit the earth" (Matt 5:5). Jordan points out that the English word meek has come to mean little more than weak or harmless, and claims this is a long way from what Jesus means. In the Bible it is used, for example, to describe both Moses (Numbers 12:3) and Jesus (Matt 11:29), neither one of whom shows the least sign of being weak or harmless. But if they are indeed "meek," what does meek *really* mean in the Bible?

Jordan goes on to say that "meek" in Scripture refers to persons who "have surrendered their wills to God and learned to do God's bidding." Because they are meek before God and dependent upon his sufficiency, they are strong in the face of those forces that oppose his compassionate kingdom. When Peter and the other apostles are dragged before the Sanhedrin in Jerusalem for continuing to preach the gospel after previously being told to stop immediately or suffer the consequences, they say, "We must obey God rather than human beings" (Acts 5:29). They blatantly risk their lives. Gamaliel, a member of the Sanhedrin, senses the possibility the council is dealing with men who are courageous because they are meek, surrendered to God. He advises caution, so the Sanhedrin spares their lives, giving them only a flogging and another warning, and releases them. The truly meek are strong, not weak when obedient to God and committed to his upside-down kingdom of love (Clarence Jordan, *Sermon on the Mount*, 12–13).

Perhaps Christians best learn this powerful meekness with difficult people within their own congregations or with difficult neighbors. Jesus calls his disciples to be courageous in resolving problems with another person. Better than relying on a third party or a person with official authority to settle a matter, go to the person himself, says Jesus, and seek reconciliation and resolution (Matt 5:25–26). If such compassionate engagement fails because the other person will not engage and the issue must be resolved one way or the other, mediation may be needed. Either way, the disciple of Jesus is called to compassionate forgiveness.

Jesus invites us, his disciples, to be compassionate enough to engage, even where engagement is most difficult, and to do it in humility and with sensitivity. He invites us to trust the strength of his love. He invites us to quit pretending there is no real concern or issue when there is. He invites us to quit tiptoeing around difficult issues, or even worse, gossiping with allies about the matter, trying anything except engaging the person or persons directly involved. He wants us to trust courageous love, wherever it may take us.

There is no guarantee the other person will be willing to respond in kind. We may be rebuffed in our attempt to be reconciled. We are not responsible for the failure, however, if we have done our best with honesty and compassion, and if we have left the door of reconciliation open. What we *have* done is practice courageous love. We have given testimony to the way of Jesus by risking reconciliation. We have done something that, with love, endures. This is why we never give up on love. And this is why one day we may take a very public stand that happens to insult the smug and uncaring by forcing them actually to see those who suffer from exploitation, poverty, racism, or sexism—even if the price we pay is huge.

Chapter 33

Loving Confrontationally

Phyllis Tickle writes that early in her Christian journey she was somewhat perplexed by Jesus' directness, especially when it comes across as, well, outright rudeness. "Why do you call me good?" he snaps at how one seemingly sincere questioner addresses him. "No one is good save God alone." To one eager disciple who dares to object to Jesus' prophecy about his future suffering, the Rabbi launches a searing missile: "Get thee behind me, Satan!" These are among the more extreme examples. There are many more examples of Jesus' startling directness with people, his willingness to confront head-on.

The reason Tickle gives for her difficulty with this directness is that it seems not to be consistent with that quality of Jesus' character she found so attractive: his humility. She "had always seen these two threads of tradition—the humility and the directness—as contradictory of one another. . . . a kind of de facto schizophrenia that one had to accept to be a Christian and that one was better off spiritually to leave alone." Into her adulthood she was forced to rethink her position. "Were directness and great humility wedded in the personas of those choosing and chosen of God? Apparently so, I concluded."

Over time, she concludes that "like most holy paradoxes, this one is more apparent than real. Loving and believing oneself beloved of God makes one a citizen in a country apart. It confines and blesses one with both loyalties and responsibilities that are unlike those of one's secularly-enfranchised neighbors" (*The Shaping of a Life*, 257). For disciples of Jesus, there is a time for humility and a time for confrontation. There is no hiding behind humility to avoid confrontation, as there is no hiding behind the need to confront to excuse the absence of humility.

JESUS' MINISTRY DID NOT go smoothly. Yes, the people often "heard him gladly." At other times they were perplexed, even belligerent. The religious establishment seems to have been against him almost from the beginning as they quickly perceived his gospel called into question their narrow view of the world and finely honed, complex righteousness. Time after time they went on the attack and tried to draw him into arguments. His religious practice, or lack of it, perplexed them. His messianic claims irritated them. His blasphemy in claiming a too familiar closeness to God himself appalled them.

How does this Jesus, this incarnation of God's love (John 3:16) respond? First of all, it is important to observe that he always does respond, in one way or another. He does not pretend there is no confrontation nor ignore the tension that is obviously there. *How* he responds seems to depend both on the nature of the issue and on the way the issue is framed. Sometimes he changes the question because he thinks it is falsely premised (for example, Mark 2:13–17, 23–28). Sometimes he answers the question or faces the challenge directly, usually giving an unanticipated or even shocking answer to the challengers (for example, Mark 7:1–13; 9:38–41). Often, realizing the question is designed to trap him, he turns the trap into ironic truth (for example, Mark 11:27–33; 12:13–17). And near the end when so much has already been said and the profile of his mission has been drawn, there is little need of words in responding to challengers. Here there is mostly silence or simply assent, and behind both is the answer (Mark 14:53–65; 15:1–5). The only challenge yet to be met is a cross on a hill outside Jerusalem. No answers, no defense. The answer hangs there for all the world to see: love confronting the full force of evil and prevailing.

What enables Jesus to respond in these incredible, revealing ways? Why does he seem never to be ruffled or ill at ease? It isn't just his brilliance and his profound knowledge of Scripture and of the human heart, though these do help him enormously. It is also his compassion. We do not really understand what motivates and informs how he deals with confrontation and conflict unless we recognize it in each case as an act of love. He is not concerned with someone getting the best of him or outsmarting him. He is interested in guiding every question asked of him to the answer the questioner must personally confront, though it changes the question itself. Unlike the person in the witness stand in our courts who is required to answer the specific question asked, Jesus usually changes or redirects the question to confront the inquirer or accuser with the life-changing decision he or she must make in order to find life.

A good example is the rich young ruler who asks Jesus, "What must I do to obtain eternal life?" The man has done just about everything the law requires. Jesus, however, puts his finger on the one thing keeping him out of the kingdom of God: his idolatrous attachment to his wealth. Jesus invites him to share it with the poor. Jesus is telling him the real question he needs to ask is: What about my horded wealth? Jesus confronts him with this most sensitizing and loaded question, and the most important answer of the man's life is unavoidably set before him. The proud man is, I imagine, terribly embarrassed in the presence of the gathered crowd. The props of his calculated righteousness have been pulled out from under him, for all the world to see. Has Jesus won some kind of battle here? Not at all; he isn't interested in that. He wants to love this man into his kingdom, and love of money, or the god called Mammon, has him in its thrall. The real captivity has to be named. Love must be willing to do the unpleasant thing to help a person find his soul and save his life (Mark 10:17–22; Matt 19:16–26; Luke 18:18–23).

Sometimes love calls us, Jesus' imitators, to do the same. We confront by listening to someone's question or challenge and allowing ourselves to be attentive and sometimes to hear a different question or discern a better challenge. Love invites us to allow the Holy Spirit, the Spirit of Jesus himself, to hear and see deeply, to look into the person's own heart, beyond the issue raised or the challenge issued. And then, with great sensitivity and awareness of what we are risking, love invites us to confront.

In the matter of *how* we confront, we need to read between the lines consistent with the attitude of Jesus. The confrontations of Jesus are not attacks, other than where he confronts someone who is exploiting or abusing those who are more vulnerable (for example, Mark 11:15–17; Matt 21:12–13; Luke 19:45–48; John 2:13–16). Nor are they attempts to justify himself or win arguments. They are love on the offense, trying to find a way into the heart of a matter, to no end other than to free someone from his abusive or self-destructive course. They are love in action.

Many Christians seem to hold the view that those who follow Jesus are supposed to be nice people who don't confront. There are indeed certain kinds of confrontations that have no place in kingdom-of-God living, though they do and will occur because discipleship is a lifelong journey in which we sometimes fail to act like ourselves as a people created in and redeemed in the image of God. Sometimes we allow ourselves to be drawn into ridiculous squabbles (or even cause them!), or fight out of fear, or dump on someone else, unaware that our anger at the time really has to do with something else. Sometimes we do need to confront a person, but we do it so poorly we only escalate the situation. All these, and all other poor, unpleasant, and ineffective confrontations are occurrences that Jesus our Rabbi calls us to learn from, repent of, and if need be, seek forgiveness for. He does not ask us to retreat into a place of complacency where we refuse to confront wrong or fail to encourage another person to deal with the deeper issues of his life. He asks us to trust love for courage and wisdom.

Sometimes love leads us to confront a Christian brother or sister. In Matthew's Gospel, Jesus addresses a specific situation of this kind and gives clear direction on how to proceed when a fellow believer "sins against you" (Matt 18:15-20). Jesus does not say to go to someone else to complain, or to ask them to talk to the offending person (triangulation), nor does he say to stew in the pain of it (self-pity). He says, "Go to and correct them when you are alone together. If they listen to you, then you've won over your brother or sister." In other words, confront one-on-one.

We go in love, not with accusation but with honest reporting of what we have experienced. *Then*, if the person refuses to take any responsibility for what has happened, expand the possibility of resolution by bringing in one or two other witnesses. If that brings no resolution, then, if the matter affects the whole congregation, bring it before them. This is not like some court of law; it is a court of love. The object is not to make someone pay for something but to bring reconciliation. Jesus invites us not to even scores, but to seek to restore broken relationships. Confrontation with this in mind is far more likely to bring a good resolution.

Jesus expresses great confidence in the ability of the congregation of his disciples to resolve such matters. As we all know, however, a Christian congregation can sometimes become something other than a reflection of the kingdom of God. It can, in fact, become polarized, prejudiced, and occasionally even vicious. Sometimes the church fails to *be* the church. In such circumstances a congregation is unable to be a catalyst for reconciliation, as Jesus invites them to be in this passage. The apostle Paul describes such a failure when he tells the church in Corinth that Christians taking their disputes among themselves to civil court is to abandon the gift of discernment and to give false witness to the world (I Cor 6:1-11). The Holy Spirit has given the people of God the discerning gift to "bind and loose on earth," to make good judgments in disputes between disciples that God will honor. Obviously, this must be done in humility and love, lest we prove ourselves guilty of not paying attention to our own blind spots (Matt 7:1-5; Luke 6:41-42). (Note: In situations within a congregation where there is strong reason to believe that a crime has been committed, reporting to civil authorities must not be suppressed. The church must never shelter those who have been involved in criminal acts.)

Jesus puts his finger on why we so often have great difficulty in dealing with confrontation. The difficulty lies in our hearts where motive and motivation guide our actions. In the Sermon on the Mount he takes up the commandment against murder and expands it far beyond the physical act of killing someone. He does it by going beyond the brutal act itself, into the brutality of the heart (Matt 5:21–26). The heart can harbor pain, self-pity, and fear, and turn it into hatred of the ones who caused the harm, or even a generalized hatred of a group of people who are convenient targets of generalized hatred for any reason hatred is looking for. The hatred resides in the heart. The heart is a victim of the fear that holds it captive. The only freedom from this captivity is a surrender to the transforming love of Jesus, the "perfect love [that] casts out fear" (I John 4:18).

In this instance of Jesus calling attention to the heart, we are given profound insight into why we struggle with confrontation: We are afraid of what our hearts may unleash or perhaps what we know we're unwilling to touch upon. As the old gospel song says, "Oh what needless pain we bear." Jesus invites us to deal with some of the painful burdens we carry in our hearts. Usually the best way to do that is with the help of a friend, a pastor, or a counselor, with the support and prayer of the body of Christ. It may be a long process, but as progress is made, we begin to be free to trust the love of Jesus residing in our hearts. We begin to have the freedom to confront with both honesty and compassion.

Chapter 34

Loving Prayerfully

Jesus pours out his life over the course of an intensive, three-year ministry. It is an immense labor of love. How does he do it? Where does the capacity and the strength come from? We could give a facile answer by simply saying, he is God. No limitations. When all of us would get tired, he simply draws on the energy storehouse of his divine nature. Period. That's it. That's how he does it.

If we do that, we have just called his humanity into question. We have suggested his divinity was some hidden storehouse of power he called on when his human resources gave out. We have said he wasn't fully human because his divine nature enabled him not to have to live with the limitations we do. How, then, can we be like Jesus, our Rabbi, if we don't have the trump card of divinity as part of our very nature? And how can we tell when, in the Gospels, he is being human and when divine?'

We could ask this question in the language of the apostle Paul in Philippians 2:6–7. Paul says Christ Jesus who "was in the form of God," let go of his "equal[ity] with God," and "emptied himself by taking the form of a slave and by becoming like human beings." How could he have "emptied himself" if he could conveniently call on his divine power when he was at the end of his human resources? It would mean that Paul is mistaken. We know, however, he isn't, because we know the gospel story.

So how could Jesus, the God-Man, have emptied himself of his equality with God and still have been God? Good question. It may be helpful to see it and answer it in this way: Jesus emptied himself of the privileges and prerogatives of God, but not his divine nature. Divinity can limit itself; humanity cannot make itself unlimited. In Jesus God became fully human, accepting our limitations so that he could reveal and exemplify our full humanity. As the writer to the Hebrews likes to put it, "We don't have a high priest who can't sympathize with our weaknesses, but instead one who was tempted in every way that we are, except without sin" (Hebrews 4:15). If Jesus was not "tempted in every way that we are," then he had not divested himself of his divine privileges and prerogatives. The truth is that he was vulnerable, just as we are. He had to rely on the grace and strength of his heavenly Father, just as we must. He had to cultivate his relationship with the Father, just as we must. He needed that intimacy, just as we do. He needed to pray, just as we do.

EUGENE PETERSON SAYS THAT prayer was integral to the very life and living of Jesus. To see it as a specialty of his, or a separate gift, or an activity separate from his ministry, or as his spiritual battery recharge, or as a necessary respite for him, or as needed escape to another world, is to miss the mark. Prayer is engagement with God, who is in the world seeking to draw us in at every turn (*Tell It Slant*, 206–7).

Consider Jesus' prayer in Gethsemane (Mark 14:32–42; Matt 26:36–46; Luke 22:40–46). It is the most honest, engaging, soul-searching prayer we will ever find. It reveals a self-exposure and a human determination that is surely a model for us all. It is a matter of life and death. Peter, James, and John, whom Jesus asked to be his sentinels and prayer supporters that night, are so "overcome with grief" over what they fear is soon to happen, they escape into sleep. Meanwhile Jesus is on his knees, sweating blood, pleading with the Father. He the Father's beloved, the Father his beloved, confirming three times their love for each other and their love for the world, a love that will break the Father's heart and the body of Jesus. It is a prayer from the depths of saving love, a mystery so strangely powerful it can never be fully understood save by someone who can only confess and respond in a way that would later be echoed by Charles Wesley, "Love so amazing, so divine/ Demands my soul, my life, my all." For what purpose is this total demand? The purpose is twofold: intimacy with God and compassion (suffering love) for the world he loves. It's all there in the Gethsemane prayer story, Jesus and the Father exposing their hearts to each other and facing the reality of where their love will lead them.

There were certainly times when the disciples saw him praying alone. Luke records that on one occasion the disciples overhear him praying and ask him to teach them how to pray (Luke 11:1–4; Matt 6:9–15). Jesus answers with a model prayer; Matthew contains the fuller version and Luke contains the abbreviated one. In this prayer Jesus is teaching us to pray his prayer with him, to see and address God the Father as he does, using the more intimate name, our *Abba*. With our Rabbi Jesus we connect with God on this more familiar level, seeing what he sees, hearing what he hears, saying what he says, and aligning ourselves with his will. Let's follow the progression:

We acknowledge his holiness and ask him to reveal it to the world ("uphold the holiness of your name"). We seek the growth and prosperity of his kingdom of love ("Bring in your kingdom so that your will is done on earth as it's done in heaven"). We acknowledge our utter dependency on him, even for life's most basic essentials ("Give us the bread we need for today"). We ask for his forgiveness for our own sins, recognizing that it means nothing if we do not forgive others in turn ("Forgive us for the ways we have wronged you, just as we also forgive those who have wronged us"). And then we return to acknowledging our utter dependence on him, this time by confessing our inability to see our way clearly without him and to rescue ourselves from the insidious deception and dangerous captivity of evil ("Don't lead us into temptation, but rescue us from the evil one"). Prayer is the glue of our love affair with God, with one another, and with the world. It is a call to action based on that love affair. In prayer we engage with God and he engages us with the world he is working to save.

The Lord's Prayer teaches us that prayer is a community event—always. When we pray we are in community with God, our brothers and sisters in Christ, and all humanity. This is true when we pray with a community of believers, and it is true when we pray alone. When we pray together we pray for each other and for the church, as Jesus did with his disciples (John, chapter 17). We also pray outside the circle of Christian faith, for those without faith and those of other faiths, and of course for our enemies. The same holds true for our personal prayer, where we pray for ourselves and beyond ourselves, as did Jesus in Gethsemane.

Jesus also teaches us that we can make a sham of prayer. Some use prayer in public to draw attention to their piety, which should only be practiced in private (Matt 6:5-6). Some public prayers are only a flow of empty words (Matt 6:7) or a display of one-upmanship (Luke 18:9-12). These prayers, Jesus says clearly, will not be heard (Luke 18:14b). They reveal an unhealthy self-love and little concern for anyone else. To update the words of a nineteenth-century poet, "He prays best who loves best."

Turn the phrase around, and it is still true: he loves best who prays best. Sometimes loving someone is difficult. No matter how hard we try, we just can't do it. Perhaps the person gets to us in a way that throws us off love's course. Perhaps we have gotten defensive or even angry at the person. Jesus calls us to pray for those who harass us (Matt 5:44b) or mistreat us (Luke 6:28), even though we find it hard to pray for them in love. He expects us to bring those persons and our inadequacy to deal with them into the presence of God. Prayer creates a different context for the difficult situation. It helps us to see our adversaries through the eyes of God, and just as importantly it enables us to see ourselves honestly, see our own resistance to loving them. And perhaps it even helps us to begin to understand and confess something in us that needs to be owned and confessed. In fact, Jesus does tell us to forgive anyone we have something against *before* we ask in prayer for forgiveness for our own sins (Mark 11:25).

This kind of prayer is powerful because it includes the one praying in the formula for needed change. In this prayer we expose *ourselves* before God, asking him to change us even before we ask him to change the other person or the difficult situation. In this way prayer is essential if we are to love others in the way our Rabbi Jesus calls and commands us to do. It's amazing how barriers to loving people weaken and begin to crumble when we start with the barriers in *us* that the grace of God can reveal through honest, seeking prayer.

Prayer, according to Jesus, is not a peculiarly religious exercise, something we do to feel or be more spiritual. It is of a piece with the minutes of our day, the flow of our lives, the varied expressions of our love, the paths of our different vocations. This is why Jesus speaks of praying continuously, like the persistent widow seeking justice (Luke 18:1–8), echoed by the apostle Paul (I Thess 5:17). Prayer is a relationship essential to anyone who follows Jesus. As it is with Jesus who prays regularly, not just in crises, so it must be with those who seek to imitate his life. He knows we are human; so was he. He knows our vision and discernment of his kingdom can fade, our righteousness can be compromised, our capacity for love can dwindle, our strength to give ourselves to others can be exhausted. So he invites us to pray with him often and regularly, even in the heat of our battles.

As we engage ourselves in this persistent prayer, we are in company with God, with ourselves, and with others. A study of Jesus' prayers shows that for him and for his disciples, prayer has nothing to do with our private prosperity. It has only to do with the prosperity of God's kingdom in the world and in people's lives, with how we (those who pray) can live better as citizens of this world-claiming kingdom. All this to say, prayer is finally missional. It aligns us with God's heart, his deep love for the world, and his incarnation in Jesus to save it. And it calls us all to be his extraordinary lovers of the world for which he died.

Section Three

Jesus on Witnessing
Finding Our Calling in the Everyday

JESUS CALLS ALL HIS disciples to be witnesses. All of them. No exceptions, no passes, no excuses. In the Gospels not only does he send out the twelve as well as the seventy (or seventy-two) during his ministry, but in the last verses of all four Gospels, the resurrected Jesus, in one way or another, commissions his disciples to be his witnesses and continue his mission:

- Matthew concludes with the well-known command to his disciples to "go and make disciples of all nations [ethnicities]" (Matt 28:19).

- Mark has Jesus saying, "Go into the whole world and proclaim the good news to every creature" (Mark 16:15). Now that command is part of a concluding section not found in the earliest manuscripts of Mark. Either it was part of the original manuscript and was lost and later found or it was added later. If it was added later, perhaps compensating for an original ending lost, it is certainly consistent with the "sending out" by the resurrected Jesus in the other Gospels.

- Luke's concluding sections focus at first on the resurrection of Jesus and its foretelling in Scripture. The text then moves on to record Jesus explaining what follows: "A change of heart and life for the forgiveness of sins must be preached in his name to all nations, beginning from Jerusalem. You are witnesses to these things" (Luke 24:47–48).

- John records the resurrected Jesus appearing to a very anxious group of disciples, twice giving them the blessing of peace for their troubled spirits, and then challenging these only-moments-before fearful followers with a bold commission: "As the Father sent me, so I am sending you" (John 20:21). He invites them to leave their place of fear and cowardice and obey his call to mission.

One of the modern misinterpretations of these passages is the view that this call to mission is a select calling for only some Christians. It goes something like this: There are Christians who have been especially gifted for witnessing and reaching out to others. They may be very outgoing. They may be comfortable with engaging people in different or unfamiliar settings. They may have the ability to reach across social boundaries or cultural barriers. They may have the gift of evangelism or social service or political action, for example, and are therefore well suited for these opportunities for witness. The rest of us are called to live out our discipleship by serving the church, caring for other Christians—and, of course, praying for those who do the outreach.

Some of the church growth literature of the last century encouraged this kind of separation between people who were "gifted for mission" and those "gifted for maintenance," those whose ministry would take place outside the church or in the world and those whose ministries would take place within the church. It is certainly true that 1) there are disciples of Jesus who have specific gifts that naturally lead them to fulfill important missional roles, and 2) their apostolic service is crucial. It is also true, however, that Jesus does not call them to carry the entire weight and responsibility for his mission. In fact, were the mission of Jesus being carried out as he intended, these disciples with special gifts for outreach would be carrying a much smaller role in fulfilling it than they are now. I remember hearing Billy Graham remark once that his form of mass evangelism was fully insufficient for the requirements of the Great Commission.

The Great Commission is a call to all Christians. Jesus calls all his followers to give witness to the gospel with their transformed lives, their timely words, and their compassionate action. That, and that alone, is the fulfilling of the Great Commission. One does not need to be a gifted evangelist to touch the hungry heart of a seeker after God, nor a qualified social worker to share the compassion of Christ with a not-yet disciple. One need only be willing to take the risk with people and trust the guiding Holy Spirit of Jesus.

How, then, do we describe this witness to which Jesus calls all of us? We imitate our Rabbi, and we obey his call. We investigate the Gospels and allow the Jesus we meet there to teach us how to live the life he gives us. And what we discover is that he also gives every one of us disciples an extraordinary calling. We cultivate a life with Jesus, and that life itself, by its very nature, becomes a mission that influences beyond our calculation.

The life of the disciple of Jesus is foundational for any real influence that the disciple will have in the world. This influence is what we call mission. Our life and our mission are inseparable from each other. The Christian life without life-changing influence in the world is a contradiction, as are formal mission projects without compassionate disciples.

So we will examine how we cultivate a life of strong witness and influence for the kingdom of God. Again, Rabbi Jesus is the teacher and his life the model. We shall call this section of our study "The Cultivation of a Life." We shall then listen to Jesus' command to go public. With Jesus as our model for public action, we shall explore the ways and means by which we reveal Jesus in the smaller and the larger worlds where we live. We shall call this final section of our study "Bearing Public Witness."

The Cultivation of a Life

Chapter 35

Intimacy with Jesus

My memory of Eunice McCrae goes back to when I was about twelve. I was in the first year of my church's six-year Bible and leadership training course for junior and senior high school students. At one of our meetings, Eunice McCrae was invited to share her journey with us. Eunice was a Salvation Army officer and single. Her appointment was to operate a home for unwed pregnant mothers and be pastor to the young girls who found themselves in what was considered then to be a publicly embarrassing situation. She was nearing retirement and had much to say, but she was aware of the short attention span typical of our age group. She spoke only of the matters she felt would carry weight with us. I distinctly remember a certain beauty in how she spoke about her life, although I don't remember most of the details.

What I do remember clearly is what she said about being single. I was growing up in a two-parent family and acquiring the unspoken assumption that people naturally got married when they grew up. Now here was Eunice McCrae telling us of her chosen path to the single life. That intrigued me.

Eunice talked about not marrying as a very conscious and important choice she made. (Is there really a choice here? I remember thinking.) And then she said something with a firm gentleness: "I feel I've become married to Jesus." As a twelve-year-old, I took that in without knowing what I was taking in. I saw the institute of marriage as a social norm, but I also had inklings of a very intimate side to it—namely the sexual—and the way Eunice talked about being married to Jesus had the feel of intimacy. How could she be intimately married to Jesus? I had been taught in church that a Christian was a follower of Jesus who tried to be like him. But intimate with him? I had much to learn.

WHEN IT COMES TO our relationship with Jesus, imitation without intimacy will not do. It would be a sham. Remember, Jesus calls his disciples, first of all, to "be with him" (Mark 3:14), and the risen Christ promises continued intimacy with his disciples just before he ascends to the Father: "And surely I am with you always, to the very end of the age" (Matt 28:20).

"I am with you always." Our response to that assurance might be: That's great, he's got my back. I can get on with my calling. I can do my work. There's so much to do. Stay close to me, Jesus, and we're going to build this Kingdom of God!

Not exactly. The issue is not so much whether Jesus is with us. (He is.) It is whether we are with him. Remember Mary and Martha (Luke 10:38–42)? Mary is spending time at Jesus' feet, Martha is busy in the kitchen seeing to needed meal preparation. Mary seeks intimacy with Jesus, Martha seeks to serve him. Both aspects of our relationship with Jesus are important.

One way to understand the story is to recognize we all have both Mary and Martha in us: We all want and need intimacy, we all want and need to serve. For all of us, it seems, one of the two is more available to us than the other. Some of us are comfortable spending time in relationships, others are more comfortable doing things. For many of us, the Martha in us is more available, and we don't give the Mary much of a chance. Most churches probably tend to reward the Marthas more than the Marys. We applaud the people who get things done, those who have a spirit of service. Why is that? Are we ill at ease around those who seem to spend an inordinate amount of time (in our opinion) in conversation or in worship and prayer and solitude?

Jesus gives us no reason, no blessing, to run ahead of him with our good works and great plans. He gives us plenty of reason, and his blessing, to follow him. And there is no following him without knowing him, no imitation without intimacy, no discipleship without relationship, no calling without communion.

At the conclusion of his prayer for his disciples (John 17:24–26), Jesus speaks of knowing God in a way deeper than the factual and intellectual. It is a personal knowing, a true intimacy. "The world," says Jesus (obviously using "world" here to mean the fallen world), "didn't know you [the Father], but I've known you." They do know, however, that the Father has sent Jesus (v. 25). In other words, says Jesus, whereas fallen humanity does not know God in the intimate sense or does not have a close relationship with him, they do have a strong sense of Jesus having been sent by God; and they are right.

Jesus becomes a kind of continuing conduit through which those who follow him (his disciples) connect with God. Jesus claims he reveals the

Father to us; "I made your [the Father's] name known to them, and will continue to make you known" (v. 26a). Elsewhere he goes even further by claiming an extremely close intimacy, saying that he and the Father "are one" (John 10:30). In John, chapter 17, however, he connects (we could almost say he merges) his intimacy with the Father with his intimacy with his disciples. Or as the text says, "[I] will continue to make [your name] known so that your love for me will be in them, and I myself will be in them" (v. 26b). In other words, we can receive and experience the love of God in Jesus. The Father's love for Jesus, the God-Man, in some astonishing way becomes his love for us (humankind).

However, Jesus goes further than the claim that he is the conduit of God's love. He claims he *is* God's love. Receive God's love and we receive Jesus; receive Jesus and we receive God's love.

In this prayer shortly before his crucifixion, Jesus speaks of this intimacy with him in the context of his disciples' life and calling in the world (John 17:6–23). The words of intimacy are his final words in the prayer. As you read these verses, do you think he is saying: Above all, as you go into the world as my disciples, as you follow your calling, you do so with me in you and in the power of the Father's love? I think so.

Just how intimate is this intimacy with Jesus? As intimate as branches are with the vine. (John 15:1–17.)

All true intimacy, and the honesty and self-disclosure that come with it is always a scary thing. Remember when Jesus compares himself to the bread we eat and the water we drink, which physically then become part of us and sustain and energize our life? "Whoever eats my flesh and drinks my blood remains in me, and I in them. . . . so whoever eats me lives because of me" (John 6:56, 57b).

Do you remember what follows after Jesus says this? Many of his disciples say, "This message is harsh. Who can hear it?" And later John writes, "At this, many of his disciples turned away and no longer accompanied him" (John 6:60, 66).

Intimacy is a wonderful thing, and it is a threatening thing. We long for intimacy, and at the same time we are afraid of it. We can keep Jesus at a distance and be shallow Christians, maybe even good surface imitators. Or, we can draw near to him and experience the joy and the pain of letting his life enter us so that we can become like him. It is the most fulfilling relationship in the world, and also the most unsettling as we can never be the same after we enter it.

For many of us, the idea of intimacy with Jesus is hard to get our minds around. He is not here in the flesh. It seems as if we are talking to the air, speaking to ourselves. How do you dialogue with someone who is not there physically, or not even available by phone or internet? How is such a relationship even possible?

The only way it can begin is to know that Jesus is always there, even during the times when he is hidden. He is there when we take in the stranger, commune with a friend, journey into solitude, or feel utterly abandoned. When we welcome the stranger we welcome Jesus. When we share our heart with a friend, it is Jesus who opens the door. When we risk solitude, Jesus speaks in the silence. When we are utterly alone, the Jesus who felt forsaken by God as he hung on a cross includes us in his cry of dereliction. Jesus comes to us in these moments, inviting us to intimacy.

Brother Lawrence teaches us something further. He says that this intimacy does not have to come about in occasional or unique moments apart from the practical tasks of the day; it can be a way into them. He is not speaking of living in a kind of otherworldliness disconnected from reality, but of connecting with reality through the heart of God and with the eyes and ears of God. It is what he calls "the schooling of the soul to find its joy in His Divine Companionship" in the world around us (*The Practice of the Presence of God*, 70). The Jesus who companions with us does not leave us on our own as we live the day. Our ever-present Rabbi walks with us to draw us to the reality of God's presence and work. "The trivial round, the common task/ will furnish all we ought to ask/room to deny ourselves, a road/to bring us daily nearer God," says a verse of John Keble's hymn ("New Every Morning," *Hymnbook 1982*, v. 5, 10).

Disciples of Jesus pursue their calling in the world in his intimate company. All three Synoptic Gospels record an occasion when Jesus, along with Peter, John, and James, goes up onto a mountain (Mark 9:2–13; Matt 17:1–8; Luke 9:28–36). To say that he goes simply to pray does not seem adequately to capture his intention. He seems to be going to seek the face of God, to encounter his Father at an intense level of intimacy and blessing. The appearance of his face changes, his clothing becomes luminous, and Moses and Elijah appear in a similar splendor, conversing with Jesus. The conversation centers on something that will happen in Jerusalem at the conclusion of Jesus' ministry, something described as a "departure" (Luke 9:31).

The disciples have been dozing off, but the light and the talking arouse them. They now see and hear it all. They don't know what to make of it, but Peter wants to capture it in some way. Not really knowing what he is saying, he impulsively suggests erecting three commemorative booths or shelters. A thick cloud or mist suddenly enshrouds them, and a voice from heaven says, "This is my Son whom I dearly love. I am very pleased with him. Listen to him!" The mist lifts, and they find Jesus alone. The disciples don't know how they are going to explain all this to the others, so they keep it quiet for a while.

There are aspects of this story reminiscent of Moses on Sinai, where he receives the Ten Commandments, which become the heart of Old Testament law (Exod 34). Before Moses ascends the mountain, he begs God to be present with him as he leads the Israelites toward the Promised Land, and God agrees. Then he asks God, "Please show me your glorious presence." God answers that He will allow His goodness to be seen, but not His face. It would be more than Moses can bear. He is promised only a back side glance (33:12–23).

When Moses goes up the mountain, there is a thick cloud and the voice of God. The voice announces who God is: compassionate, gracious, slow to anger, abounding in love and faithfulness to thousands, forgiving wickedness, rebellion and sin, and yet holding us, his beloved, accountable for our lives; a God who makes covenant with us, his beloved. The terms of the covenant are then revealed to Moses, the way of life that will define the Israelites as a people living faithfully in this covenant with God. When Moses comes down from the mountain (forty days and nights of fasting later), his face is aglow because he has spoken with the Lord. Then he shares with the community what the Lord has said to him.

The story is not lost on the apostle Paul, who, in his second letter to the Corinthian church, compares this encounter with God to the access to God we now have because of Christ (II Cor 3:7–18). The glory (or glow) on Moses' face is far inferior to the glory (or glow) on the faces of those who have encountered Christ. Moses had to wear the veil, meaning that the law cannot provide full reconciliation with God; we can be law-abiders and still have no intimate relationship with God. "But whenever someone turns back to the Lord [Christ], the veil is removed." The glory of this is the freedom that then comes from the Holy Spirit, the Spirit of Jesus, and the glory is now reflected in our faces, our countenance. This is not some mystic glow, nor some pretended, legalistic holiness. It is the fruit of a genuine intimacy where by the closeness and the openness of that relationship we are being transformed into Jesus' likeness.

Jesus ascends the mountain to see God, and the glance into the Father's face transfigures him, encouraging and equipping him even further for the radical love that will end in crucifixion. We glance into the face of Jesus and see the loving Father who wants to transform our lives through His Jesus. He is inviting us to put aside our ambitious plans for self-improvement, our petty goodnesses, and allow Him to take us further than we want to go and make us more like Jesus.

What Peter, John, and James see and hear on the Mount of Transfiguration is beyond what they can fully comprehend. It will take time as their memory continues to be interpreted by what happens later. What they do not forget is the luminous Jesus speaking with the likeness of Moses and Elijah, the three of them looking into the future, to his departure in Jerusalem. But mostly they remember the voice from the cloud, saying, "This is my Son, my chosen one. Listen to him." And then Jesus standing alone, with his intimate Companion the Father unseen but present, and the world before him.

Discipleship is not first of all about the laws we keep; it is about the company we keep. We now live in the company of Jesus. We have heard God say, He is my Son, my Beloved (Mark 1:11; Matt 3:17; Luke 3:22). If you want to be my people, walk with him. Live with him and listen to him. He stands alone, the sole source of life, the full embodiment of our true humanity, the astonishing enfleshment of God's love for us. He invites us to get intimate with him, so that we can be like him, and in that closeness we begin to cultivate the life he came to give us.

Chapter 36

Feasting and Fasting

I've never been very consistent about fasting. Feasting is another matter. I am very fond of eating, and I consider tasty, nutritious food to be one of God's many gifts, which I reason it would be ungracious of me not to accept. Keitha and I have sporadically fasted, abstaining from solid food for a day. When we do, we're often amazed at the clarity of mind it brings toward the end, even sometimes a sense of spiritual clarity.

I wonder, however, if it may be helpful to see fasting and feasting in a much broader sense. What if we see the meaning of fasting beyond the literal sense of abstinence from food in particular and feasting as more than the enjoyment of food in particular? Can we understand fasting best if we see it as a metaphor for a wider range of experiences that can be described as an emptiness; and can we understand feasting best if we see it as a metaphor for experiences we describe as a fullness? In this sense our lives seem to play out in the back-and-forth of feasting and fasting, fullness and emptiness. At one time we seem to be feasting, we sense a fulfilling or a fullness. At another time we seem to be fasting, we sense an emptying or an emptiness. Perhaps that is exactly how our lives should be. Life could not be sustained if we knew nothing but emptiness, nor could there be any motivation for growth if we knew nothing but fullness. Either way, there is no moving forward; and when life does not move forward, it declines.

Let's explore what Jesus has to say on the matter and what his own life teaches us.

WE WHO ARE DISCIPLES of Jesus live our days and pursue our callings in his presence. On this journey we discover times of feasting and times of fasting. We experience the presence of our Lord as joy and generosity; these are times for feasting. And we experience his presence as different or even distant; these are times for fasting. Sometimes Jesus is present up close; sometimes he seems further removed, though still present. Both experiences are valuable to our discipleship. The feasting is when we experience God's nearness and lose ourselves in adoration and gratitude. The fasting is when we long for the nearness and set out to find greater spiritual depth or perhaps even a new orientation.

In the days of Jesus as in our own day, literal feasting and fasting correlate with contrasts in one's spiritual experience. The question of when to feast and when to fast comes up a number of times over the course of Jesus' ministry. On one occasion the people ask Jesus, "Why do John's disciples and the Pharisees' disciples fast, but yours don't?" Jesus answers, "The wedding guests can't fast while the groom is with them, can they?. . . . But the days will come when the groom will be taken away from them, and then they will fast" (Mark 2:18–20; Matt 9:14–15; Luke 5:33–34). Weddings are a time for feasting, and Jesus is inviting his listeners to a wedding banquet called the newly arrived kingdom of God. When we experience his absence or feel ourselves to be outside his kingdom, it is time for fasting. In our journey with Jesus, there are times for both.

When Jesus tells his disciples that his mission will lead to his suffering and death, and then his resurrection, they object. They are in denial. But over time, as he keeps telling them, and as they are aware of the growing opposition to his mission, they begin to grasp that his life may well be cut short. They may lose him. And so they begin to allow themselves a kind of fasting, wondering what his absence will mean for them and how they will be able to keep what he came to bring them when he is gone. They grieve (Matt 17:22–23).

We see Jesus practicing *feasting* on a number of occasions. He goes to parties and celebrations, even when the guests are of questionable repute (Matt 9:10–11). He speaks of the kingdom of God as a huge international banquet feast (Luke 13:29). By miracle he feeds the hungry thousands in a great outdoor feast (Mark 8:1–9a). Jesus shares meals with his disciples, and we can be sure many of those occasions are suffused with a joyful closeness and intimate prayer. In fact, Jesus' love and enjoyment of feasting is proven by the religious establishment's harsh criticism of him for it (Luke 7:34).

Feasting is also a broader metaphor for the experience of sharing Jesus' intimate presence. Jesus himself actually speaks of feasting on *him* (John 6:41–71). The language is so physical and intimate that people are offended and take their leave. If we could catch their thoughts, here's what we might hear: "Let's not allow our religion to take on real flesh and blood. Let's not allow Jesus to touch our lives up close where we are most vulnerable. Let's certainly not allow him to enter our bloodstream and enflesh himself in us.

Let's keep him at a safer distance." Sitting down to a meal with someone carries overtones of a more intimate relationship. Some do not feast with Jesus because their faith has no place for the joy and pain of intimacy. Jesus, the feaster, the host of kingdom-of-God banquets, invites us to draw near and feast with him and imbibe his very presence like a meal both sweet and spicy.

We also see Jesus practicing *fasting*. Before he launches his own messianic mission, he is led by the Spirit of God into the wilderness where for forty days he fasts (Mark 1:12–13; Matt 4:1–11; Luke 4:1–13). There seems to be a definite connection between his fasting and his freeing himself from the threefold temptations of the devil to divert him from his true mission. On the week of his death he prepares himself in the Garden of Gethsemane with fasting prayer, denying himself sleep and pleading for grace for the coming day that even he felt would be beyond his human resources. Finally, the Cross is the ultimate fast of deprivation: "My God, my God, why have you left me?" He lets go, he fasts, of everything.

His experience teaches us that fasting can lead to the purifying of heart so essential to fulfilling our calling. It can be a journey inward to find the center of who we are as sons and daughters of God and true disciples of Jesus. Fasting is a deprivation that helps us shed some of the distracting bulk and baggage that is not part of who we really are in Christ, or to settle unresolved issues relating to our discipleship. Having begun to open our eyes to the reality of our transformed selves, fasting leads us to confess our need to move forward, further into radical discipleship, and to receive grace for that journey. Fasting can help to free us to get a better grasp on what is truly significant in the kingdom of God, and it can empower us to find and pursue our true calling, as it did with Jesus.

The Jesus we meet in the Gospels is a feaster and a faster. He invites us, his disciples, to live our lives feasting and fasting in his presence. We must, however, understand this spiritually. Feasting and fasting are metaphors that describe our relationship with Jesus.

Consider what it means to *feast* with Jesus. We can say that the sacrament of the Lord's supper, or a love feast, or a community meal is a participation in the life of Jesus, but it is so only if *we* participate, if we are present with Jesus and therefore with all who are gathered there. Time shared with a friend in the presence of Jesus is a feast. Time shared in solitude in the presence of Jesus is a feast. These and all feasts of Jesus are deep joy.

Consider what it means to *fast* in Jesus' presence. These are times, not of fullness but of emptiness. We are not filled with joy, we are filled with longing. We long to know Jesus more, or we long to be better disciples. We recognize we are not fully prepared for the journey to which he is now calling us, so we fast in penitence and preparation, or we fast by purifying our hearts, or we fast by seeking a spiritual depth we have not yet explored.

Perhaps the journey of Mary, the mother of Jesus, can help us understand. Mary loves Jesus deeply, and yet she has to come to terms again and again with Jesus moving ahead of her understanding of his calling, requiring of her a shift in spiritual insight and perhaps her own personal change. It begins with Simeon's prophecy over the infant Jesus: "And a sword will pierce your (Mary's) inmost being too" (Luke 2:35b). This leaves her with a mystery far beyond her own optimism about her son's future. Twelve years later, without telling his parents, Jesus stays behind in the temple in Jerusalem. When his absence from the returning caravan is discovered and his parents return to Jerusalem to find him in the temple engaged with learned teachers, Mary is again perplexed and criticizes Jesus' unannounced separation from them as inconsideration: *Jesus, how could you?* "Didn't you know that it was necessary for me to be in my Father's house?" responds Jesus (Luke 2:49b). He is pulling ahead of her, and she will have to deal with it.

Years later, Jesus leaves home, family, friends, and occupation for his calling, and Mary does not know what he is about to do. When he later returns to his hometown, most of the people reject him and his calling (Luke 4:14–30). What does Mary make of this? And what does she make of Jesus' startling statement when the family visits him in a town nearby? "Who is my mother? Who are my brothers?. . . . Whoever does God's will is my brother, sister, and mother" (Mark 3:31–35; Matt 12:46–50; Luke 8:19–21). And finally, there is Mary at the foot of her son's cross, seeing his filial love for her in her son's face, but still pondering in her heart, still not fully understanding, feeling the distance between them, the mystery of this strange redemption. Perhaps, however, she is moving closer to grasping, though still not there for now.

In all these, and probably other instances, Mary is letting go of a "familiar" Jesus and having to come to terms with a still unfamiliar Jesus, who is the true Jesus. Mary's experience teaches us that along with the rich fellowship and joy of Jesus' presence, there are also times when we feel his absence. He has not *actually* left us, but he is allowing us to feel and know that he is moving ahead of us, not to leave us but to beckon us further on our journey as his disciples, perhaps to a certain purification of the heart, perhaps to a further fulfillment of our calling. Again and again Jesus' disciples think they have figured him out and know what he is about; then Jesus shows them they have not, forcing them again to become learners. For the disciple of Jesus, fasting is the experience of clearing the mind, calming the heart, and moderating the body, so as to heighten the sensitivity of the spirit to the beckoning Jesus, who has more to teach us, more ways to stretch us, and more love to give us. All so that we can be with him, be like him, be him in the world.

Both feasting and fasting are ways into God's presence. They are essential parts of the journey for all who are disciples of Jesus. We *fast* so as to shed our dependence on the non-essentials, the temporal, the shallow, so that we can search our hearts, own our compromises, and seek a purifying. Through fasting we acknowledge an emptiness in order to seek the presence of Jesus in a new way. We *feast* to celebrate and grow in his presence. It happens in many different ways: in the intimacy that can be experienced in solitude, in the fellowship of each other, in the joy of life, in the fullness of the world around us, and in the sheer delight of simple pleasures, like a meal together which Jesus promises to grace with his presence.

As with so many important experiences in discipleship, both feasting and fasting can become unhealthy exaggerations. Some Christians believe that the Christian journey should only consist of a string of spiritual feasts. They try to move from one high to another. They manufacture successions of mountain-peak experience. They fear the valleys. They resist looking within at their own shallowness, getting in touch with their deeper hunger, looking at the Jesus who beckons them to take an honest look at themselves. They do not allow themselves to confess their shortcomings and sin to free themselves to move forward. They are afraid of the fast of humility and honesty. Without the fast, however, they are stuck in their ever-increasingly forced and empty feasts. Their denials close all doors to following the Jesus who beckons them beyond their complacency. They would do well to hear the honest words of Thomas à Kempis: "I have never found a man so religious and devout that he had not sometimes a withdrawing of grace" (*Imitation of Jesus*, 80).

Some other Christians believe that the Christian journey should only consist of a string of spiritual fasts. By compulsive fasting (i.e., various and sundry forms of self-abnegation) they parade either their unworthiness or their righteousness. The metaphor of sackcloth and ashes speaks to them of the only way they see leading to personal validation. Fasting becomes an end in itself, the glorification of non-indulgence, their source of pride. They cannot see that true fasting leads to feasting, the emptying to a filling, the self-denial to a fullness. They miss what God truly desires for them.

Disciples of Jesus live in the counterpoint between feasting and fasting. The experience of God's fullness dominates some days, the awareness of our emptiness dominates others. Our calling does not ask of us that we live in denial of these fluctuations. It asks of us an honest response to the reality of both the fullness and the emptiness. Both are gifts to affirm and cultivate. The feasting strengthens and nurtures us for the times of emptiness. The fasting deepens, humbles, and prepares us for genuine feasting to follow. Our lives are enriched and our callings are built upon both.

Chapter 37

Trust

Sometimes people assume that when good things come their way, or bad, God is rewarding or punishing them for something they have done. The rich man who believes in God may suspect God is rewarding him, and the poor man that God is punishing him. Poverty, however, is manmade, and wealth is often a matter of chance or chicanery. Parents with an exceptionally endowed child may suspect they have been especially blessed by God, and parents with a child of very limited capacity that God has chosen not to bless them. Birth endowments are certainly not matters of divine arbitrariness. We are guaranteed no exceptions to fortunes or misfortunes of this kind. Jesus says of his heavenly Father, "He makes the sun rise on both the evil and the good and sends rain on both the righteous and the unrighteous" (Matt 5:45). In a popular phrase, sometimes bad things happen to good people.

What, then, does it mean to trust such a God who guarantees neither financial security nor good fortune? What's the point?

JESUS INVITES US TO trust in a God who listens and responds to us. "Ask, and you will receive," he says. "Search, and you will find. Knock, and the door will be opened to you. For everyone who asks, receives. Whoever seeks, finds. And to everyone who knocks, the door is opened." Jesus goes on to ask if our son were to ask for bread, would we give him a stone? If he asked for a fish, would we give him a snake? "If you who are evil know how to give good gifts to your children, how much more will your heavenly Father give good gifts to those who ask him?" (Matt 7:7–11).

Perhaps an important key to understanding these words of Jesus is to consider the phrase "good gifts." There is a lot of gift giving going on in the world. People "gift" others for various reasons. Often it is to obligate the recipient, and it often works because we don't like to disappoint some-one who has gone to this trouble for us. In these cases the gift may be very nice, but the motive is self-serving. The gift comes with strings attached and is therefore no gift at all. Sometimes we are given gifts that by their very nature, if not their appearance, are not at all good for us. The gift may be degrading, demeaning, or addictive. It may even be destructive. The giver has a more sinister purpose. Or, the gift may be good in and of itself, but it serves to distract us or divert us from dealing with deeper issues in our lives. And sometimes we ask God for specific gifts that he knows will not prove to be for our good. God's gifts are for our good and for the good of what he has called us to be.

What does Jesus mean, then, when he invites us to trust God to give us "good gifts"? We know some bad things will happen to us. So what are the good gifts we can rely on God to give us?

Perhaps an important part of the answer lies in Luke's recollection of these sayings of Jesus (Luke 11:9–13). Instead of "good gifts," Luke re-calls "the Holy Spirit." This gives a very different interpretation of what Jesus means—or perhaps it sheds important light on what he does mean. The Holy Spirit is not a dispenser of material rewards; he is the bestower of the fruit of the Spirit (Gal 5:22–23) and the endower of spiritual gifts (I Cor 12:4–11). Also, when we suffer and are rendered weak, when we face the frustration of our limits and the reality of our inadequacies, the Holy Spirit comes alongside and intercedes for us with the Father (Rom 8:18–27). The Holy Spirit does not wave a magic wand to make everything better or to eliminate suffering or to fix our problems for us. The Holy Spirit *is* the "good gift," the true blessing. Through the Holy Spirit Jesus is present with us. The Holy Spirit is the Spirit of Jesus (John 16:12–15; Rom 8:9; Gal 4:6; Phil 1:19). The Jesus that God gives us (John 3:16) is present in the gift of the Holy Spirit.

How, then, do we see the good gifts God is eager to give us? And how does that determine our trust level with God? If we cannot trust God to guarantee our freedom from harm, our avoidance of pain and suffering, and the success of our plans, what *can* we trust Him for?

That question looms over the cross on which Jesus hangs dying, and it is posed by the chief priests, the teacher of the law, and the elders who stand by mocking: "He trusts in God, so let God deliver him now if he wants to. He said, 'I'm God's Son.'" And God is silent. A few hours later Jesus cries out, "My God, my God, why have you forsaken me?" (Matt 27:43, 46). Then he dies.

Does God let Jesus down? Does he let you and me down when he does not suddenly appear and rid us of our suffering and pain? Matthew's Gospel concludes with assuring words from the resurrected Jesus: "Look, I myself will be with you every day until the end of this present age" (Matt 28:20b). The promise we are given is the promise of presence. Jesus never leaves us or forsakes us. The Holy Spirit, ever present, is the Spirit of Jesus, re-presenting him to us and empowering us to become more and more like him. And this likeness gives the heavenly Father pleasure.

Notice what this trusting is not. It is not God spoiling us with more than we need. We are tempted to identify his good gifts in materialistic terms: We read the "green pastures" the Lord makes us lie down in (Psalm 23:2 NIV) to mean endless plenty and provision. We picture verdant mountain pastures stretching all around, when, in fact, there was no such setting in Palestine then or now. (The more suitably modest CEB translation of the phrase as "grassy meadows" brings us closer to the reality.) All the valleys were rocks and sand with only small tufts of grass growing in the shelter of rocks, which protected enough of the scarce moisture to allow meager growth. It was enough for the day as the sheep had to be led on by the shepherd to another valley the next day. The valley did not provide wealth for long-term provision, only food sufficient for now.

This trusting for today is not expecting God to fix everything for us, endorse our ideas and plans, or produce the miracles we think we need. Nor is it making our life easy or, on the other hand, cheering our overworking selves. Such a God would be so easy to believe in and trust. But he would not be the God of the Bible, not the God Jesus trusts. The God Jesus trusts does not make things easy for his own Son, does not even save him from the horror and suffering of a cross. Jesus does not trust his heavenly Father to fix things; he trusts him to be faithful in all things. He does not trust the Father to exempt him from suffering; he trusts him to see him through it. He does not trust the Father to produce miracles on demand; he trusts him to surprise the world with miracles every day.

Jesus our Rabbi is our model for this trust in God's faithfulness. He calls us, his disciples, to cultivate trust: to trust the God who is with us, surprising us beyond prediction, enabling us beyond our resources, and gracing us beyond our deserving. To trust *this* God in *this* way is to be in a place where we can hear his call and do his bidding. A life of such trust speaks volumes to this distrustful world.

Chapter 38

Obedience

One of the earliest survival techniques we learn as children is to obey our parents and other lawful authorities. As we mature, of course, we become more capable of making decisions on our own. As we approach the teenage years we may sometimes suspect our parents lack sufficient rationale for what they are telling us to do. We begin to ask them, "Why do I need to do this?" They usually respond with an explanation of some sort, which we may consider to be insufficient rationale. We push further, and at that point the response will vary depending perhaps on the emotional state of our parent at the time. I remember a few such occasions when my dad was either at a low point or had become exasperated with my persistence. "Because I said so" was his response to my questioning. I don't remember having said that to our two daughters during their growing-up years, but I confess I may well have. You would have to ask them.

During the latter part of the last century a new movement in child-rearing became popular with some parents. It was premised on the conviction that childhood obedience as a rigid and consistently enforced principle had gone too far, inhibiting the innate creativity and evolving competencies of children. A suppression of the minors, if you like. Parents converted to this way of thinking sometimes went to the opposite extreme, seeing their role as doing nothing to stand in the way of what their children wanted to do and refusing to provide guidance or direction, and sometimes even boundaries. The extremities of both high-control and no-control parenting have each delivered unfortunate outcomes.

How our personal freedom and our conformity to laws, customs, and authorities work themselves out continue to be the challenge of a lifetime. It is especially a challenge in matters of how we live out our faith. We are poignantly aware of this as we confront the reality of practitioners of one religious faith seeing it as their sacred duty of obedience to their God to exterminate those of other faiths who refuse to convert. (Lest we feel smug about our Christianity in this regard, we should not fail to remember that over the almost 2,000 years since Jesus was crucified many Christians have believed themselves led by God to do the same.) Obedience to one's God can mask a political, economic, social, or psychological agenda which may have nothing whatsoever to do with the nature or intent of the God whose interests the perpetrators are claiming to be furthering. To be sure, we are using the example of an extreme religious fanaticism, but it does illustrate the dilemma of obedience. If Jesus is our Lord and Master, how do we determine our obedience of him? And what is it that motivates us to obey?

THERE ARE TWO WAYS the Bible speaks of obedience. One has to do with obeying a law or a moral principle; the other with obeying the wishes of a person. Jesus models them both, and teaches us to do the same.

First, there are laws to be obeyed, teachings to be followed. In a prayer to the Father, Jesus says, "I have revealed your name to the people you gave me from this world. . . . and they have *kept your word*" (John 17:6, italics added). We disciples take Jesus' teachings seriously. We believe what he teaches, and we do what he asks us to do. "Whoever loves me," he says, "will keep my word (John 14:23a)," as "I [Jesus] do just as the Father has commanded me" (John 14:31).

The Bible is saturated with teachings to be obeyed. Some of them were given in a historical context in which their purpose and usefulness were relevant. For example, we can look at Old Testament instructions about sacrifices in this way. Or some of the New Testament guidelines about the place and role of women in the church, crafted carefully for a culture not yet prepared for—and largely radically opposed to—the leadership gifts available from over half the Christian population.

Other teachings are refined or even superseded by the teachings and example of Jesus. For example, Jesus carries the law against murder further, saying the harboring of anger against one's brother is a sin for which a person is also to be judged. Jesus seems to be suggesting that though not carried out in action, it is a form of murder performed in the heart (Matt 5:21–22a). Or, Jesus supersedes the command to keep our oaths by saying we must not make any oaths by swearing, implying that we simply speak truth, let our "Yes be Yes and our No be No" (Matt 5:33–37). In a shocking replacement of Old Testament law, Jesus takes the "eye for eye, tooth for tooth" principle of the Old Testament (Exod 21:23–25) and identifies it as no longer valid for his disciples. Instead, here is how they are to deal with personal injury:

"Do not resist an evil person. If someone strikes you on the right cheek, turn to him the other also. And if someone wants to sue you and take your tunic, let him have your cloak as well. If someone forces you to go one mile, go with him two miles. Give to the one who asks you, and do not turn away from the one who wants to borrow from you" (Matt 5:39b-42).

Across the spectrum of contemporary Christianity there are teachings considered as sacred and even scriptural which are actually not commanded in Scripture. For example, some groups claim their form of church government is the only one consistent with the New Testament, when, in fact, more than one form of church government is followed in the New Testament church, depending on culture, context, and social norms. Some denominations claim their particular theology and practice of the Lord's Supper is the only one consistent with the teaching of the New Testament church when, in fact, it is unclear that there was any kind of developed theology of the Supper, nor prescribed ritual of its practice, in the New Testament church consistent with contemporary practice. Sometimes claims are made on behalf of a teaching on this or that practice that are presumed to be based on clear scriptural teaching, when the body of evidence is ambiguous; for example, observing the Sabbath by doing, or not doing this or that thing. In a day when rules for Sabbath observance were prescribed in detail, Jesus, in fact, sows great confusion by saying that the Sabbath was made for humans and not humans for the Sabbath, and by allowing for Sabbath compassion to override Sabbath rules (Mark 2:23–3:6; Matt 12:1–14; Luke 6:1–11).

All this to say that for the disciple of Rabbi Jesus, every teaching must be affirmed, revised, conditioned, superseded, or even eliminated by what Jesus says. He is the Teacher, the source of truth, the standard by which all teaching and teachers must we weighed and measured—and this brings us to a second kind of obedience.

Both the Old and the New Testaments also see obedience in this other way. This interpretation goes beyond obedience to specific teachings or laws, to a deeper personal understanding. Here obedience is experienced as a direct response to the will of a loving God. The priest Samuel confronts King Saul with his disobedience, but he expresses it not in terms of disobeying a law or failing to offer proper sacrifices, but in not obeying *the Lord himself* (I Samuel 15:20–23). This disobedience is personal. It has more to do with violation of a covenant relationship with another person than with not following prescribed orders. It is a failure of love rather than a violation of law.

For the disciple of Jesus, the key to the second kind of obedience is the opening phrase of John 14:23: "Whoever loves me will keep my word." This obedience is more than following a teaching; it is following our Teacher, our Lord, our Lover. Our obedience is an act of love, returned to him who first loved us and gave his life for us. Discipleship is not checking off items on an obedience to-do list. It is following Jesus wherever he leads us.

Obeying Jesus is an act of love. This is where the Martha in us is helpful. She is ready to express her love for Jesus with action. She has doubts and uncertainties, but she doesn't let them stand in the way. Jesus says to her as she mourns the death of her beloved brother Lazarus, "Your brother will rise again." And you sense Martha saying in her heart: Okay, Lord, I don't get it, don't understand it, but I'll go with it. Wonderful Martha, letting her love become her obedience (John 11:21–27).

Obeying Jesus sometimes (or perhaps often) means being willing to listen without fully understanding. Martha listens to Jesus and trusts what he says even though she can't get her mind around it. Jesus takes Peter, James, and John to the top of a mountain, where they witness his transfiguration into a shining countenance (Mark 9:2–13; Matt 17:1–13; Luke 9:28–36). This is no Hollywood visual effect; something is being revealed about who he is. His glory is further enhanced by the company of Moses and Elijah. Peter sees this as a spectacular spiritual event and compulsively suggests it can be captured by erecting three commemorative shelters or booths. Immediately the cloud of God's presence envelopes them all, and they learn what this is *really* all about. The voice from the cloud says, "This is my Son, whom I dearly love. Listen to him!" Peter has jumped the gun in his rush to obey the impulse to get something done right away. The voice of the Father stops him short: Wait a minute. Don't go running off half-cocked with your plans. You stand in the presence of my beloved Son in whom I take pleasure. He is your Rabbi-Lord! *Listen* to him!

The terrified threesome have fallen face-down on the ground. Jesus touches them and tells them not to be afraid (Matt 17:7). They get up, and all they can see now is Jesus. As they descend the mountain, they listen to him, they listen to God's beloved. They listen to him who is also *their* beloved, and they spend the rest of their lives listening to him, and over time, from their listening to this Rabbi-Savior who loves them comes the obedience of love returned.

We must admit, however, that some of what Jesus requires of his disciples seems far too extreme. He talks about leaving home, or spouse, or brothers, or parents, or children for him and the gospel (Mark 10:29–30) or for the kingdom of God (Luke 18:29–30). On another occasion he speaks in hyperbole, extremely exaggerating to make a point: "Whoever comes to me and doesn't hate father and mother, spouse and children, and brothers and sisters—yes, even one's own life—cannot be my disciple" (Luke 14:26).

Did Jesus hate his own family? Of course not. The Gospels paint a very different picture. Does he expect us to hate our families? Of course not. He is clearly exaggerating to make a point. And the point is this. Those closest to us cannot define, control, or map out our calling. We love them, but as disciples of Jesus we do not give them final, absolute obedience. This is our final, absolute obedience: to carry our cross and follow him (Luke 14:27). To carry our cross means to surrender our life to Jesus, all of it, come what may. Even burn those bridges that may take us in the wrong direction.

Here's the amazing thing: When we do that, we then begin to learn how to love those closest to us in the way that is healthiest and best. Jesus gives them back to us so that we can love them in the deepest way as true family.

One of the great ironies of discipleship is this: Jesus says to us, "Do as I say," and we obey our way into freedom.

Chapter 39

Humility

We know of the extraordinary humanitarian work of Nicholas Winton, an English stock broker during World War II, only because his wife came across a scrapbook in the attic almost fifty years after the war. The secret the scrapbook revealed was that Nicholas had secretly saved 669 Czechoslovakian children, most of them Jews, from being sent to concentration camps with their parents following Hitler's invasion of Czechoslovakia. A friend had made him aware of the plight of these children, and Nicholas quickly decided to find a way to bring them to safety. His strategy was to go to Czechoslovakia with forged passports for the children and to place them with British citizens willing to take them into their families. The first eight trainloads succeeded in their mission. The ninth trainload was stopped after Britain had declared war on Germany. Those children were never heard from again.

Nicholas did not speak of his courageous mission of compassion. At the beginning it was a secret he kept to insure its success. What is so striking is that after the war, right up to the time the scrapbook was discovered, Nicholas never talked publicly about what he had done. He passed away in 2015 and would otherwise have gone to his grave with the secret had his wife not discovered the scrapbook. She later said he had forgotten about it.

Forgotten about it? How could he not have dropped a few hints along the way, secretly hoping the truth would come to light and he would be given the acclaim he deserved? Well, with the discovery of the scrapbook his plan for anonymity as the savior of those hundreds of children did not succeed. He had to accept Queen Elizabeth's knighting him and Czechoslovakia giving him their highest medal of honor. He was gracious in accepting these recognitions, but what clearly brought him joy during these ceremonies was being able to meet so many of those whose lives he saved—half a century later (*60 Minutes*, April 27, 2014)!

We can easily celebrate Nicholas Winton's extraordinary mission as an act of courage and compassion. We need also to recognize it as an expression of profound humility. His secretiveness enabled its success at the time, but his silence over the succeeding decades demonstrated a purity of motive. Humility is compassion's friend and mentor. For the follower of Jesus, it is perhaps the most important gift to cultivate.

CONSIDER THE ACCOLADES JESUS' followers bestow on him. For example, John the Baptist saying such things as: "I'm not worthy to untie [Jesus'] sandal straps"; "Look, the Lamb of God who takes away the sin of the world!"; and "He must increase and I must decrease" (John 1:27, 29; 3:30). That kind of adulation can go to your head.

Jesus didn't seem to let it. "He emptied himself," says the apostle Paul. He let go of his equality with God (Phil 2:6–8).

Jesus knows he has to be lifted up so that "everyone who believes in him will have eternal life" (John 3:14–15). But he doesn't lift himself up. He humbles himself. He is lifted up on a cross by those who seek to destroy him and his kingdom. And in allowing this to be done, ironically and fortunately he makes his Kingdom available for us all, and thereby, actually and strangely glorifies himself (Phil 2:9–11).

It is astonishing how Jesus makes his grand entrance on that last Sunday before his death. He rides into Jerusalem . . . on a donkey! A donkey, a lowly donkey. A king confidently claiming his kingdom, a non-violent messiah on the lowliest beast you can ride. A startling marriage of confidence and humility.

Earlier in Jesus' ministry a crowd gets so excited about Jesus they want to make him king right away. As soon as they say it, he sneaks away, escaping the honor they (and we) want to bestow on him. (John 6:15) He will have nothing to do with our "honors."

Jesus says to us, his imitating disciples: Pick the lowest place; humble yourselves; wash feet (Matt 18:1–4, 23:8–12; Luke 14:7–11, 18:9–14; John 13:1–17). He contrasts the humility of his disciples with the pride of power of the Gentile leaders (Matt 20:25–28; Luke 22:24–27). He strongly criticizes many of the religious leaders who glory in their spiritual superiority (Mark 12:38–40; Matt 23:1–7; Luke 20:45–46). At every step of the way, Jesus calls his disciples to stay low, or as the apostle Paul would advise: "Do nothing out of selfish ambition or vain conceit, but in the humility of Jesus consider others better than yourselves." In other words, just empty yourselves of the pride of unmerited or merited status. Imitate Jesus (Phil 2:1–5a)!

Some see humility or meekness as a sign of weakness. Indeed, there is a kind of false meekness that is really weakness. Someone once wryly quipped, "The meek will inherit the earth: they're too weak to refuse." True meekness is the refusal to define one's importance by, seek after, or hide behind power over others. It is inner strength without exploitation. The humble do not manipulate and cannot be manipulated by power.

Jesus prepares himself for the wilderness temptation by humbling himself through fasting and prayer. Then he is ready to face the temptation of arrogance and power. The three temptations attack the humbling, as if Jesus had gotten it all wrong, had missed the point of power and position. Satan tries to correct Jesus' "misunderstanding" and get him on track to take advantage of the opportunity that now lies at the Galilean's fingertips: power and control, the realm where Satan excels.

The wilderness temptation is fear-driven. Satan tells Jesus he can really "show his stuff" if he chooses the way of power. Consider, for example, the first temptation. It is deeply deceptive because it offers easy compassion: Use power to feed all the hungry. Let that be your mission, to give easy satisfaction to everyone's needs. Why pour out your own life? Why suffer yourself? Do you really want to bear all the pain? Are you really up to so much rejection and abuse? Be a heroic provider, not a humbled savior. I'm offering you the easy path to glory. Then you have nothing to be afraid of.

Fear drives the lust for power, and Satan uses it to tempt Jesus to bring in his kingdom by force and fiat. Even his disciples expect, at least at first, that Jesus will somehow establish his kingdom in that way. Jesus himself mentions those who are trying to advance his kingdom forcefully following John the Baptist's mission ("From the days of John the Baptist until now" [Matt 11:12]). Against his own objections, some were seeing John as the liberator-leader of a new kingdom of power. In contrast to such messianic expectations, Jesus trusts the power of love's meekness.

We disciples of Jesus better hold on to our hats, because he is calling us to trust this same power, the power that robs us of a triumphalist Christianity and gives us a cross, takes away our religious greed and gives us unselfish Golgotha, invites us to find the only glory worth having by lowering ourselves. Jesus is looking for disciples with the spirit of humility. He does not need disciples who have a better idea or an easier proposal, disciples who like to bask in the importance of their clever plans for a calling and their manageable goals for a mission. He is not looking for disciples who want to fashion a calling to their liking and a mission based on leveraged market share. He is not looking for disciples described by the prophet Isaiah as having "chosen their own ways" (Isa 66:3e). Instead, says the Lord, "here is where I will look: to the humble and contrite in spirit, who tremble at my word" (Isa 66:2b).

Humility is the heart-set and mind-set of the disciple of Jesus. It is the source of his quiet strength and the vehicle of his compassion. The Rabbi who starts this revolution called the kingdom of God is "meek and lowly." What does that say to us, his imitating disciples about how we live our lives and follow his calling?

The humbling of Jesus was necessitated by his mission, not his condition. He did it for us and for our salvation. Our own humbling does begin with our condition; we—all of us—are sinners, called to be humbled to repentance. We do not begin, or continue our lives as disciples of Jesus under the mistaken notion that we were chosen because of our righteousness. Jesus does not call his twelve disciples because of their spiritual qualifications or achievements. A quick study of the Gospels proves the point well. They are chosen for reasons only God knows; there is so much to be done with such raw and damaged material. Perhaps Jesus wants to prove we can all qualify! Again and again these twelve trainees have to be humbled for their misguided motives, their misunderstandings, their selfish ambitions, their cowardice, and worst of all, their denial of their own Rabbi Lord.

These humblings are the humblings of repentance, the admission of spiritual and moral failure, the surrender of lies, the relinquishment of arrogance. In the company of Jesus, his disciples are humbled again and again. Reduced to a spiritual nothingness, they repent, and God embraces them with grace. What the apostle Paul later puts in his more theological language ("All have sinned and fall short of God's glory" [Rom 3:23]), Jesus says in a more concrete way. He says it in response to someone mentioning a catastrophe that happened to a group of Galileans while they were sacrificing and another that happened with a tower collapse in Jerusalem. He is being tested on the widespread belief that personal catastrophes are God's signaling punishment of those who have sinned against him. Jesus simply asks, Do you think these unfortunate victims are more guilty of sin than anyone else? And then he answers his own question: "No, I tell you, but unless you change your hearts and lives, you will die just as they did" (Luke 13:1–5). Without exception, those who follow Jesus must live in the humbling of repentance where grace abounds.

In this place of grace we disciples are being prepared for our calling to follow Jesus in the world. This is the second humbling, the humbling of our mission. Jesus invites us to take up the yoke of our calling. It is a yoke that is easy, a burden that is light—precisely because it is not a yoke of our own making! Our self-made yokes are heavy because we want to prove ourselves.

His yoke assumes we have nothing to prove; the proof lies with him. We humble ourselves to take up his yoke. It is a course in humility, a course taught by a Rabbi who tells us to "learn from [him]," the one who is "gentle and humble" (Matt 11:28–30).

Jesus calls us, his imitator-disciples, to humble ourselves, be servants of him and one another. Ah, but here's the rub: he doesn't want us to make anything at all of it, doesn't want us to want to be recognized or rewarded for it. He tells the story of a servant who's been working hard all day plowing the field and looking after his master's sheep. When he come home in late afternoon he's tired. Wouldn't it be nice if the master said a few kind words of appreciation? Sure it would; we should always show appreciation.

Well, maybe so, maybe not. Should the servant expect it, asks Jesus? No, no. Being who we are, servants of our Master, is enough. But isn't recognition for our humble service how we are encouraged to be humble ourselves—a kind of positive reinforcement? No, no. Because then we would wear ourselves out being humble, always serving here, always serving there—all the while looking out of the corner of our pleading eyes for the grateful word or the slap on the back. We would miss the joy of genuine humility, the deep pleasure of serving God, each other, and the whole world—doing it for no other reason than *that is who we really are: servants.* That is the only way to *be* who we are. To live as a disciple of Jesus is to serve, not in order to be recognized or rewarded but in order to be real. Truly human. Holy.

If we cultivate that kind of humility, we will probably find our way to a compassionate life. With our eyes on the humble service of Jesus, we can cultivate the life of his disciple and prepare to live his life in the world. We can learn to lower ourselves. In that humble state we will open the door to the kingdom of God Jesus is bringing into the world.

Chapter 40

Spiritual Power

No matter what Christian denomination we may be members of, power and how it is exercised in our denomination or congregation is an issue that must be recognized and addressed. In the early days of a new movement of Christian believers, before it becomes an institution (a denomination), power tends to be exercised in more fluid ways and conflicts are more upfront. The conflicts may be very intense, but they're usually in the open and deal with important issues about the future (doctrine, mission, church government, authority, leadership, and so on). The early issue over whether Gentile converts should be required to follow Jewish practices is an example. It was a heated debate, but finally and decisively resolved.

Once the movement becomes institutionalized, boundaries are defined, positions of power are fixed, practices are formalized, and membership is regulated. Inevitably the spontaneity is diminished or brought under some form of organizational control. Now there are rules aplenty. Now institutional power is vested in a particular leadership position or leadership group. And now comes the greater temptation—native to all institutions, it seems—to play power games. This can be done in two ways, both of them damaging to the body of Christ. One is for a member to be driven by a lust for power and therefore seek a position in the congregation or denomination that will enable that lust to be satisfied (if it ever can). If such persons do attain positions of power, they will probably abuse it. The other way is the underground option: The member works behind the scenes with a demeanor of concern to undermine formal leadership by building a secret coalition or simply by spreading gossip.

In the church power can be helpfully exercised both formally and informally if it is open to input and respectful of others, is consistent with the Gospel of Jesus, and is aimed to help the church change hearts and cultivate holy lives. This is spiritual power, or the power of love, and it is very different from the power exercised by those who love power.

The Gospels are suffused with power. It is not the power of an irresistible force but of life over death and love over fear.

Consider the miracles of Jesus. None of them is simply a raw display of force nor over-wrought proof of divine authority and power. All of them are demonstrations of concrete help to humans in need, of healing to those who suffer from disease or handicap, or of peace to those taken by fear. Whenever Jesus is asked to perform a miracle to authenticate who he is, he refuses (for example, Mark 8:11; Matt 12:38; Luke 11:16, 29). That refusal is grounded in the wilderness temptation at the beginning of his mission (Mark 1:12–13; Matt 4:1–11; Luke 4:1–13). The miracles of Jesus reveal the heart of a compassionate God, not the muscle of a controlling deity. Jesus knows that miracles on demand are the enticement of the devil.

Luke tells us that after the forty-day wilderness temptation, "Jesus returned in the power of the Spirit to Galilee." The Greek word for power used here is *dunamis*, which means power in the sense of the ability to do certain things. With the aid of an Isaiah prophecy, he announces his messianic mission in the synagogue service of his hometown Nazareth. The hometown folks are skeptical. Who does this Jesus, son of humble Mary and Joseph right up the street from us, think he is? Jesus perceives their skepticism, and perhaps jealousy, and puts it into words. I know what you're thinking: Can you "do here in your hometown what we've heard you did in Capernaum?" They want neither gospel nor healing. They want spectacle. Jesus has no heart whatsoever for that. He slips away through the crowd (Luke 4:14–30).

Luke's narrative continues with Jesus returning to Capernaum. In a synagogue service there he is confronted by a man possessed by "the spirit of an unclean demon." Jesus perceives the suffering of a person torn by the plurality of confusing voices that tear away at his soul and confuse his mind. The man never asks for healing; all we hear are the multiple demonic voices accusing Jesus of an intention to destroy them. They are right. But Jesus is not listening to their loud voices. He seems to hear only the unspoken or muffled cry of a suffering man. Then he frees him of the foreign inhabitants of his mind. There is no display; it is spiritual power motivated by compassion (Luke 4:31–35).

On and on it goes, Jesus releasing enormous spiritual power, but only for healing and hope. It is always directed at the enemy's success in attacking the integrity of the soul, the heart, the mind, the body, the community.

Another Greek word used for power in the Gospels is *exousia*, which carries the sense of authority. It is power authorized for specific purposes, authority to do specific kinds of things and not just anything. It is power given to Jesus. Jesus says he has "authority on the earth to forgive sins" (Matt 9:6; Luke 5:24). When he teaches in Capernaum, the people are "amazed by his teaching because he delivered his message with authority" (Luke 4:32). In his prayer just before his arrest, he speaks of the authority the Father has given him "so that he could give eternal life to everyone [the Father] gave him" (John 17:2b).

Spiritual power is also given to Jesus' disciples. To all who receive Jesus, to those who believe in his name, Jesus authorizes (gives *exousia*) to become God's children—children "born not from blood [natural descent] nor from human desire or passion, but born from God" (John 1:12–13). Salvation by God's grace through faith. At the invitation and authorization of Jesus, we can become his disciples in the new kingdom of God. And there is more. When he calls his twelve disciples to him, he gives them "authority over unclean spirits to throw them out and to heal every disease and every sickness" (Matt 10:1). When he sends them out on their mission, he again gives them "authority over unclean spirits" (Mark 6:7).

As disciples of Jesus we are given authority and power to participate in his mission to proclaim the gospel and bring healing. He commissions us as he commissioned his first disciples: "I've received all authority in heaven and on earth. Therefore, go and make disciples of all nations, baptizing them in the name of the Father and of the Son and of the Holy Spirit, teaching them to obey everything I have commanded you" (Matt 28:18–20a).

The spiritual power comes with the presence of the resurrected Jesus: "Look, I myself will be with you every day until the end of this present age" (v. 20b). It is the power of life over death, wholeness over sickness, love over fear. It is the power of a new life called discipleship, a new way lived in obedience to Jesus. These are the true miracles of the kingdom of God.

As all temptation is temptation away from the authentic and real to the false and counterfeit, we disciples of Jesus must be diligent not to be drawn in or seduced by our own man-made miracles. Mega-churches may see their phenomenal growth as definitely God's miracle. The success of service programs in the congregation may seem to prove that God is miraculously at work. The achievement of a congregation's goals may be assumed to be the act of God. The questions in all this are: Has any of it come about at the expense of gospel integrity, the call to discipleship, and obedience to Jesus Christ? Are we too easily assuming that our measurable success is God's miraculous intervention, or have we even wondered about that? Are we simply building our own kingdoms overlaid with a patina of gospel?

In the days of Jesus, it seems, miracle-workers of one kind or another are plentiful. Some of them are impressive enough to have a following. Exorcisms take place; people are freed of the demons of the moment. Ah, but where do they go from there? What comes after the miracle? Even Jesus' miracles alone cannot bring repentance and life-change. Jesus looks at his ministry in Bethsaida and Capernaum, where he had done his greatest miracles, and laments that the miracles did not bring about a change of the people's hearts and lives (Matt 11:20–24).

Jesus may well have this question in mind when he tells that interesting story of the man who has an evil spirit depart from him, leaving him looking like a house that has just been swept clean and put in order. The place is spotless and nice to look at. However, something is clearly lacking: houses are meant to be lived in. In fact, a house not lived in is an empty place and vulnerable to foreign occupation. As Jesus' story suggests, there are plenty of evil spirits around, interested and ready to occupy. The story ends with the evil spirit not only re-occupying, but bringing with him "seven other spirits more evil than itself. They go in and make their home there." The man is worse off than he was before (Matt 12:43–45; Luke 11:24–26).

What does the original miracle—the exorcism of the evil spirit—lack? The exorcism is a good thing. Our evil must be excised, our sin forgiven. Why, then, is he so vulnerable to a worse occupation by the evil spirits?

We can certainly draw two conclusions from the story. First, it is clear that miracles alone cannot overcome our fallenness, our failed lives. Miracles and miraculous conversions cannot stand on their own. They release us but they do not reform us. They make us converts but not yet disciples. How many times have we seen new converts to Christ stumble and fall because the new house remained empty, and vulnerable?

The second conclusion we can draw from Jesus' parable is that the power of the kingdom of God does not so much lie in external drama as in deep change. The apostle Paul is a good example. He has a rather dramatic conversion (Act 9:1–19), but he apparently goes off for three years, combining an early witnessing ministry with a retreat and training in discipleship. His "house" was being occupied with the presence of Jesus and re-outfitted with the gospel of the kingdom of God (Gal 1:15–18a). His agenda is to leave no space for re-occupation by the evil spirits of his old ways. He allows himself to receive from Jesus not only the release from the past but also the spiritual power to become a disciple and a missionary for the rest of his life.

The gift of Jesus is not simply the drama of miracle, whether the drama is exorcism, high-profile conversion, or a rapidly growing new Christian congregation. The real gift of Jesus is the new and liberating kingdom of

God and the spiritual power to live in it as his disciples. There is no evidence he intends less.

The first disciples were commanded by the now resurrected Jesus to "stay in the city until you have been furnished with heavenly power" (Luke 24:49b). He invites us to do the same: to stay for the real power of the Spirit and resist the power of our own cleverness, pride, and ambition. Like Jesus, we will probably go through a desert experience, a confrontation of our particular demons and their seductions, before we are ready to follow him in the power of the Spirit (Luke 4:13–14). Perhaps we will have more than one desert experience along the way. There may be a number of illusions about ourselves and presumptions about our own spiritual understanding to be expunged from our hearts in order for us to continue to move forward on the journey. As we give up these personal impediments, draw nearer to Jesus, and follow his lead, there will be spiritual power sufficient for the way ahead.

Chapter 41

Confidence

We live in a world of credentialing. Each successive generation ups the ante on qualifications. Once upon a time a high school diploma was a sufficient credential for many respectable occupations; now it's a college degree—at least! As professions become more and more specialized, so does the required credentialing. There's clearly good justification for most of it. We would not want a doctor without specialized training in the field to be operating on our brain. On the other hand, the proper credentials alone do not necessarily make for an effective brain surgeon. There is something deeper—perhaps a passion to heal, maybe a profound respect for life, or simply a focused mind and a steady hand—that makes the difference.

When it comes to our Christian faith, where does our authority for the proper practice of it reside? We certainly have our credentialed experts in the church: biblical scholars and doctors of theology on the faculties of divinity schools, well-trained preachers in the pulpit, clinically schooled pastoral counselors on staff. Where does that leave the rest of us who lack this credentialing? Where is our credibility for representing Jesus, and how can we be certain we're following him in the right way?

We do well to remind ourselves that Jesus' credentials were frequently questioned: Isn't he a Galilean? How can the Messiah come from such a place (John 7:41)? Isn't he only a carpenter, the son of Mary and Joseph (Mark 6:3; Luke 4:22)? So where did he get his wisdom and these miraculous powers (Matt 13:53–57)? What are his credentials? By what authority is he doing these things? Who gave him this authority (Luke 20:2)?

JESUS' CRITICS—AND THERE WERE many—want to see credentials: the name of a school of thought that endorses what Jesus is doing, some other famous rabbi's referral, a PhD perhaps. They are looking for some institutional authority that gives Jesus legitimacy. In their desperation to de-legitimize Jesus, some Pharisees resort to accusing him of being demon-possessed. Who else but the prince of demons could have power to drive the demons out of a person possessed (Matt 9:32–34)? As if acts of compassion are merely the subtle manipulations of an evil mind to impress the gullible.

It's interesting that the common people are not as concerned about the credentials as are the credentialed people. The Evangelist Matthew notes, perhaps with a touch of humorous irony, that "the crowds were amazed at [Jesus'] teaching, because he was teaching them like someone with authority and not like their [credentialed] legal experts" (Matt 7:28b-29).

How does Jesus respond to the insistence on credentials by the credentialed? He refuses to give them anything! "Neither do I tell you what kind of authority I have to do these things" (Luke 20:8). What he *does* say on another occasion is this: "He who sent me is with me. He doesn't leave me by myself"(John 8:29a). Evidently, he is confident that this is the only back-up he needs. Like the prophet Jeremiah, whose prophetic credentials were also questioned over and over again (Jer 1:5), Jesus appeals not to external authority but to God's call.

Our confidence comes from the same source as did Jesus': "the one who sent me." The legitimacy of our calling as Jesus' disciples comes from our having been sent by God, not our qualification by virtue of institutional endorsement or personal charisma. We are on someone else's mission, not ours. Disciples of Jesus may be housewives or househusbands, full-time community volunteers, lawyers, social workers, field workers, carpenters, ministers, physicians, students, teachers—name whatever way any of us may spend most of our day. Hopefully, each person is fairly good at whatever he spends all this time doing. In most all these occupations there are minimal requirements of competency, though recognizably some develop their competencies more diligently and practice their vocations more passionately than do others. What the disciple of Jesus knows is that his discipleship is lived in *these* places, as well as at church or in the privacy of his family or with close friends. Wherever he is, he is sent there by Jesus. He doesn't invent his own life there; he is sent there to find out what God is trying to do and to get on board with it. He has been appointed there by the one who is already there, the Jesus who says he goes before us and will never leave us alone. Our authority, and therefore our confidence, comes from him, whether or not we carry organizational credentials.

This is not an appeal to devalue good credentials and competency in whatever vocation a disciple of Jesus may be pursuing. In fact, our Rabbi Jesus would be insulted and saddened to learn that one of his disciples was not giving his best to the practice of his vocation. Rather, this is an appeal not to hide our discipleship behind official endorsements, institutional credentialing, and the security of our positions—whether in the church or in secular occupations. That is a breeding ground for discipleship complacency. True disciples are always asking: "Why have I been sent here today?" They see beyond the practice to the purpose. Every day they are on a mission for their Rabbi.

Almost all of us are given authority of one kind or another, whether by the organization or denomination for which we work (even if as volunteers) or by society at large or a group in which we are involved. Jesus calls us to exercise it responsibly but not to hide behind it, not to exploit it, not to build our fragile egos with it. He calls us to exercise it as his sent disciple with an authority and a confidence deeper than any institution can assign to us.

In the Gospels, when Jesus appears to his disciples who are in a confused or fearful state, his first words are often: Don't be afraid. Don't be afraid: "Whatever you ask in prayer, believe that you have received it, and it will be yours" (Mark 11:24). Don't be afraid: "You will do greater things than I have done" (John 14:12). Don't be afraid: "The Holy Spirit will testify about me so that you can testify" (John 15:26–27). Don't be afraid: "I have conquered the world" (John 16:33).

Jesus invites us to pursue our calling with confidence. This is not confidence in the authority invested in us by virtue of our official position or authorization. Nor is it confidence in our illusions about personal adequacy. It is confidence in the crucified and resurrected Lord who has overcome the world. And it is confidence in what he means to do through us—wherever we are from, whether or not we have degrees or pedigrees, and however much we have made a mess of our lives in the past. None of this matters to the One who has overcome the world. What matters is faith in him expressed in love (Gal 5:6). He is the One who calls and sends us, and he is the One who grants us spiritual authority, not to build large congregations and successful businesses, but authority to proclaim the kingdom of God and heal the broken and sick (Luke 9:1–2).

Where does the disciple of Jesus get the courage to claim, stand by, and live out a way of life that clearly stands over against an adversarial culture around him? How can he declare that the new kingdom of God has come and is now reality, when it is often so hard to see and so embarrassing to live by in this present world order? Jesus himself indicates that though the kingdom of God is now present in the world, it is often hidden and must be found, exposed, and nurtured (Matt 13:44–46; Luke 10:8–9, 21:29–31). He says his disciples are those who believe it, receive it, and live it. They must risk today the future they see coming in God's time. This they do in the power of the Holy Spirit. "The community of the Spirit," says Martin L. Smith, "lies under the authority of the future."

The *authority of the future* gives confidence for the radical discipleship of the present. Followers of Jesus are not passive believers waiting faithfully and quietly for the kingdom of God to come in all its fullness. They are active believers living faithfully the life of Jesus, discerning the emerging presence of the Kingdom of God in the world, and risking their lives and reputations on its reality. Their confidence to do this comes from the One who gives them authority to do it, the One whose kingdom is even now bearing fruit on the way to the rich harvest of eternity.

Our calling as disciples is to follow the Jesus who goes before us, to trust him to lead us well, even though he sometimes takes us where we do not want to go. He is our Rabbi. He calls us to trust him.

Sometimes, however, he calls us to trust him by trusting ourselves. The decision to become a disciple of Jesus is not a decision to trust Jesus by distrusting ourselves. Our Rabbi does not hover over us, dictating our every step. He shows us the way and empowers us to walk in it. He shapes our soul and trusts our emerging humanity in God's image. He revolutionizes our thinking and releases us to make decisions according to what the apostle Paul calls "the mind of Christ" (I Cor 2:16b).

Throughout the Gospels we see twelve disciples following their Rabbi Jesus. Sometimes they find it difficult to keep up with him, especially at the end when their Rabbi is arrested, tried, tortured, and killed. The following is hard enough. The leading is hard, as well. When Jesus sends out the Twelve (as well as the Seventy) on their own, as it were, I imagine they have a serious attack of nerves. It is clear they have not even grasped the full message of Jesus at this point (Mark 6:6b–12; Matt 10:1–16; Luke 9:1–6, 10:1–12). Jesus sends them out anyway. He trusts them with all their imperfections and confusions. Sometimes they let him down (Matt 26:36–46). Still he trusts them.

And what happens when they let him down? The answer is clearly given as we look in on the post-Resurrection appearances when the resurrected Jesus never criticizes the disciples' pathetic showing during the last three days of his life and after his death. He appears to ten of them huddled in fear behind locked doors, gives them the blessing of peace, commissions them for his continuing mission, and then breathes Holy Spirit on them (John 20:19–23). A week later, he appears to eleven of them (now with Thomas), again giving them the blessing of peace, this time finding Thomas in particular and giving the doubter, not rebuke, but every reason to believe (John 20:24–29). By the Sea of Tiberius he appears to all of them, where he gives them a huge catch of fish and a cooked breakfast, and then comes to

Peter, whose courage had completely failed him when Jesus could have used it. He looks at Peter with forgiving compassion and asks him if he loves him more than any other. When Peter, sensing Jesus' forgiving love, says "Yes" the three times, Jesus entrusts his flock to him (John 21:1–19).

Jesus trusts us beyond all logic. We stumble and sin, and he lifts us up and says, This is not you, not the you I'm helping you discover, not the real you. He keeps trusting us, showing us, breathing Holy Spirit into us. We keep on living in that trust, and before we know it we are ready to receive the gift of confidence, confidence to follow our Rabbi and be his disciples where he sends us.

The cultivation continues.

Chapter 42

Willingness to Fail

In a success-driven world, failure represents what we fear. There is nothing worse than being a failure. What failure actually means is defined by the culture of comparison which seems to have us in its grip. I'm a failure because someone is better in my tennis league, or someone else got the top position in our firm. We're failures because another football team rather than ours won the championship, or our party didn't win the Presidency. Of course, there are comparisons within comparisons. It can be very disappointing for my football team to lose the championship game, but it's downright shameful to be at the bottom of the league when the season is over. The culture of comparison precipitates seasons of soul-searching, although the soul actually has nothing to do with it. Our sense of failure in these cases has to do with the self, not the soul. It has to do with the profoundly insecure part of us that has been made stupid by the myth that our value as a person is measured by competitive success. Being more successful than someone else (or a whole bunch of someones), is based on arbitrary measurements that have no enduring reality whatsoever.

Let's turn this culture of comparison on its head and ask: Can failure ever be a good and fortunate thing? Well, we know that failure can motivate us to work harder to master a skill, or gain a position, or win a championship. We are still, however, totally orienting ourselves by a culture of comparison based on arbitrary values; still trying to be the best this, that, or the other.

So, is there a kind of failure that has nothing to do with the culture of comparison? And if there is, how do we understand it— and does it have something important to teach us about living?

LOOK AT JESUS FACING failure. He tries to bring his mission to his hometown of Nazareth, and he is spectacularly unsuccessful (Mark 6:4–6; Matt 13:53–58). Early in his ministry he can already say a prophet is without honor in his own country (John 4:44). There's the time he speaks of himself in a way the people are not prepared for, and they abandon him (John 6:66). There are times when he is preaching to deaf ears, blinded eyes, and deadened hearts (John 12:39–40).

In many ways Jesus' mission is a failure, and his death on a cross as a criminal signals at the time to almost everyone, including his disciples, the failure of his mission. Everyone does not accept with open arms his strange new kingdom, nor his messianic claims. Nor do they support the strategy of redemptive suffering, the way of the Cross.

How does Jesus deal with this failure? He accepts it. He accepts it because he knows success is hidden in the failure. He knows our plans may fail but his love wins. He knows his suffering and death will release the saving love of God in the world. This enables him to face the reality of immediate failures without allowing them to persuade him to give up or to overcompensate with easy successes. One instance of this is recorded in Matthew 11:16–19 and Luke 7:31–35 where Jesus speaks of the many who have rejected both his message and that of John the Baptist. He compares John's message to a dirge, but no one has mourned. He compares his own message to the more graceful sounds of the flute, but no one has danced. John comes with a lifestyle of self-denial and fasting, but he is dismissed as demon-possessed. Jesus comes accepting invitations to parties and banquets, but he is dismissed as a glutton, a drunkard, and a friend of tax collectors and sinners. Jesus' mission is not made successful by success; it is made successful by the power of his love and the cost of his life.

Perhaps we are just too afraid of the pain of failure, so we play it safe. And Jesus says to us: Fear not. Don't be afraid to fail. God will use your "failure" in ways you never imagined.

Yes, we sow seeds that sometimes don't sprout. Sometimes, promising beginnings end in failure. Sometimes, our efforts are choked by contrary forces. (Jesus once told a parable about that.) And sometimes we throw out onto the field a tiny seed, not expecting much to come of it, holding out little hope for an outcome, and a few years later—a huge, lush, healthy tree!

God is full of surprises. He turns what we normally expect upside down. And sometimes, what we see as our most unpromising efforts, as well as some of our worst failures, turn out to be our greatest successes. A success-driven life can yield momentary euphoria, but a life lived fully in the new kingdom to which Jesus calls us yields a life of eternal consequence.

Failures are under-rated by a culture obsessed with success. Disciples of Jesus do not set themselves up to fail, but they measure success by a different standard than the forced outcomes achieved through our obsession with comparisons, numbers, strategies of manipulation, and our cleverness. Their measurement of success is the life lived by and the love shared after the pattern of Jesus. They do not plan and then set out to do their own mission: Their mission is not self-initiated, and therefore not judged by their carefully considered expectations. Rather, they go *to* their mission: Their mission is to follow Jesus into the world in order to be with him, be like him, and do what he does. How do you measure success by that? Not on a statistical printout, rather by lives changed. God is not honored by our expansionism; he is honored by the contagion of Jesus, the spreading of his love, the transformation of heart, the imitation of his life. Where this happens, we free ourselves from our pathetic obsession with not failing. And sooner or later the success, whatever form it may take, will take care of itself.

Disciples of Jesus do not institutionalize their mission, pursuing success as the advancement of their congregation or denomination, though this may well occur, or not. Their mission is to follow Jesus with all their hearts, to discern what he is doing and give themselves over to it. This will lead to some outcomes deemed failures by people who can grasp the idea of success only in materialistic ways: increased attendance, bigger budgets, power leveraged in the community, and the like. The outcomes worth pursuing are those to which Jesus calls us. Of themselves, they may carry little aroma of worldly success; the aroma of their lives is rather a permeation of God's love (I John 4:7–21), a fragrance, says the apostle Paul, of life over death (II Cor 2:14–16). A spiritually dying church can expand by time-proven expansionist policies and strategies and thus keep alive the appearance of vitality and keep at bay the ghost of failure. A spiritually vital church can face its failures and learn from them, and even more importantly, see in some of its failures a deeper success, seeds sown for outcomes not measurable by market standards but by what proves over time to grow the kingdom of God in people's lives, the harvest of eternity.

We must learn from Jesus' failures and from his losses. They have given us fullness of grace from which comes "grace upon grace" (John 1:14–16). Rabbi Jesus rescues us from the oppressive culture of comparison and from the drive it demands of us. To follow Jesus is to be freed from our fear of failure and to be encouraged and empowered to take risks for the kingdom of God. Who knows?—some of our failures may prove to be our greatest successes!

Chapter 43

Self-Denial

Self-denial is not particularly in vogue these days. It is often associated with extreme acts of self-deprivation undertaken by misguided people. Think of a member of a religious order who may carry the expectation of personal discipline to a self-punishing extreme in the belief that their actions merit the favor of God. Or the parents who martyr themselves (and make much of it!) for the "good" of their child. Or the extreme case of the mentally deranged person who cannot help inflicting harm on himself. None of this leads to good.

There are, however, other acts of self-denial that are commendable, even redemptive. We rightly admire acts of heroism where the hero has risked his very life for the sake of another person, or a cause, or his country. We may wonder what goes through the minds of these heroes that leads them to the actions they take. In many such cases, decisions must be made quickly. Maybe a profound humanity rises to the surface when called on suddenly, when the opportunity for further reflection might allow a preventing fear to intervene. On the other hand, maybe the humanity is recovered after an initial panic followed by a deeper reflection. Maybe what brings the person to the act of self-denial is the further reflection of a disciple seeking to imitate his self-giving Lord. Perhaps the compassionate act brings him closer to who he really is.

David Guy reminds us of a decision of 6,000 nineteenth-century mill workers in Manchester, England. It was a time, says Guy, when "Christian faith was robust in the English working classes." These workers made the decision to write a letter to Abraham Lincoln "urging him to continue the fight for the abolition of slavery even though the Civil War had resulted in their own unemployment because no cotton was reaching the mills where they were employed." Lincoln was deeply moved, and in reply to their letter he called their self-sacrificing act "sublime Christian heroism."

There is a self-denial that is motivated by a holy humanity. How does Jesus help us understand it, and live it?

THE JESUS WE MEET in the Gospels calls us to surrender our self and gain our soul. This is different from the metaphor of fasting we discussed earlier. Fasting involves giving up this or that thing in order to position ourselves better to draw closer to God. Self-denial is giving up something we are pretending to be in order to become who we really are in God's image.

Jesus is our model for self-denial, as he is for our fasting. On one occasion he takes his disciples to a private location for the express purpose of clarifying what is going to happen over the coming months: " . . . the Human One [Son of Man] must suffer many things and be rejected by the elders, chief priests, and the legal experts [i.e., the religious establishment]," all of it leading to his killing and then his resurrection three days thereafter. Peter is incensed over these words. They don't fit the script as he understands it. He takes hold of Jesus and corrects him with scolding. Responding to Peter, though probably sensing, as well, that all the disciples are unwilling to endorse such a future for the one they believe to be the Messiah, he turns to them and tells them they aren't thinking like God, but like fallen humans (Mark 8:31–33).

Jesus believes they *will* get it eventually. True compassion (love willing to suffer for another) is counter-cultural, even in many religious establishments. Easy love is more to our liking and our religious practice. But Jesus' disciples will come around when they see compassion in action and in outcome, on a cruel cross and in an abandoned tomb. For now, it's time to teach the crowd what this means for the life to which he is calling all who decide to be his disciples. Having shared with the Twelve the deeper mystery of his suffering and death, according to Mark's Gospel he calls this larger crowd to hear what he has to say next. The Twelve have been given the mystery of salvation through an abused and murdered Messiah, the mystery of redemptive, life-giving suffering. It's too early, however, for this radical, strange gospel to be announced from the rooftops, perhaps because it would precipitate too much too soon. There is a *kairos*, a right time, known only to God. Jesus must live out the full life and message of his calling. It is not yet time for everything to be revealed.

It *is* time, however, to be clear to those listening to the Messiah about the life he is offering to those who would be his disciples. He has delivered sermons about the ethics and behaviors consistent with his new kingdom, told parables to reveal secrets of this kingdom through understandable analogies from everyday life, and healed many sick people, demonstrating restoration to wholeness in the kingdom. By and large, these were all very much to the people's liking. More and more were coming to hear him and to receive his healing touch. It was too big and irresistible a give-away to pass up!

But now comes the appalling clincher. It's a give-away all right, but it works the other way around, as well. Jesus is giving away everything to those he asks to give away everything. The give-away works both ways. Here is the other give-away—ours—in the powerful, unavoidably memorable words of Jesus himself:

> "All who want to come after me must say no to themselves, take up their cross, and follow me. All who want to save their lives will lose them. But all who lose their lives because of me and because of the good news will save them. Why would people gain the whole world but lose their lives? What will people give in exchange for their lives?" (Mark 8:34b-37). [Note: the Greek word translated as "life" here is translated as "soul" in some other translations.]

This is not just giving back, it's giving away! The kingdom of God is not just about receiving a new life; it's also about giving away an old one. No one likes to lose to begin with; we would prefer to gain the whole world and then decide to give away what we would like. We want to act from a position of strength; Jesus calls us to begin with losing our lives. Only then, he says, can we get a life. This call does not compute with the logic of the world around and within us. We are world-trained acquirers, self-aggrandizers, seekers after success, builders of empires of one sort or another. We are "selves" and therefore self-centered. A "self" needs to prove itself, it strives to bring everything under the gravitational pull of its own personal world.

But we are not selves; the self is a fiction. We are *souls*. Our soul is our true identity: it is centered on God and created in and for community. The self as our true identity is a fiction because it defines itself by itself, without God and without the other. It is a lie, but an attractive one to a human race desperately seeking a meaning to life after having separated itself from God and having profoundly weakened community. Acquisition promises life after bringing everything and everyone within one's orbit; it invites a desperate feeding frenzy. But it does not give life, only death. The way to find life, says Jesus, is to give yourself away so that your God-given soul, your true identity, your life, can live.

The call to self-denial is paradoxically a call to fullness of life. How do we reconcile Jesus' call to fullness of life (John 10:10) with his call to lose our lives by taking up our cross and following him? One seems life-affirming, the other life-denying. We may tend toward one or the other. Some see life as a perpetual self-indulgence, a seeking after self-affirmation and advantage. Others see life as given value and meaning only by an incessant put-down of themselves, finding virtue and worth in self-abnegation itself. Both these extremes are self-centered. Identity is found here either by selfishly indulging life or by proudly negating it. In both approaches, the self is front-and-center.

How can Jesus' call to lose our lives be life-affirming? The answer is found in what we are *actually* losing: what we have taken onto our identity that is not really *us*. It is part of our false self, something that is not of our soul.

As with those first disciples who had to give up not only their false ideas about the kingdom of God but also their presumptions about themselves and their compromised motivations, so we must begin letting *our* false selves die, *our* arrogant dreams, *our* sin. Then we can begin to find our souls and live soul-fully. We may make this crucial decision in a dramatic moment, but over a lifetime we will be discovering anew what it means to die so that we can live. In this place of self-denial we are cultivating a life worth living and a calling worth pursuing.

Chapter 44

Keeping Focus

Do you fight distractions as much as I do? Do multiple choices and novel ideas ever get you thinking in too many directions? Some possibility pops up, some opportunity presents itself, and we so easily jump to it without asking the question, much less praying: Will this advance the mission to which I have been called, we have been called, our congregation has been called? All too often we go along with it, only to realize over time it was a diversion. Then slowly, or suddenly, we see we have gotten off track. We have been dealing with matters that prove trivial or have gone down paths that lead nowhere. We may have even lost the way. And our Rabbi beckons us back.

THE JESUS OF THE Gospels knows his calling. He keeps his sights on his mission. "He steadfastly set his face to go to Jerusalem" (Luke 9:51b, KJV), the completion of his three-year journey. Never was a life more focused.

Jesus calls his disciples to live and serve with no less a focus. When he sends out the seventy-two disciples to an array of cities and towns, he tells them not to be distracted along the way by people and issues intended to divert, nor to keep moving from one house to the other. The mission on which he is sending them is to spread peace, accept hospitality when it is given, heal the sick, and proclaim the coming of the kingdom of God (Luke 10:1–12). Today this is still the mission of Jesus' disciples. Each of us is called to do the same, each in his or her own way. Anything we do that doesn't support or that serves to detract from that mission blurs our focus and diverts our journey.

It is tragic when we allow distraction to keep us from our mission. Sometimes we allow ourselves to be drawn into *distractions of the mind*. We become fascinated with questions of doctrine that are either not that important or are invitations to endless speculation and debate over matters that cannot be solved or resolved this side of eternity. One example is the attempt by Sadducees to trap Jesus over the logic of the resurrection (Luke 20:27–40). One sometimes wonders what is really going on beneath such debates. Convenient diversion from matters of real substance and Christian living? Engaging mind games? Winning arguments? Our Christian doctrines are important, but they exist to give us more clarity and depth in understanding the gospel story. They do not exist to give us fine points over which to argue or to separate us into opposing schools of theology. Sadly, for some Christians doctrinal positions become straightjackets of the mind and distractions from the gospel and its mission.

Sometimes, *another person or other persons* become a distraction. Disciples may fight over positions in the kingdom of God in comparison to other disciples (Mark 10:35–40; Matt 20:20–28). At the very end of John's Gospel, Peter is having quality time with the resurrected Lord, and he notices another disciple, John, is following them. He whispers to Jesus, "Lord, what about him?" Jesus basically cuts him off and says to Peter, "What difference does that make to you? You must follow *me*" (John 21:2–23. Italics added).

Of course, in the best of families—and churches—there are disagreements, jealousies, and even fights that sour the heart. We should not pretend otherwise and live in fantasy land. Jesus calls us, in the power of the Spirit, to work through them, to bet everything on the reconciling power of Christ's love. It is no good hiding our heads in the sand, hoping that Christ (without us) will fix the problem—and if he doesn't, we can just hunker down till glory. Cancers, left to themselves, grow, and growing cancers undermine the life and purpose of the body. Jealousies, left to themselves, blur our focus on our calling and diminish our readiness for mission.

Something else that can lure us away from our mission is *work*. Perhaps we should call it work addiction. Jesus was no stranger to hard work. When you see his typical daily work load, you wonder how he did it. He did not, however, work for the sake of working; he worked in ways that advanced his mission. And he rested when he needed to. Furthermore, he invited his disciples to come to him when they were wearied and burdened, and he would give them rest for body and soul (Matt 11:28–30). The work addict, of which we have our fair share in the church, sees value in work for its own sake. He may see his work obsession as a path to personal and public worth, or as escape from important matters of life and the intimacy he refuses to face—or both. Disciples of Jesus can lose themselves in their work, and in doing so take their eyes off their Rabbi and the real mission to which he is calling them.

In our day a new form of distraction is firmly in place: *the internet*. A valuable information tool, it becomes an addiction when we cannot resist its lure. And now that we can carry the portable version in our pockets or purses, even take it to bed, it is sufficiently placed to shape the agenda of our lives twenty-four hours a day. Why do we not turn our cell phones off when we sit down to dinner with a friend or a spouse? Are we begging for distraction from intimacy? When our dinner partner excuses him- or herself to visit the restroom, do we grab our phone to check messages, or a football score, or any kind of new information to give us the next fix? The agenda of the internet is a universe of information. It prospers by creating endless informative distraction. The disciple of Jesus can lose his way and also his mission in an internet world he fails to control.

I wonder if Jesus' metaphor of the narrow gate and the wide gate and broad road speaks to this focused life to which he calls us. Most people manage to do some good here or there. Perhaps just about everyone. And I'm sure all of us, even those most admired for their goodness and good works, manage from time to time to do wrong or harm to themselves, or another. And further, some of us divide our commitments or loyalties in so many directions that focus is next to impossible. Whether our loss of focus is due to trying to cover the landscape of our lives with a thin layer of goodness everywhere, or it is due to a compromised goodness where we pursue just sufficient enough good actions to outweigh our omissions or our wrongs, we are missing the point. We are trying to enter the kingdom of God by way of the broad road and wide gate.

The point, says Jesus, is simply this: "Follow me, your Rabbi. Keep your eyes steadfastly focused on me. I'm calling you into my new kingdom. I'm teaching you, showing you, helping you live in it. My kingdom is not just any old thing, or any new thing you want to make it. It's not about a compromised life (a broad road) and it's also not about an oppressive life (an impossibly difficult road). Not about doing just enough goodness to get you through, nor about a flood of hyperactive good actions that will carry you right into a kingdom you then think you more than adequately deserve. It's about realizing I'm letting you in now! You're family! And I'm your older brother Rabbi responsible for leading and training you, mostly by showing you. Stay close to me. See what I see, do what I do, be who I am. And don't let yourself see, do, and be something else. Keep your focus. Set your hand to the plow and don't look back."

And if Jesus sees us lose our focus and stumble onto that broad road, he calls us to repentance, as he did with Peter more than once. We learn from our distractions and get our lives refocused.

After Jesus' death, when his disciples think they have lost their mission, they decide to go fishing, the work with which they're familiar and comfortable. They work hard all night on their *distraction*, and they catch nothing. (When all is said and done, distractions yield nothing for the kingdom of

God.) The resurrected and living Lord appears in the morning light, and the light dawns on them (and us)when he says, "Throw your nets the other way, get back on course. Get yourself—get your congregation—back in focus."

"It's the Lord!" we shout.

"Come and have breakfast," he says.

And we do.

The refocusing begins.

Chapter 45

Traveling Light

The Christian church has been around for a long time. It has survived for the two millennia since Jesus' death, in one form or another. Its long history has been spotty, blessed by acts of compassion but also marred by politics both insidious and brazen. It has undergone division after division: some breakoffs the result of a genuine desire for faithfulness to Jesus, others of a less honorable drive for power. Today the United States is flooded with traditional denominations and new, competitive upstarts. The established denominations have for the most part been declining over recent decades, and most of the upstarts will over time become more organized, evolving into institutions increasingly concerned about strength of membership, success in member recruitment, and corporate conformity—becoming, that is to say, denominations.

What are we to make of this varied assortment of people called Christians? For the present we'll limit ourselves to this one observation: Each well-established church calling itself Christian probably has organizational baggage created largely by the drive for denominational integrity, distinctiveness, success, and survival. Each denomination—and most congregations, for that matter—feels it has an integrity to preserve and a distinctiveness to celebrate. The felt need both to survive and succeed necessitates implementing strategies of planned growth and recruitment, along with acquiring increased resources. It all adds up to larger staffs, more departments, standardized programs, and increased internal activities. What is all this complexity accomplishing?

The church has become heavy, and the weight of denominational and congregational life may be weighing down members' ability to travel in their world as disciples of Jesus. Mission is not helped by an over-busy congregation of Christians who enjoy and are fully satisfied with each other's company. Ironically, the congregation itself can be an obstruction to its member' life outside church, the places to which Jesus calls all his disciples. Jesus calls us to be members in his body, the church—so that we can be prepared to be mobile missionaries, scattered throughout the community in obedience to our Rabbi Lord.

Add to this congregational self-absorption the lack of mission focus discussed in the last chapter, and we disciples of Jesus have a significant challenge in cultivating our lives in the world after Jesus and giving convincing witness to the kingdom of God.

JESUS SENDS OUT THE twelve disciples (seventy-two in Luke) on a mission (Mark 6:7–13; Matt 10:1–15; Luke 10:1–12). He tells them: *Take with you only a staff, the clothes on your back, and the sandals on your feet. Take no bread, no carry-bag, and no money. Rely on people's hospitality.* In other words, *travel light.* And here is what happens on their mission:

- They preach and people repent.
- They drive out many demons.
- They anoint the sick with oil and heal them.

We get the impression that traveling light is one of the keys to their success. Are the Gospels teaching *us,* their readers, to follow the same instructions? Is Jesus teaching us to simplify, to rid ourselves of the weights and burdens we unnecessarily carry and think we can't live without? Does our cluttered life stand in the way of our living the life of a disciple and following a clear calling? Do we hide behind the heavy demands of our incessant busy-ness and multiple preoccupations, including church life, in order to escape our calling and avoid our mission?

Fast forward to the Last Supper. Jesus asks his disciples gathered around the table, "When I sent you out without wallet, bag, or sandals, you didn't lack anything, did you?"

"Nothing," they answer (Luke 22:35). Nothing.

And in that free-moving state, they are soon to change the world around them.

The early Christians had practically nothing, and started a revolution that turned the world upside down. When you and I start lusting after the latest thing—whether equipment, good promotion, more money, or any of the props that make us feel more secure—we would do well to remember those disciples returning after an immensely successful mission, telling Jesus: We lacked nothing.

It is inevitable that over time all movements, including Christian movements, become institutionalized in various ways. For example, the eighteenth-century Wesleyan Revival becomes the Methodist Church, followed by an increasing number of denominational versions, each one with its own organizational interpretation of Wesleyan faithfulness. A nineteenth-century movement to reach the poor of London expands to other cities and countries, and for the sake of unity and uniformity The Salvation Army develops a system of governance, orders and regulations, and standardized processes. A similar development takes place in every denomination, though some might want to object and claim otherwise. Every expression of Christian faith and community that survives over time becomes institutionalized, adopting norms, practices, procedures, elaborations, and complications—and thereby creating behavioral diversions. Its doctrines also become more carefully defined and enforced, with oversight, resulting in increasing time spent in insuring a doctrinal orthodoxy. All this can—and usually does—lead to less time, energy, and thought given to a calling in the world where members spend more than 90 percent of their time!

It would be an over-generalization to suggest that in and of themselves these kinds of developments are detrimental to the original mission of the movement. They are quite natural and in fact unavoidable over time. This is why it is important for any organization to keep its core beliefs and practices under scrutiny: to make sure that institutionalization does not seriously weaken mission. It is true that as a movement is becoming an organization, there is very real danger that it can evolve into something quite different and, despite its overt claims to the contrary, begin focusing more on itself and less on its mission. A certain level of internal focus and concern is essential in order to keep the movement together and even to assure accountability for mission faithfulness and effectiveness. In the case of the church, the reality is that mission begins with the nurture and training of a community of disciples, the very nature of which motivates, equips, and supports their mission. However, when internal concerns increasingly focus on 1) organizational survival and issues and 2) position and status within the organization, the mission is well on the way to having been forgotten or replaced by institutional programs and promotions. The organization has become elaborate, activity is losing mission focus, non-essentials are becoming essentials.

The movement launched by Jesus looks different. It is focused on reaching people, teaching them about the kingdom of God, inviting them to this new way of living, bringing healing to those who suffer, discerning the times, and making disciples. *These* are the mission actions to which disciples of Jesus are called.

A disciple of Jesus may come to realize this mission is being weakened by his congregation's preoccupation with internal concerns. Suppose he decides to keep his focus on mission, humbly living out the life to which his Rabbi has called him. He allows the Rabbi to direct him into "the fields . . . already white for the harvest" (John 4:35b), a world in need of the compassion of Christ. His actions are genuine, his life authentic, his bottom line selfless. Over time other members of the congregation begin to see that *this* is surely what their Rabbi is leading them to; this is *their* mission, as well. The church politics, the doctrinal squabbles, the worship wars, the power struggles now begin to be seen as heavy baggage that detracts and de-energizes. A congregation finds a certain freedom (and its true mission) when it looks beyond itself to the world for whom Christ died, and to which they now see themselves to be called.

The person who realizes he is first called to be a disciple of Jesus understands this calling means looking at his whole life in terms of this vocation. It means honestly identifying the things worth not doing in light of the calling. It means giving up distractions and diversions that weigh him down and drain his energy to no good end. If he is a member of a congregation that is embroiled in organizational issues or, worse, political infighting, he refuses to be drawn into these futile skirmishes and poisoning exchanges. Instead, he chooses to think and act out of his calling. Traveling light, he keeps his journey with Jesus as his primary and defining concern. He may even become a model to his church family of what it looks like to travel light, see beyond congregational concerns, and discover mission.

Chapter 46

A Faith Private and Public

The spiritual life has a face both private and public. Some Christians are more comfortable with the private face. They see their spiritual journey as a very personal matter, something between them and God, not to be put on exhibit nor to be subject to the religious scruples or directives of one group or another. They may attend and appreciate public worship, but they experience it and take away from it only those blessings or challenges they feel are pertinent to their own spiritual needs. Others are more comfortable with the public face. They more agreeably express their spirituality in the open. They embrace the fellowship of worship. They may allow themselves to be in an accountability group. They may push for an aggressive form of public witness, perhaps a prophetic voice in the community as well. They may urge their congregation to engage in social outreach or service to the underprivileged.

We could call those who are most comfortable with the private face "contemplatives," and those most comfortable with the public face "activists." If you think that is too rigid a way to distinguish Christians, you are right. The reality is that the best contemplatives are compelled to bring the wealth of their contemplation to share in the public arena, and the best activists are compelled to bring their activism to the realm of prayer and the counsel of contemplatives. The best mystics bring their depth to the horizons of activism, and the best militants bring their strategies, along with their successes and their failures, to the insight of mystics. Better still, mystics themselves become activists, and activists mystics.

How does this happen? How does a disciple of Jesus live out his faith well in both arenas?

JESUS PROVIDES US WITH the answer: *humility.* Humility is the key to being his disciple in both the public and the private arenas. It keeps our good works secret and our public life from being self-serving. In Matthew 6:1–18 Jesus addresses some important faith practices: compassionate giving, prayer, fasting, public witness, and public repentance. Let's consider what he says.

Compassionate giving

When we *give to the needy*, we must do it privately, without any of the public announcing that the hypocrites like to engage in. Metaphorically speaking, our left hand must not know what our charitable right hand is doing. But how could we do something good like this unselfconsciously? Of course we know we're doing a very commendable thing.

Where is Jesus trying to lead us here? Perhaps he is trying to lead us to a place where compassion is natural behavior, and not a self-conscious act to help us feel good about ourselves and elicit God's approval. If we avoid commendation or recognition for our charity, we will eventually get used to the joy of non-recognition. Compassion is the "quiet normal" for Jesus' disciples, and Jesus invites us not to let it be sullied by praise. (vv. 1–4) Whatever good you do, do with silent humility.

Prayer

What about our *prayer* practice? We must go into our closet, says Jesus. Again, it seems Jesus is being unrealistic. Is he suggesting we are not to practice public prayer but pray only in private? That would not make sense, as he himself prayed in public on occasion (for example, Matt 11:25–26). Not to pray in public would privatize ourselves before God and undermine the very thing Jesus came to restore: our humanity in God's image, to which our life as a community of faith is essential. From beginning to end, Scripture describes God's people coming together as a body in public worship and prayer (for example, Acts 1:24–25; 12:5). Public prayer is normal Christian behavior.

What, then, does Jesus have in mind when he commands us to pray in private? Clearly he is attacking prayer as public display (Matt 6:5–8). Our prayer *piety* must be private.

What does Jesus say about public prayer? He says when we do pray in public get to the point and do not gush on "as the Gentiles do" (v. 7) and do not make a self-conscious display of your spiritual erudition. One is reminded of the wise advice of the Teacher: "The more words increase, the more everything is pointless. What do people gain by it?" (Eccl 6:11). Jesus also clearly has in mind some of the self-righteous teachers of the law who "to show off . . . say lengthy prayers" (Mark 12:40b). Their objective seems to be being heard and admired by others rather than speaking with God himself. Public prayer is not a time to display personal piety or spiritual superiority. It is a time to speak with God on behalf of those gathered together in God's presence and to draw them to the place of listening for God to speak.

Jesus gives us a gift: a model prayer, a pattern for our public praying. It is centered on our heavenly Father, his Name, his Kingdom. It then moves to simple, straightforward requests: Give us bread, forgive our debts as we forgive others theirs, lead us not into temptation and deliver us from the evil one. There is no place in such prayer for self-conscious performance or public display, nor for telling God what he already knows. There is only place for adoration, praise, and total dependence.

Fasting

What about our practice of *fasting*? The traditional Jewish practice of fasting required putting ashes on one's head as a sign of grief, penitence, or self-denial. It was very public. Jesus commands a very different way to appear in public when we fast: Look normal, comb your hair, put on your usual make-up. Don't look any different than you normally do. In other words, hide your fasting in public. Keep it completely private. Jesus is saying that fasting is a discipline of the spirit expressed in the denial of the body, and it has no place in public faith (Matt 6:16-18).

In all three of these examples of private Christian practice—giving to those in need, personal prayer, and fasting—Jesus is saying that to allow or encourage them to become public is to turn them into an ungodly carnival of self-righteousness. By their very nature, these private practices cannot be done to be noticed or paraded or postured without losing their authenticity and their benefit.

Public Witness

On the other hand, *Jesus does invite us to express our faith in public ways.* Jesus, the Light of the World, tells us, his disciples, that as his followers *we* become the light of the world, like an exposed lamp in a room. He tells us: "Let your light shine before people, so they can see the good things you do and praise your Father who is in heaven" (Matt 5:14–16). Jesus is now talking about a publicly exposed faith, a faith expressed not to enhance our profile but to demonstrate how the Spirit of Jesus transforms human life.

Faith is publicly expressed in such a way that people see the acts of God. Testimony is given so that people can see the miracles and moving of God in the world and in people's lives. Prophetic words are spoken to help people discern how God is at work to establish his kingdom, and to invite repentance and radical change in light of it. Some forms of public prayer and even fasting may be engaged to call attention, not to those who are praying or fasting, but to those who are being exploited or abused, or those who are following a dangerous delusion.

Sometimes the influence of extreme individualism discourages us from a public faith. It may tempt us to see our faith purely as a private matter, not up for public display: We should not interfere with each other's faith; it is private domain. The result is that many Christians do not risk prophetic insight, nor publicly expose their faith, nor call attention to God at work in the world when they see evidence of it. They sometimes do not even share their private faith journeys with their faith communities. They fail to see, for example, how in the Acts of the Apostles, the Holy Spirit works primarily through a group of some kind, a community small or large.

Public Repentance

Disciples of Jesus must take the public expression of their faith seriously. One example is public repentance. Some Christians seem to affirm only the legitimacy of a private repentance. The idea of a community or even a crowd humbling themselves before God bears no legitimacy for them. They hold this view, however, over against the witness of Scripture. The Old Testament has numerous examples of public repentance (for example, I Kgs 8:46–51; Ezek 14:6). John the Baptist calls the gathered crowd to respond to his message in repentance (Mark 1:4–5; Matt 3:1–6). Jesus himself calls the crowds to repent (Matt 4:17; Luke 13:1–5). In obedience to him, his disciples follow suit (Mark 6:12; Acts 2:37–41).

Jesus call us, his disciples, to a public corporate repentance: to humble ourselves before the world and confess a failure to follow him, perhaps by a settled complacency by which we have allowed ourselves to overlook our personal sin; or by complicity in social, political, or economic injustice; or by our hidden exploitation of others; or by our shallow self-promotion or subtle competitiveness for missional "market share"; or by our frequent failure to embody or give witness to the Kingdom of God in our community. He calls us to a full and rich expression and response of our faith, not only in repentance but in every aspect of our life as a community. Our personal faith must go public as the body of Christ stands together to build each other up and give witness to the world.

Jesus calls us to a faith both private and public. Our private faith molds us, our public faith mobilizes us. Each brings us to the other. The disciples of Jesus are called to live their lives in this synergy, as did their Rabbi.

The Influence of a Life

Chapter 47

Living

One of the congregations my friend Jim pastored had a member that we'll call Bert. Bert, says Jim, did not fit in very well with his fellow congregants. It probably had to do with his awkwardness, as well as the food stains on his old clothing. It would have been nice if Bert had used a good deodorant, given his aura, but he didn't. Brushing his teeth would also have been appreciated by those who sat next to him, but oral hygiene was not his priority.

The members of the congregation valued consistent church attendance, but Bert was sporadic. When he did come, he made his presence felt. In Sunday school class his questions and comments were usually long and rambling. During the Sunday morning sermon he would invariably raise his hand for a question about what had just been said, or not said. Bert was just plain awkward and embarrassing.

When Bert passed away, Jim conducted the funeral. The membership of the congregation were not well represented. A few of them were present just to show support and prevent the unfortunate situation of one of their members having no one come. A small number of chairs had been put out for attendees.

Then other people started to file in. More, and then more chairs had to be brought in. The shocked members of the congregation wondered who these people were and where they had come from. After a couple of hymns and prayer, Jim began his brief message. A woman in the back interrupted Jim by raising her hand and asking to speak. Jim thought to himself, "Hmm, the tradition lives on."

Jim allowed the woman to say what she wanted to say. She was followed by one voluntary speaker after the other, none of them members of the congregation. These were people the members didn't know. They had not come to hear the sermon. They had come to talk about their friend Bert. It turns out that

Bert, the member who didn't fit into his own church congregation very well, came every day to check in on an old lady in the neighborhood to make sure she was okay and had food for the day. Bert was also the man in his neighborhood who fixed plumbing problems, cleared roof gutters, and repaired the children's bicycles and tricycles. He was the one man in his neighborhood who had time to listen to the teenagers that everyone had given up on as lost. Each person from Bert's neighborhood who spoke concluded his or her comments with almost identical phrasing: "Bert showed me what it was to be a real Christian."

THERE ARE MANY WAYS we witness to the gospel. But there is one way of witnessing that all disciples of Jesus must take, and that is living the life of Jesus 24/7. Bert, in all his awkwardness and lack of sophistication, was pretty good at it.

Jesus calls us to a life. When we become his disciples, we enter the kingdom of God. This kingdom is what we are made and redeemed for, from here to eternity. In the Gospels Jesus comes preaching this kingdom and inviting us to enter it in the only way we can: By faith we accept both his lordship and his invitation to become disciples. Under his lordship we are *freed and empowered* to live; as his disciples we learn *how* to live; in the community of his Spirit and in our life in the world, we do the actual *living*.

Whatever else our witness as disciples of Jesus is, it is, before anything else, the life we live everywhere and all the time. Our witness is never only something we do; it is who we are in everything we do. When Jesus speaks of "a city on top of a hill [that] can't be hidden" and tells his disciples they are "the light of the world" (Matt 5:14), he is not referring to occasional openings for blurbs or testimonials. When he asks us to "let [our] light shine before people" (5:16a), he is not suggesting we turn on a switch called witnessing only when certain advantageous opportunities come along or we implement a strategic witnessing plan. The light switch *stays* on. The way we live our whole lives is the essential witness. Our witness has credibility when what the apostle Paul calls "the fruit of the Spirit" (Gal 5:22–23a) is making headway in our actual living (however imperfectly). Otherwise, our intentional witnessing and our well-planned evangelism mean little. It will be salesmanship without sufficient product proof.

Consider the mission of Jesus. The Jesus we meet in the Gospels does not come to pursue a political campaign, recruit party members, or win an election. He does not come to overthrow a government and set himself up as king or president. He does not come to start a new school of religion or philosophy and earn a place in our religious or intellectual history. He does not even leave any sacred or scholarly writings behind.

He comes to show and give us life in all its fullness (John 10:10b). Jesus is about living. The living is an ever-evolving experience of grace. We don't *fully* master it in this life, but we are learning from our Rabbi, getting better at living by growing and maturing as his disciples.

It is in the living that we find our witness—the total living of our lives. As we get better at the living, we get better at the witnessing. Our witness emerges as we are living the life of Jesus. Witnessing happens on the way. It is not the "doing" part of our lives separate from the "becoming." The witnessing happens as we are growing in grace and becoming who Jesus redeemed us to be. The mission to which every disciple of Jesus is called is first and foremost a living out of the kingdom of God in our own lives.

People are drawn to Christians for the right reasons when they witness lives unaccounted for by social norms, self-advancement, and self-protection. The best witness, the most effective and enduring mission happens when Christians are living the life to which Jesus calls them and for which he enables them. Our witness is basically what happens as we are living the life of Jesus. The world is drawn to Jesus when they see him reflected in the life of his disciples.

Sadly, we disciples sometimes or even frequently forget this. We have "a way of life" alright, but all too often it is self-constructed, driven, or shaped by a culture other than the kingdom of God. It may even be put together with sincere intentions. Sooner or later, we discover we have a lifestyle, not a life.

The self-constructed way of life has its own priorities and scale of values. We measure our success this way or that. We say this action has more value and that action less. Then we congratulate ourselves that we have preferred one over the other, we have invested ourselves in what we think is more important in the eyes of God. Perhaps we have prayed over the matter and truly believe God is smiling on our undertaking. He may well be. We may have made a wise choice.

God certainly honors wise planning to accomplish the mission to which he calls us—so long as we do not presume to confine his freedom or impede his gracious action by our too-narrow plans, our too-inflexible strategies, and our actions too short-sightedly pursued. Plan we must, so long as we do not worship the plan and believe the plan is the key to our calling or the guarantee of our effectiveness in helping Jesus build his kingdom in the world and in people's lives.

This flexible attitude requires humility. Indeed, humility must reside in the planning of Jesus' disciples. Humility is a way of saying whatever the outcomes *we* desire and anticipate for the kingdom of God through our plans, the gracious work of God will often come in surprising, unpredictable ways, above and beyond our intentions. In fact, we live humbly in that expectation. At best our plans become fertile ground for grace at work in ways we cannot fully anticipate and that sometimes shock us with God's power through our next-to-nothingness. So many miracles happen simply by the way, or on the way. Eugene Peterson points out that most of Jesus' witnessing takes place while he's on the move, not in pre-planned gatherings or sermons or testimony times. In fact, he has to be very disciplined just to carve out time for personal prayer, so available is he to others on the spot or on the way. Peterson cites Luke 9:51 through 19:27 as containing, one after another, the most astonishing examples in the Gospels of situational witnessing, witnessing that happens as life is lived, witnessing that follows the course of our days, embedded in our common life. He calls it "informal conversations [that] arise from incidents and encounters with one another that take place in the normal course of going about our lives in families and workplaces, on playgrounds and while shopping for groceries, in airport terminals waiting for a flight and walking with binoculars in a field with friends watching birds. . . . the comings and goings of our ordinary lives" (*Tell It Slant*, 9–14). The humble places of our day are open doors for people to see the kingdom of God at work. God is there all around us, not just in our pre-planned evangelism. Jesus' own life and ministry teach us about this.

Jesus gets off a boat after a harrowing voyage to Gennesaret on the Sea of Galilee. Word gets around quickly about his location and the sick are brought to him. There are too many of them, too many for individual attention, so their caregivers beg Jesus to let their sick simply touch the hem of his garment. A quick, passing touch, and they are healed, their lives changed in ways they never thought was possible (Mark 6:53–56; Matt 14:34–36).

What should we make of this? It seems so quick and casual. So superficial, even theatrical. It is not so with those who are healed. A quick, casual encounter can change someone forever, especially and particularly when God is in it. The healing of hundreds was part of no organized plan, save possibly in the heart and mind of God. He seems to enjoy performing miracles when life is happening, not necessarily (perhaps rarely) when we are planning for them, and often outside even our brilliant plans or our well-executed church programs.

Our witness as disciples of Jesus is not something we construct; it is a life we live. As we faithfully live the life of a disciple, witnessing unfolds and mission happens. Yes, we have plans and strategies, but they have more to do with living authentically and intentionally in such a way as to take seriously the kingdom of God, the compassion of Jesus, and the presence of the Holy Spirit. Our "strategies" have more to do with losing our lives (in the words of Jesus) or emptying ourselves of ourselves (in the language of the apostle Paul), so that not only will we save our souls but we will also see better what *God* is doing, how he is calling us to live, and what he is calling us to become and do. The living and the doing are one. Our mission is not something we reserve time for, a church program we participate in. It is the life we live, the kingdom of God we embody, albeit imperfectly, wherever we are.

After Jesus speaks of losing our lives for him and the gospel, he goes on to speak of his return, when he will "repay each one for what that person has *done*" (Matt 16:27b, italics added). What does he mean by this? What are these things we are to *do*? If we interpret his meaning by the context, the doing he is talking about is losing ourselves, refusing to save our self-constructed lives, taking up the cross of compassionate living, whatever the cost, and following him. Strangely, *this* is the path to true living; it is life-affirming because as we peel away the exterior of our gaining and grasping, we begin to discover and free our souls for real living (Mark 8:34–37; Matt 16:24–27; Luke 9:23–25).

According to Jesus, living is not going after all the gusto we can get. It is not measured by the level of excitability or self-satisfaction. It is finding ourselves by losing ourselves, surrendering our self to discover our souls, which amounts to loving God and our neighbor with everything we are and have. And according to Jesus, this is the non-negotiable part of our witness. Whatever gifts, skills, resources, or training we bring to our witnessing as disciples, none of them amounts to any eternal good if we are not living the life of Jesus. None of them is a substitute for, or a way around, sold-out discipleship. However impressive our performances, our gift displays, our devotion to the ministry of our church, without a whole-life witness these things alone will prove in the end to be an unfruitful witness. We are called, above all, to live the life of Jesus. Our witness, our mission takes place *in this living*, not outside it. By this measure, Bert did pretty well. We needed only ask his neighbors.

Chapter 48

Belonging

I was born and raised in the South during the forties and fifties. I did not have Southern roots. My father was born in England, and my mother was born soon after her parents immigrated to this country from England. They both came quickly to love the South. I and my siblings were cradled and cultivated with a touch of England and a deep immersion in Southern culture.

The South taught me the beauty of belonging, the importance of tradition, the strength of families, the durability of values, and respect for the past. It also taught me the evils of a social system, some of the curses of a tradition, the narrow-mindedness of racist families, the durability of hatred, and the inherited oppressions of the past. As I matured I began to be aware that underneath the undeniable charm and graciousness of Dixie there was a horrible exclusion.

We never talked about it, weren't made aware till later, for example, that the reason there were no African-American children in our school was that they were all bused out of town, studying in far more humble school buildings and using our old textbooks. I remember traveling in a bus when a very elderly man got on board and saw that the only empty seat was in the very back, where African Americans were forced by law to sit. He stood by me and said, "I ain't going back there with them n.....s." I told him I didn't mind at all and gave him my seat. As I went to take the seat in the back, I wondered why separation from these particular fellow human beings was so important to the man. Afterwards, a close acquaintance told me I had better be careful about saying and doing such things in public. During my college years I had a summer job driving a mail truck. I once stopped to get a quick lunch at a downtown diner, only to be thrown out by the white manager, who told me this restaurant was for colored people only. Once after a long mail run from the downtown post office I went in to the first men's rest room I saw in the station. As I stood at the urinal, the supervisor came running in to tell me I couldn't take care of business there—it was a "colored bathroom."

During those years I was being schooled in the rules of a racist social order. I witnessed the social exclusion of a racially lower class, and I experienced my own exclusion, as racially upper class, from association with the racially lower class. I further witnessed that most Christians I knew supported the divide and refused to acknowledge the sheer evil of it and the day by day abuse of African-Americans it inevitably perpetrated. Fortunately, there were a minority of prophetic Christians around who saw the divide as a violation of the kingdom Jesus preached and lived, and who at great personal risk opposed the denigration of a race of fellow humans. A lingering question for me is how "Bible-believing Christians"—so easily it seemed—gave in to such an inhumane social order, or at least lacked the courage to reject it. What was missing in their reflection on the life and mission of Jesus? And did they think the great kingdom-of-God banquet would be racially divided?

It's worth looking at the whole gospel enterprise in which Jesus was engaged to understand how radically inclusive his mission was.

THE INCARNATION OF GOD in Jesus of Nazareth was not a foreign occupation; it was a homecoming. The Creation stories in Genesis, chapter 1–3, depict a God who loves this good world he fashions. He enjoys walking in the Garden with Adam and Eve. He is at home on earth. And then something terrible happens. There is a separation, a sin, and the fall of humanity. God becomes distant from us, or we, in our sin, see him that way, and we become distant from one another. We now live on one side of a great divide, perpetuating belief in an inaccessible God and fueling hatred between people. We are lost. The Gospels, however, begin with the announcement that in Jesus, God has not only closed the gap, he has made himself right at home. He's become a man.

In what sense, then, is Jesus, God incarnate, a man? In every sense, as the writer to the Hebrews reminds us again and again. God did not become a man in appearance only, divinity masquerading as humanity, though some early Christians, uncomfortable with their God being tempted in every way we are, embraced the heresy that Jesus was not really fully human; he only seemed to be. The doctrine of the full humanity of Jesus, however, won the day. Full humanity means many different things. One of them is the need for community. Every human being needs to belong. Including Jesus.

We see this in Jesus in two ways. First, he enters into our world and becomes a part of our community. Second, he invites us to enter his world, both the world he calls the kingdom of God and the world of those living in close relationship with him, the community of his disciples. The first is an identification with humankind, the second an invitation to humankind. Both are essential, not only to his mission but also to the mission of his disciples.

Identification

The die is cast when God becomes a man, a truly human being. He makes himself at home with us, beginning with a family, then a neighborhood in Nazareth where he grows up, then a gathering of disciples-in-training, then placing himself with this or that group of common people, and finally on a cross where he identifies himself with all sinners—i.e., all humanity. He insists there is no place he doesn't belong, while most religious people think there are places he shouldn't be seen. The identification with us is total. No group of humans is left out.

He makes that clear in choosing to be baptized by John the Baptist. Why does he do this? He does not need to signify the old man has died and a new man born. He *is* the new man. He steps into the churning waters of the Jordan as if entering the morass of the human condition where divine intervention is so desperately needed. He totally immerses himself in our life. He is saying, I totally belong with you. I am profoundly affected by your desperate situation, and I am not going to separate myself from it. I'm here to stay, to give you life, to show you the way.

Every time Jesus comes into a new situation, he is entering the turbulence of our sin. He never refuses to enter the world of a sinner when invited or needed. It can be a Pharisee, a member of the Sanhedrin named Nicodemus, or tax collectors named Matthew or Zaccheus. It can be the marginalized and despised: thieves, zealots, prostitutes, publicans, adulterers, and Samaritans. It can be the Gentiles and lower-class Jews being exploited by money-changers in the Court of the Gentiles outside the temple proper. He belongs with all of them.

Jesus also understands and honors the profound ways in which we are connected to one another. One striking example is the time four men go to great lengths (including coming through the roof!) to bring their paralytic friend on a stretcher to Jesus. Jesus sees *their* faith and heals the man. On another occasion a centurion comes to Jesus on behalf of his sick servant back home. Jesus recognizes the *centurion's* faith in Jesus' healing, and the servant is healed. He knows something we Western worshipers of individualism find it difficult to accept: We can have faith for another person; our faith can strengthen his; our faith can be a pathway to transformation in his life. As we belong together, so we can be empowered together. A later convert to Jesus, Paul the apostle understood this as well and expressed it by describing the church, the community of Jesus' disciples, as one body in which what happens, good or bad, to one member affects the others (I Cor 12).

As God made us social beings ("It's not good that the human is alone" Genesis 2:18a), so his incarnate Son comes, not as an outsider but as a human as much in need of a community as we are. In fact, he comes as a creator of a new community, one that breaks barriers and excludes no one. Jesus is the great Belonger. Every group, every ethnicity, every class are his people. As we saw earlier in the book, when Jesus preaches his first sermon in his hometown of Nazareth, the people are thrilled when he says that the year of the Lord's favor has arrived. But everything changes when he goes on to point out that at a time of great drought, Elijah chose a *Syrian* widow for a miracle of food provision, and at a time when many Israelites suffered from skin disease, Elisha cleansed the diseased skin of only the *Syrian* Naaman. When they hear this, says Luke, everyone in the synagogue is filled with anger. They chase him out of town and attempt, unsuccessfully, to throw him off a cliff (Luke 4:16–30). Jesus has gone too far. He thinks "the year of the Lord's favor" is for everyone. It eventually gets him killed: fallen humanity wants to keep up the barriers, practice exclusion, look down on "the other," the different people.

His true disciples imitate him in this inclusiveness as well. They exclude no one and they belong to everyone. Anyone who claims to be a Christian who is not going in this direction, not actively working to defeat the prejudices, personal and social, that exclude or diminish other persons, groups, ethnicities, races, or religions, is resisting the identification with all humanity that Jesus models for us and calls us to emulate. Jesus does not belong just to us; he belongs also to them. His true disciples belong far beyond their own borders and barriers.

Invitation

The belonging of Jesus moves from this radical identification with all humanity to an open invitation to all humanity. The invitation he extends, in fact, is possible only because of the identification. He invites everyone into his kingdom because he now *belongs* to everyone. No one doesn't belong, so Jesus doesn't know a stranger. No one has more right than another to belong to his kingdom, and no one has less an invitation to the banquet. Jesus invites into his kingdom family those he has already identified with. Everyone.

Jesus' invitation to vulnerable little children to come to him is given by someone who once belonged to that company. The invitation to a Gerasene demoniac, a woman taken in adultery, a blind man, a Syrophoenician woman, is given by someone who also knows what it is like to be an ostracized outsider. To a member of the Sanhedrin named Nicodemus, and to a devout rich young ruler the invitation is given—given by someone who is also profoundly serious about his Jewish faith. The Gospels do not picture a God who issues an invitation from afar to join his family and be his people. They give witness to a God who joins *our* family to bring us home. Only home looks very different from what we have made it: a narrow, exclusive conclave of people just like us—whether "like us" means doctrinal conformity, living standard, culture, ethnicity, race, or nation. For Jesus, home means a radically inclusive community, held together not by bland sameness but by unity-in-diversity.

How can we fallible humans align ourselves with such a radically inclusive Jesus? How can we get beyond our own prejudices and biases— we *all* have them!—and issue invitations beyond the circle of people with whom we are comfortable for conversation and relationship and faith sharing? Imitation of Jesus here looks very difficult.

The Gospels provide three important keys to our doing so, all of them challenging. The first is to join Jesus fully as a member of the human race. Why is this a challenge? We *are* fully members of the human family, aren't we? In theory, yes. But in fact, we all probably have residual barriers to certain individuals or groups of people whom we, consciously or unconsciously, look down upon or exclude. Some people just don't seem as suitable for Jesus as we are. We find it hard to identify with them. For us to reach out to them with this condescending spirit, however, would be de-humanizing. We must, like Jesus, humble ourselves and refuse to let ourselves see anyone in any way other than on a level playing field with us. Jesus calls us to reach out to the other as if he were a brother, she a sister, even though we do so with some personal discomfort. He shows us that this other belongs as much as we do.

The second key helps with the first. John the Baptist models it when Jesus walks by him and two of his disciples, and John says to them, "Look! The Lamb of God!" (John 1:36) The two leave John and follow Jesus. One of them is Andrew, brother of Simon Peter, and so it goes as John keeps deferring to Jesus. A little later John is point-blank with his disciples: "He [Jesus] must increase and I must decrease" (3:30). Lest any of us, unlike John, get intoxicated with our popularity in the narrow world of our own following and think we can identify who is and is not allowed into the Kingdom of God, let us remember that Jesus, and he alone, is the host and says who is invited to the banquet. He is the one to blame for the indiscriminate guest list. We just need to confess the inadequacy of our inclusiveness and ask him for the grace we need to open our hearts.

And this leads to the third key. Knowing we are inadequate to the task of this radical inclusiveness, we can admit it and pray for the enabling grace of Jesus. And when we stumble over our narrowness, we can ask for the kind of forgiveness that doesn't wallow in weakness but gifts us with new strength and a heart widened and deepened by compassion. And in one way or another, perhaps over time, maybe step by step, Jesus will give it to us.

Chapter 49

Telling

Are all of Jesus' disciples called to be tellers? To witness to the gospel with words of persuasion?

Some people are good tellers. Words come easy, perhaps with an eloquent flow or convincing logic. Some people struggle with words. The best words are hard to find, the flow of thoughts falters. Some are at home speaking in public, others are nervous, even threatened, by it. If we go by the logic of these observations, we would expect that Jesus does not call all his disciples to be tellers. But there is more than one way to tell.

WHEN WE LOOK AT what Jesus actually says in public, as reported in the Gospels, it is basically *announcing*, and then filling in the details. We can summarize what he announces as follows:

- The kingdom of God is here. (See, for example, Matt 4:17c; and Jesus' dramatic announcement in the synagogue service in Nazareth, Luke 4:14–21.)

- I, Jesus, am the Messiah sent by God the Father to bring it in. Just open your eyes and ears to what is taking place (Matt 11:1–6; Luke 7:18–23).

- I, Jesus, invite you now to enter the kingdom of God through me (John 14:6), and I am giving my life to make it possible (Matt 20:28).

- What you must do to enter this kingdom is "change your hearts and lives" (Matt 4:17b) and lay down your life and follow me (Mark 8:34–35; Matt 16:24–25; Luke 9:23–24).

- I am showing you *how* to follow me (see, for example, Matthew, chapters 5–7).

Everything else Jesus says is filling in the details, mapping out what this new kingdom looks like, and what it *doesn't* look like—and he doesn't fudge on what it will cost him, and us.

Think about the times Jesus sends his disciples out on a mission (Mark 3:13–19; 6:6b-13; Matt 10:1–15; Luke 9:1–6; 10:1–12). Announcing or preaching the nearness of the kingdom of God ("kingdom of heaven" in Matthew's Gospel) is essential to that mission, along with healing and the expelling of demons. There are two ways we can read this. We can see those twelve disciples as specially gifted for that ministry—in this case, for preaching—and that is why Jesus is entrusting this mission to them. The preaching or announcing, then, is the calling of those who have this special gift. It is true that certain Christians are called to preach, and others are not. Without denying the importance of this special calling (The church does need gifted preachers!), another way to see Jesus' charge to the twelve disciples to preach the kingdom of God is to see it as a charge to *all* his disciples.

It may be helpful in this regard to look at the sending out of the seventy (or seventy-two, according to some Greek manuscripts) disciples in Luke 10:1. It is unlikely that all seventy or seventy-two were gifted preachers! Notice this group of evangelists is not told to preach, or proclaim, or announce (all meanings of the Greek word *kerusso* used when Jesus sends out the Twelve) the kingdom of God, but to "say (Greek *lego*) to them, 'The kingdom of God is near you'" (v. 9). The act of *saying* does not presume a large or even smaller audience. It can refer to a one-on-one encounter. This telling, then, is the telling to which all Jesus' disciples are called. It happens in everyday interactions, in normal, unforced ways.

It is possible we can get too caught up in strategies for witnessing, formulas by which we present the gospel, how we can make someone feel they need to be saved, even how we can get them to feel guilty over their sins—and we lose the beauty of what we have to tell. It's as if we were salesmen trying to pressure someone and close the deal *now*, rather than good sowers of seed, making sure as best we can that the seed being planted can grow in cultivated soil ready to receive it.

Our line is not "Do you know where you're going to spend eternity?" (the fear factor). It's more like: "I see things so differently from how I used to. It's like entering a new world. Jesus has given me hope. He's given me a new life. He's given me himself." Now that's an announcement! And if a person is interested, we can say what Jesus says to Andrew and what Andrew then says to Simon Peter, "Come and see" (John 1:39). Or we can do what the man from Gerasa does after Jesus frees him from his demons. He simply goes home and does what Jesus commanded him to do. He tells the people around him what Jesus has done for him (Luke 8:38–39).

We don't need to make people feel like terrible sinners. When we try to make someone feel guilty, or exploit the guilt feelings they already have, it is a questionable, unhealthy guilt. When we leave it to the Holy Spirit to convict, the guilt is authentic and can lead to repentance. We need simply to tell our story and describe what Jesus has done for *us*.

Let our announcing be *good* news! Let our testimony, both in speaking and in living, give witness to the kingdom of God, new life in Christ, and the joy of God's kingdom! This is what disciples of Jesus do. They tell, not with cleverness but with honesty and openness. Their good-news (evangelical) mission is not to manipulate someone into a decision but to tell the truth and open the door to him who *is* "the way, the truth, and the life." He is the subject and object of our telling, the focus of the whole gospel story, the one who must increase while we decrease in the telling, like John the Baptist when he directs his own disciples to Jesus and then fades into the background (John 1:35–37).

And let us make one final observation: Sometimes the telling comes in our *silence*. There are times when Jesus does not speak. When his words have provoked anger, he leaves (Luke 4:28–30). When everything has been said, and there is nothing more to say, he says no more (Matt 27:12, 14). He cautions his disciples against a flow of empty words to impress (Matt 6:7). When imprisoned John the Baptist sends messengers to ask Jesus if he is in fact the Messiah, he does not answer so much with words as with the events that have been visibly observed (Matt 11:2–5; Luke 7:18–22). Actions speak. Events reveal. Often, very little needs to be said.

There is another kind of silence that speaks volumes. It has to do with a disciple's acts of mercy and compassion. Jesus says they reveal his kingdom only if we do not speak them in public or even to ourselves. This wordless telling is probably the most convincing and enduring witness to the presence of God's kingdom in our lives. When we seek or expect public affirmation for our good deeds (Matt 6:2–3), the credibility of our motives is severely weakened. Even if we are self-conscious about our laudable good works toward the less fortunate, we are calculating our righteousness in our own eyes rather than sharing God's compassion from the heart (vv. 3–4). The actions of a disciple must speak for themselves, devoid of ulterior or exterior motive. The world will take notice of such unfamiliar authenticity, and God will be pleased.

Chapter 50

Doing Good

"Good" is a word that can be used in multiple ways. As an adjective its meaning is made clear only by the noun it's modifying. The Gospels speak of a good tree, good fruit, good soil, good salt, a good portion, good tidings, good will, the good shepherd. In these instances, good means that the thing or person it is modifying is being what it is supposed to be, or the very best expression of it. A man or a woman is called good in relation to any number of things. For example, their moral standards (a good, upright woman), their attentiveness to other people (a good caregiver), their job performance (a good, reliable worker), or their professional competence (a good lawyer).

What we think something or someone is supposed to be, however, may vary. To say that a certain meal is good assumes certain expectations of what a meal should be, and those expectations may differ between cultures and even persons. A child may be called good on the basis of a person's own standards of what a child is supposed to be. Some parents may believe the standards are defined in terms of obedience to them, others by the expression of freedom and creativity, still others as a more flexible combination of the two.

Make "good" a noun, however, and things are different. It stands alone. It isn't defined by something it modifies or that modifies it. It just is. So how do we understand what we mean by "the good we do," or the quality of "goodness" in a person? We may call a person good because we have observed actions that suggest a consistent pattern of good deeds. A person who does good presumably has an inner goodness from which his good actions have sprung.

As followers of Jesus, who, according to his apostle Peter, "traveled around doing good" (Acts 10:38b), we rightfully want to know what the nature of that goodness is. The answer to that question is important because it is his goodness that we, his followers, seek to emulate or at least approximate; and there is no question that this emulating is crucial to both our genuineness and the credibility of our witness as his disciples.

LET'S VISIT JESUS ON a Sabbath in Capernaum. He's at the synagogue, and a man with a withered hand approaches him. He's being watched carefully to see if he will break Sabbath law by healing the man. Jesus suspects his critics are poised to condemn him if he performs the healing. Before taking action, he asks them, "Is it legal on the Sabbath to do good or to do evil, to save life or to kill?" He is asking those gathered (and he is asking us, as well) to make a choice of priority. If one has to choose between a Sabbath law and an act of healing, which way does one go? Clearly Jesus is implying that doing such a good thing for another person trumps obeying a rule of ritual behavior (Mark 3:4; Luke 6:9).

In Luke 6:32–36, Jesus introduces the question of motive behind the good done for someone. Doing something good to those who do good to you is a common and sensible practice in our world. Tit-for-tat goodness, however, is not what Jesus has in mind. "If you do good to those who do good to you, why should you be commended?" Almost everyone does that. The good works Jesus is inviting us to do is toward those who are in no position to reciprocate, especially our enemies.

Where does the capacity for these extravagant good works come from? Jesus teaches us it does not happen by accident. It springs from the heart, like good fruit borne by a healthy tree that has been carefully and generously tended (Matt 12:33–35; Luke 6:43–45).

Does this mean, however, that there are some people for whom doing such good works is not possible? Are there people (other than seriously mentally ill individuals) who are incapable of "bearing good fruit"? When we look more closely we see that Jesus speaks further of the overflow from the treasury of the heart. Do not all of us have stored up in our hearts both good and evil? We have all had both good and evil done to us, and it all lives within us as memory. So does the evil we have done to ourselves and to others. The message of the Gospel, however, is that Jesus frees us from the stain of the evil and his Holy Spirit works with us to alleviate the pain of it, so that we can nurture and release the good.

Some people have much good stored up; others, unfortunately, little. Those with little good stored up have a self-image shaped largely by a lie. They believe their lives must center on their own interests over that of others. This accounts for most of the overflow of badness. There is no surprise here. Their true humanity, however, cannot be entirely hidden and will show its face from time to time, revealing hints or intimations of a true personhood in God's image and perhaps even a clear movement toward God. If we had not a remnant of goodness, there would be no way to know our lostness, to know our distance from our true selves. The goodness within lies buried under the burden of both our own sin and the damage done to us, calling out to be set free.

The prodigal son, having buried his filial love under the weight of his own self-indulgences hears the call to home where a radically forgiving father waits to restore the lost goodness. The Samaritan woman who carries the burden of her multiple failures in the covenant of marriage unknowingly enters the presence of the Messiah, who sees her disastrous failures and points her toward a life liberated from infidelity. The Roman centurion in Caesarea, a Gentile, is attracted to the Jewish faith and begins to do the good called for by the Jewish God. He learns of Jesus and sends for the apostle Peter to help him understand how to nurture the goodness of Jesus he has already begun to live by.

In the goodness of Jesus we see our own potential for goodness. The good fruit borne by his life summons us to our own good deeds. Jesus sees the good stored up in our hearts, the goodness of which we are capable. And with great patience he keeps appealing to it and waiting for it. He did it with his inner circle, the twelve disciples, who sometimes are unable to understand and give the goodness Jesus is calling for from them. He wants to bless the children, and sometimes the disciples act as if the children are simply a bother (Mark 10:13–16; Matt 19:13–15; Luke 18:15–17). After inhospitality from the inhabitants of a Samaritan village, James and John suggest calling down fire from heaven to destroy the village. Jesus rebukes them sternly. His mission is not to destroy but to save (Luke 9:51–56). When someone who is "not following us" starts driving out demons in Jesus' name, the disciples tell him to stop. Jesus says to them, "Don't stop him. . . . Whoever isn't against us is for us." Jesus is calling for a more tolerant and expansive goodness from the hearts of his disciples. Then he goes on to honor even the simple act of giving a cup of cold water in his name (Mark 9:38–41).

Toward the end of Jesus' life, when the disciples are probably now hoping that he will soon establish his kingdom, James and John ask for a favor of privileged position in the kingdom, one of them on the right and the other on the left of Jesus. The lust for power has trumped the longing for goodness. Their motives are still compromised, the inner treasury sullied. Jesus responds with a kind rebuke: "You don't know what you're asking!" He means, of course, he has no privileged positions of status to offer, only the suffering radical goodness brings (Mark 10:35–45). Most amazing of all is the disciples' lack of goodness when the chips are down at the end: They leave Jesus standing alone to receive the horrible cruelties. Even after that, Jesus still calls forth goodness from their hearts, the goodness of character being remade, the goodness that will give credibility to his mission they will continue and the church they will lead.

In the Gospels there's an interesting ambiguity about the relationship between our goodness and our eternal inheritance. On the one hand, Jesus says things that seem to suggest that specific and enduring confession of him as Lord is what qualifies a person for eternal life (Matt 10:32; Luke 12:8). On the other hand, he says, "Those who did good things will come out into the resurrection of life, and those who did wicked things into the resurrection of judgment" (John 5:29). Are all those who do "good things" enabled by the living Lord, whether or not they know about Jesus by name or consciously follow him? Do those who insist that eternal life is only for those who specifically confess Jesus as Lord tend to undervalue goodness when seen in a non-Christian? Perhaps they claim that the goodness of an unbeliever must by nature be shallow, superficial, or self-serving, or that it unfortunately has no eternal value.

These are tough questions for some. What seems clear is that some-times genuine goodness comes from unexpected sources, and no follower of Jesus ought to question the value or depth of it because the doer is not a person of faith. God is at work in the world, showing up in unexpected places, reveling himself sometimes in the last person you would suspect. Grace and goodness are prevenient; they are not in sole possession of the self-consciously religious.

So where does that leave the disciples of Jesus? It leaves them in a world where not only sin but also goodness abounds. Hopefully, much of it is their own good works of compassion as their Rabbi-Lord molds them toward his likeness. Much of it will also come from other sources, and Jesus' disciples, following his lead, will neither denigrate nor reject it. They will affirm it, as they will any evidence that the love of God has been let loose in the world. In fact, they may learn from it. The goodness of God is manifest in surprising places and from surprising people. A follower of the Nazarene who "went about doing good" will rejoice to see it and thank God for it. Like Peter, he will transcend his religious bigotry about Gentiles and affirm the good done by a yet-to-be disciple of Jesus. Such respect and admiration will often open a door to faith in Jesus, as it did with Cornelius.

Chapter 51

Miracles

The miracles of Jesus boggle our minds. In his day the spiritual and the physical were understood to be deeply connected; the spiritual could influence, even transform, physical reality. Miracles were commonly reported. Today miracles are questioned and doubted by a scientific worldview that assumes no connection and concedes only a vague or occasional influence. The positive attitude or the religious faith of an ill person could contribute to his healing, the argument goes, but only because such states of mind affect chemical changes in the body which themselves facilitate the healing. Where the miracle occurs outside one's own body (for example, the calming of a violent storm), the miracle is assumed to be a fabrication or coincidence.

What are the connections between the spiritual and the physical? Long ago the church condemned the heresy of a complete disconnect where the spiritual realm (seen as the good) had no real affinity with the material and the bodily (seen as the bad). The doctrine of Creation, however, teaches the goodness of all that God made (Genesis 1:31). Scripture affirms the blessings of both the spiritual and the physical. Furthermore, the physical can be ordered in such a way as to bring spiritual depth and blessing through such means as words, paintings, sculpture, music, dance, and drama. In other words, the spiritual can be conveyed by the physical. The physical can be mustered and molded to throb with the spirit's inspiration.

When it comes to miracles, however, the relationship is different still. Miracles represent the power of the spirit in healing or changing the physical. Miracles are sickness cured, the demons of insanity cast out, the threatening storm calmed. Is there such a connection between every dimension of Creation that miracles are not only possible but inevitable? Is the universe so integrated that not only does what happens here also affect what happens there, but also that a spiritual force marshalled by the power of a deep faith and a genuine love can heal bodies and move mountains? And further, can it transform the heart and change a life? We look to the life and ministry of Jesus for insight.

LET'S BEGIN BY NOTING that in the Gospels Jesus' ministry is a threefold integration: His preaching and teaching and healing are three expressions of one cohesive mission (Matt 4:23). Each aspect of his ministry is presented as part of the miracle of the kingdom of God he announced and embodied. His preaching is the announcement of the kingdom, his teaching is about the way we live in it, his miracles are what he does to demonstrate the radical changes that take place when, by faith, we fully embrace this kingdom. All of it is about the one kingdom miracle unleashed by Jesus.

The miracles we associate with Jesus' ministry are the surprising and sometimes unsettling changes we observe throughout the Gospels. They include:

- Sudden changes in the environment, like the calming of a storm to stop the terror of disciples at sea (Mark 4:36–41; Matt 14:22–33; Luke 8:22–25).

- The multiplication of a substance, like feeding thousands with a few loaves and fish (Mark 6:30–44; Matt 14: 13–21; Luke 9:10–17; John 6:5–13), or the transformation of a substance, like changing water into wine to enhance the joy of a wedding celebration (John 2:1–11).

- Casting out demons to free people from inner captivity, like the healing of the Gadarene demoniac (Matt 8:28–34) or of the fitful boy who couldn't speak (Mark 9:14–27; Matt 17:14–18).

- Healing all manner of physical sickness and debilitation (Matt 8:14–17).

- Raising the dead: Jairus's daughter (Mark 5:22–43), the son of the widow of Nain (Luke 7:11–17), Lazarus (John 11:38–45).

- The radical change of a person, described by Jesus as a complete orientation of one's heart, being (or soul), and mind toward love of God and love of neighbor (Mark 12:29–31; Matt 22:35–40; Luke 10:25–28).

All these miracles are expressions of the one miracle, the new kingdom inaugurated and embodied in Jesus.

What is there about the kingdom of God that finds expression in a miracle like *the sudden calming of a dangerous storm*? This particular miracle addresses the terror of the disciples. Fear is the enemy of the kingdom of God. It is the crippler of faith. Jesus stills the storm with a rebuke: "Silence! Be still!" He almost seems to be talking to a person rather than a force of nature, as if he has some kind of personal relationship with it. Perhaps he does. It's his Father's world, God's creation, over whom (as we sing) he is still the ruler. As our science and technology have significantly "subdued" the natural world, we tend to forget this—that is, until our careless exploitation backfires with floods and fires, and the fear comes back. How long can we hope that our Lord will calm the storms of our *own* making? In the days in which we are living, perhaps we need to claim for ourselves a part in Jesus stilling such storms.

Perhaps we need to become friends of our world so that we won't fear it like an enemy. The miracle of the stilling of the storm is certainly an expression of Jesus' compassion toward the fearful, but it also invites us to treat the world as God's good creation, to which we are called to be attentive. The Rabbi who points us to the birds of the air and the flowers of the fields also knows, however, that nature can erupt in violence, a violence which can take our lives. Nature itself shares in the disruption of evil, and God allows it. The miracle of it is that the kingdom endures even through death, as do we. And as the apostle Paul points out, the whole universe will share in redemption's ultimate sweep (Rom 8:19–21; Eph 1:9–10).

The miracles of *multiplying and transforming substances* are expressions of kingdom-of-God generosity. Loaves and fish multiplied to feed thousands are the sign of God's expansive provision through the sharing of our small store. It is God's large compassion released by a boy to become a miracle sustaining thousands. The wedding feast miracle of common water turned into the best wine in the house reverses the normal course of diminishing generosity on such occasions: Typically the worst wine is saved till last, when the guests are theoretically in no state to discern the lower quality. Here, however, is the kingdom of God portrayed as enduring generosity and joy. And John, the writer of this Gospel, comments with surprising words, saying that this miracle "revealed [Jesus'] glory." The glory of a kingdom where only the best is given.

The castings out of demons or evil spirits are miracles that address the inner captivities that plague some people. They portray evil as occupying spirits that rob us of our human freedom. Again we are struck by Jesus' recognition of the foreign invaders and their recognition of him. However we see the invaders—as demonic emissaries of Satan, or the psychological roots of mental illness, or both—the point is that they are unholy, and they rob the possessed of their God-given humanity. They cannot tolerate the holiness of Jesus, and they recognize he is out to exorcise them. They are foreign to God's kingdom and hostile to our humanity.

Perhaps we can helpfully apply this image of occupying spirits to us all, as extreme as this condition appears to be in the Gospels. Is it not true that behind every sinful act is an occupying spirit that either lures us to be someone we are not or, in the case of an extreme disorder, forces us? Sometimes the spirit can be cast out in a traumatic conversion, at other times the exorcism may require a process. Either way, the occupant's interest is to make us someone or something we are not, to rob us of God's image. When we are clear about the illegitimate occupant, we are in a position to be freed by our Rabbi Jesus' exorcizing.

The Gospels describe *a close connection between the exorcisms and the healings of Jesus*. Both are mentioned in one breath (Mark 1:34; Luke 4:40–41). What these disorders share in common is that they are both foreign to God's intention for the human race. Their cure is therefore a sign that the new kingdom of God is breaking into human history. The cure, however is not an instant cure-all. Until the kingdom comes in its fullness, we live with or in the presence of physical illness, mental illness, and insanity. Healings and exorcisms take place, but not always. Children sometimes die of illness, others have untimely adult deaths. All of us eventually die of some disease. Death is a fatal sting for all of us. Jesus, however, invites us to participate in *his* dying so that we obtain the life that endures (Matt 16:21–28; Luke 9:18–27). In Jesus the sting of death is not fatal.

The paradox of Jesus' attraction to people who are ill is his view that *illness is foreign*. Many see the unnaturalness of illness as repulsive and are therefore uncomfortable being around ill people. This repulsion to sickness even leads to the social isolation of people with certain diseases. In Jesus' day leprosy and other skin diseases are graphic examples. In chapters 13 and 14, Leviticus goes to great lengths to describe when a person with a skin disease is to be quarantined or sent "outside the camp" and to be responsible for seeing to it that no one comes close by shouting "Unclean! Unclean!" when someone approaches. The isolation is still in effect in Jesus' day. Yet, when a man with leprosy approaches Jesus, falls on his knees, and asks to be made clean, Jesus does the forbidden thing and touches him. It proves a healing touch (Mark 1:40–42; Matt 8:2–3; Luke 5:12–13). Jesus does not allow the unnaturalness of the man's condition, nor its assumed communicableness, nor its repulsiveness to deter him. The foreignness of the illness draws him, arrests him, fills him with compassion. He wants wholeness in us.

Jesus calls all his disciples to be apostles of healing. He sends out twelve, and then seventy-two to preach, teach, and heal. They do, and so does the church that springs from this beginning. Healing is God's gift to us. Disciples of Jesus take that gift seriously. Some of them have that gift and calling in generous measure. For the others, the gift is not such an obvious asset. And yet there are times when they too are healers because they see another with the eyes of Jesus, eyes that see not the distasteful or the repulsive but the yearning for wholeness. They take time to be with the sick, they trust a healing they don't fully understand. They wait in faith and pray for miracles.

Life abounds in miracles. Not only healings, exorcisms, multiplications or transformations of substances, or resuscitations. Heart cleansings and life transformations, as well. In fact, these are the most mysterious miracles of all. It's harder to locate the specific radical change. We cannot see the physical change, save in the hint of joy in a face. We do see some behavioral changes, sometimes awkward, as someone struggles to discover how to live in a very different way. We may observe a tendency to pause with another person longer, to look into another's eyes and listen to another's heart. We see life transformation over time, as it works itself out in every place, arena, and relationship in a person's life. It is the miracle, if you like, that keeps going because it is never finished in this life.

It is also the miracle that opens the door of delight to other miracles. For those with eyes to see, ears to hear, and hearts to continue to be changed, miracles abound. Author Phyllis Tickle likens these miracles to the everyday wonders of our world which are there even if we don't see them or if we have diminished the wonder of them by our explanations. Phyllis describes a day when her daughter Mary called out to her from a window where you could see almost all the back ten acres of the farm. Phyllis hurried to Mary and later described what she saw:

> The whole back pasture from the fence line halfway to the cattle pond was white with them. And they were moving as the sea moves, in undulations, curves, lifts, and falls. Never had I seen such a thing. The sheer magnificence of their whitecaps on our stubbled hay was beyond my capacity to react to. I stood stunned into silence by the sensuousness of their movement. Neither of us said anything for a full minute and a half, maybe two. . . .

In the years that followed the huge flock of mysterious birds came three or four times every fall. It was a miracle they eagerly waited for, because these unusual birds came out of nowhere it seemed, all the more mysteriously because they were unknown and un-named. And then son John came back from school one day with a nature magazine in which he found these exact birds identified and named: African Cattle Egrets that had decided to migrate in the 1930s and somehow found their way to the Mississippi

Valley in 1977. The miracle now explained and the birds now catalogued, information filled the space that before was mystery. "Miracles in general," said Phyllis, "suffer a certain loss of poetry when they become certifiable" (Tickle, *Wisdom in the Waiting* 59–62).

Just because we have a name and know the history, does the mystery have to disappear? Perhaps the mystery is in the appearing itself. When we get the information, we may think we can let the mystery go. Do the circumstances, now clarified, require we do away with the mystery? There is something in us that wants things explained, but science and rational analysis can go only so far. Miracles are not package-able in formulas and formulations. They are, as Rabbi Jesus teaches us, acts of God to get our attention, startle us, sustain us, delight us, sometimes heal us and open up a new future for us. And to what ultimate purpose? To save us (Luke 19:10)—and to give us "life to the fullest" (John 10:10b).

Chapter 52

Empowering Others

How a denomination or a congregation uses power is one of the most telling ways it reveals its true self and influences the world. There have been times when church leaders used power oppressively to instill fear and enforce conformity within the congregation or denomination. At other times they used it compassionately, to liberate, support, guide, or help. People have been drawn to the church because they found its gospel liberated them and its leaders empowered them. Others have left the church because they found its gospel subjugated them and its leaders exploited them.

How, then, can the use of power facilitate a healthy body of Christ and serve to give convincing witness to the liberating gospel? How can leaders both formal and informal use the power they have been given or assigned to empower others rather than to build their own personal power base? Again we turn to our Rabbi Jesus to see what he teaches and models for us.

JESUS IS NEVER ENAMORED of power. When the wilderness tempter asks him to perform extraordinary feats of power to impress, sway, or capture the masses, he refuses. When people demand a miraculous display, he refuses. When at the end he is taunted to try saving himself, he refuses.

And yet Jesus uses his power protectively to allay the fears of disciples when he calms the storm. He uses it generously to feed thousands of hungry people. He uses it compassionately to heal the sick, the crippled, and the deranged. He uses it transformatively to change hearts. Never to protect or elevate himself.

What do we make of this? What do the Gospels teach us about how Jesus uses power? They teach us that *Jesus uses power to empower others*:

- He empowers the sick to be whole, the crippled to walk, the blind to see, the leprous to be clean, the demon-possessed to be free.

- He empowers a woman to break a gender stereotype by sometimes getting out of the kitchen and engaging the teaching of her Rabbi (Luke 10:38–42).

- He empowers the sinner to confess his sin and begin anew (Luke 5:8–11).

- He empowers those who want to be his disciples actually to *be* his disciples (John 20:19–23).

- He empowers us all to break down the walls that separate us and learn to love one another, so that all men and women will know that we are his disciples (John 13:35).

- He empowers us to be his ambassadors in the world, giving us "all authority" (*exousia*) to "go and make disciples of all nations" (Matt 28:19).

- He empowers an impulsive, rash, and often clueless person like Peter to become a key leader in his movement (Matt 16:18–19).

Jesus is scathing in his criticism of those who are in a position to empower others and refuse to do so. Among them are some of the legal experts (scribes of Jewish law) who, having "the key of [spiritual] knowledge" keep others from entering the place of that knowledge. By doing so, says Jesus, they keep themselves out as well (Luke 11:52). When we refuse to empower others with knowledge and encouragement, we not only disempower them, we disempower ourselves. When we empower others we become stronger ourselves.

When we rely only or primarily on the power of our station or the sway we hold by virtue of our natural abilities, we increasingly manipulate and disempower others, and our credibility diminishes. People submit to us because we have power over them, or because they are addicted to the force of our persuasiveness. Institutional power and the power of popularity easily go to our heads. What is the antidote?

The antidote is a process that begins when we become disciples of Jesus. With Jesus we start anew. We begin to see reality. We begin to understand that the real power of our lives resides deep within us. It carries little or no recognizable labels, terms, or certifications. Jesus is asked by religious leaders, "What kind of authority do you have for doing these things?" and "Who gave you the authority to do them?" (Mark 11:27–33; Matt 21:23–27; Luke 20:1–8) and Jesus says simply that he's not telling. No labels, no terms, no certifications. He has no institutional power to present, and he declines to capitalize on his extraordinary natural gifts and abilities to build a power base and control people. Where, then, does his power reside? It resides in *who he is*. It emerges from the integrity of his life as a lover of others. It is there till the end when he surrenders all power to empower us all to become his disciples. We, his disciples, are those who have been empowered by our Rabbi Jesus' voluntary powerlessness. We are saved because he doesn't save himself.

The saving death of Jesus is not only the antidote that removes the guilt of our sin; it is also the antidote to our hunger for power, position, and recognition. To be sure, we all have been given more or less power or ability—*dunamis*—to make decisions that influence or control others in some way. The important question is: What is the nature of the authority out of which we exercise that power? What is the authority—*exousia*—within us that guides our decisions and actions? Is it our own fear and insecurity? Then we will use our power to bolster our public esteem, strengthen our self-esteem, build a power base, and quite possibly abuse other people who stand in our way. If, on the other hand, we are increasingly guided by a growing confidence in who we are as followers of a Savior and Rabbi who changed the world through his powerlessness, we are on a journey of radical change in how we see and use power.

We all have a measure of *dunamis*. Jesus invites us to use it without fear. We do no good for the kingdom of God when we hide our talent and fail to put the resources available to use. Unused talents are an insult to God (Matt 25:24–30; Luke 19:20–26). We may think our failure to use the *dunamis* available to us is a sign of our humility. It is not. It is a sign of our fear, born of our lack of trust in God: "I was afraid of you," says the failed servant.

Of course, Jesus forbids us to exploit our talents and advantages for ourselves and our ambitions. Our personal drive to advance and gain advantage over others is a function of our fear. We are looking to compensate for our lack of self-worth or for our lack of security. Without the position, prominence, or possessions we are driven to achieve, we feel inferior or see ourselves as failures.

He is not inferior who only seeks to share whatever talents and advantages he has to empower others. Nor is he a failure because he stays too busy doing this to advance himself. He has chosen the *exousia* of compassion over the *dunamis* of control. Whether or not he advances within the church or within society at large, of such will the kingdom of God be built.

Chapter 53

Innocence and Shrewdness

Our mission as disciples of Jesus requires the uniting of two extremes that are typically thought of as incompatible. We think of a person who embodies innocence and purity of motive as lacking in shrewdness and suspiciousness. Conversely, we think of the shrewd person as wise in the ways of the world and able to work the angles to turn things to his favor. Each, it seems, would be incapable of doing what the other does. The innocent can't bring themselves to manipulate situations to their own advantage, and the shrewd can't bring themselves not to.

So what does Jesus mean when he tells us: "I am sending you out like sheep among wolves. Therefore be as shrewd as snakes and as innocent as doves" (Matt 10:16, NIV). How does he expect us simultaneously to embrace these incompatibles? When it comes to encountering wolves, sheep are not particularly shrewd. So if Jesus is sending us "sheep" to be among wolves, how is he expecting us to be what we are not: shrewd? And why is he sending defenseless sheep out to the wolves anyway?

These are good questions, and they deserve answers. As Jesus is our Rabbi, we look to his own life and ministry for the answers. How was Jesus himself as shrewd as a snake and as innocent as a dove?

The innocence of Jesus comes from the purity of his heart. His compassion for others overrules the possibility of looking for personal advantage over anyone. The perfection of love for others incapacitates any temptation to use them for his own personal ends. His innocence is his refusal to manipulate; it is not blindness to reality. When he stands before the Sanhedrin, and then Pilate, he knows exactly what is going on, he sees the insidious script that is being played out against him. He submits to it out of compassion, not ignorance. He has no misgivings.

The shrewdness of Jesus is also grounded in the compassion itself. Compassion is not stupid. Jesus knows where his love will bring him, knows it will get him in trouble, knows it will savage his heart and his body. He loves anyway. He loves, knowing the consequences.

The shrewdness of Jesus lies in the very nature of his compassion. It is not the shrewdness of the self-seeker; it is the shrewdness of the self-giver. Jesus' shrewdness is on behalf of his redeeming mission, not some personal empire. He is shrewd for us, not himself.

We talked earlier about the rich young ruler. When he comes to Jesus, he asks if there is anything else he could possibly do to "obtain eternal life." He is a very impressive person, a leader in the community and a devout, observant Jew. Jesus could well get by congratulating him and praising his piety to those who are present. Shrewd compassion does not allow him. He refuses not to see that the man's impressive piety serves to mask his addictive attachment to his fortune. It's a cancer on his soul. Jesus will not pretend there is no killing infection. Aware that people observing this encounter are thinking that this pious, prosperous young man has everything going for him already, Jesus stuns them by saying to him, "There's one more thing. Sell everything you own and distribute the money to the poor. Then you will have treasure in heaven. Then come, follow me." To which the crowd responds, "Then who can be saved?" Oh, says Jesus, "What is impossible for humans is possible for God." This man can be saved in the same way you can be saved—by the grace of the saving God. But no one can be saved without owning up to the enthrallments that hold his soul hostage, whatever the otherwise attractive qualities of his life. Disciples of Jesus cannot have it both ways (Mark 10:17–27; Matt 19:16–26; Luke 18:18–27).

We can all be grateful for the shrewd compassion of Jesus, who will not overlook whatever seeks to destroy our lives. Of course, when Jesus confronts our hidden duplicity, we may feel insulted or angry. Strong compassion is often more than we can take and may take us where we don't want to go. It may upset our comfortable compromises. Far more upsetting to the one who truly wishes to be a disciple of Jesus is what Jesus *says* after his shrewd compassion has exposed the sin our respectable exterior has kept secret, has commanded us to let it go. He says this only—and not until—we actually do what a disciple does: *follow him.*

With the help of Jesus' shrewd compassion, we are given the courage to see and confess our compromises, bringing us closer to a true innocence. The innocence of a disciple is his putting his hands to the plow, staying focused on Jesus and his Kingdom, and not looking back (Luke 9:62). It is traveling on a straight and narrow road that has no detours and allows no deals on the way to a small gate most choose to ignore (Matt 7:13–14). It is what a Pharisee named Nicodemus has surely discovered he longs for. So he sneaks out to find Jesus under cover of night to hear what he has probably begun to suspect: that the pointless obsession with Pharisaical triviality ("filtering out gnats") is avoidance of the deeper purity of life that God desires of him. If this suspicion is right, then he must undergo a new birth, not by nature but by the Spirit (John 3:1–8). Then he, and we, are ready to be disciples.

Jesus invites us to join his mission with the innocence of doves and the shrewdness of serpents. What this invitation asks of us is a purifying and a clarifying. In the purifying our motives are being aligned with the love of Jesus. In the clarifying our vision is being aligned with the insight of Jesus. We are called to love others, not use them; and we are called to see and confront reality in our relationships with others. Without genuine innocence our journey will be sidetracked and our way lost. Without holy shrewdness our compassion will lack wisdom and our help will not be helpful.

In a passage of his letter to the Romans, Paul provides us with a helpful interpretation of Jesus' saying. He tells the Christians in Rome "to be wise about what's good, and innocent about what's evil" (Rom 16:19b). He is not suggesting they be naïve about evil or ignorant about how it insinuates itself into people's lives. In the same letter he describes in detail how sin is at work. He is saying: Study the ways of God, proclaim and live the life of Jesus. *This* is where your wisdom of life lies. Then you will see evil for what it really is: the violation of the life God has given us, the rejection of who we are as disciples of Jesus. The only study of evil is the good, and the only study of sin is righteousness. We cannot begin with evil and find our way to understanding goodness. We begin with goodness to see evil for what it is. The truly innocent are those with clear moral vision.

Leading up to this, Paul has been warning the Roman Christians "to watch out for people who create divisions and problems against the teaching that you learned. Keep away from them" (v. 17). He is saying: do not engage them on their terms, do not enter the arena of their self-serving drives—remain as innocent as doves so that you will see what is really happening and understand the damage that is being done. Then you will acquire a holy shrewdness born of compassion and become a leavening, transformative influence.

Our calling as disciples of Jesus requires a genuine innocence, a purity of heart, hand-in-hand with a shrewdness that sees reality and is not seduced by deception. Only then can compassion be helpful.

Chapter 54

Working for Justice, Living at Peace

The young policeman pulled me over in a strip mall parking lot. He calmly asked me if I knew why he had stopped me. I had no idea, and he told me my auto license had expired. I said I had sent the renewal in on time but had not yet received the renewal sticker. (Later I discovered I had unwittingly failed to include my check with the renewal application.) Technically, I was driving an unlicensed automobile. The policeman was very courteous, but wrote me a ticket and said I would still have to appear in traffic court.

Traffic court was an educational experience. The large courtroom was crowded, primarily with people of color. Almost all were poor and uneducated. The judge was a formidable woman who prevented chaos by maintaining uncontested control over the proceedings. I found an empty seat to await my turn. It looked as if I would be there for most of the day. An illiterate elderly gentleman to my right asked if I would fill out his form for him. I did, happy to do something useful during the wait.

Soon the judge stopped the proceedings to make an announcement. She said that those who did not want to contest the charge against them could line up on the left to pay their fine. Those who wanted to claim extenuating circumstances could line up on the right. The line on the right was short, and I thought I had nothing to lose by claiming that my infraction was a mere oversight and that the county should have informed me right away when they discovered the check was missing. (They had not.)

When my turn came, I began to plead my case to the Caucasian lady behind the desk and stated that the license tag fee had now been paid. With great swiftness she said something so quietly I could not understand her. I asked her if she could repeat what she had said a little louder. She leaned over closer

265

to me and repeated herself, clearly not wanting anyone in the vicinity to hear her. She said, "You may go."

As I walked out of the courtroom, my joy at getting a reprieve quickly turned to embarrassment. The person behind the desk may well have noted the color of my skin and the nature of my dress. She may well have concluded that I didn't "belong" in this court. This was a place for the poor and people of color with little or no resources. I was fortunate; they were not. I was on the privileged side of justice. The judicial system had moved me out of the courtroom as quickly as possible.

IT IS WORTH NOTING that in the Old Testament the calls for social justice and fairness by prophets and psalmists alike are aimed almost exclusively at the rich and powerful, those holding the wealth and controlling governance—those, in short, who come out on the fortunate side of the economy and law enforcement. As a class, they especially are the recipients of prophetic rage. And their salvation is inextricably tied to ceasing their exploitation of the poor and powerless. One among countless readings of the prophetic rage is Isaiah 58:6–10. The prophet mocks the hypocritical worship and fasting of Judah, and then calls them to an authentic fast: keeping the covenant and practicing justice toward the oppressed.

It isn't a matter simply of obeying certain laws insuring justice. At the deepest level it is a matter of who God is and who we are as humans created in his image. The psalmist David says that "the Lord is a safe place for the oppressed," that "he assumes his throne for the sake of justice." Who we are as his covenant people is inextricably tied to this reputation: "The Lord is famous for the justice he has done" (Psalm 9). It is a smear on God's reputation for those who worship him not only to practice injustice but also to fail to work for justice or conveniently to resist seeing and exposing it.

Jesus is clearly steeped in this prophetic tradition. Early in his ministry, attending the synagogue service in his own hometown of Nazareth, he is asked to comment on Scripture. As we saw earlier, he quotes from Isaiah 61:1–2 and 58:6 to reveal that with his coming this prophecy of good news for the poor and deliverance for the oppressed has been fulfilled. The quote points to a messianic mission that consists not only of preaching the good news and healing the blind and broken, but also releasing the prisoners and liberating the oppressed (Luke 4:18–19). Later in his Galilean ministry, quoting from Isaiah 42:1–4, he reveals that through the Lord's Servant (undoubtedly a reference to himself) "justice wins" (Matt 12:20c). On his way to Jerusalem, somewhere along the border between Samaria and Galilee, Jesus tells the parable about the unjust judge who has to be hounded again and again by a widow who has not been treated justly before the judge relents and gives her what she deserves. Jesus says, if this unjust judge finally metes out justice to this deserving widow: "Won't God provide justice to his chosen people who cry out to him day and night? Will he be slow to help them? I tell you, he will give them justice quickly" (Luke 18:1–8). Speaking to a group from the religious class, he mocks their laughable "tithe" of mint, dill, and cumin while ignoring "the more important matters of the Law: justice, peace, and faith" (Matt 23:23).

In this last quote, the call to justice is followed by the call to peace. The two are closely related; one requires the other. Without justice there is no path to peace; without justice what some call "peace" is only a rigidly enforced compliance to a repressive social order that serves only the interests of the power holders and brokers. And without peace justice is not a possibility. Those who are at war within themselves and with other persons and groups are in no frame of heart or mind to pursue justice for those they consider the outsiders. Injustice prospers where peace languishes and fear reigns.

The Old Testament prophets often diagnose a lack of peace (*shalom*) in the world around them. Messengers of peace weep bitterly (Isa 33:7). Judah has forgotten the way of peace (59:8). Prophets and priests blindly declare that all is at peace when in fact there is no peace (Jer 6:14; 8:11). Peace is simply not to be found in the land (14:19b). The Lord himself hears screams of panic and terror in a place without peace (30:5). And the wicked find that the world they have created robs them of a peaceful life (Isa 57:21).

Prophets call for the people of God to be ambassadors of peace and to live toward a future when, by God's intervention, peace will reign throughout the land. They are not to shelter themselves from the enmity that reigns in the city where they live but actively promote the welfare (*shalom*) of the city (Jer 29:7). The house of Judah is to make truthful, just, and peaceable decisions within their gates (Zech 8:16). This peaceable-ness will anticipate the coming reign of endless peace. It will be shouldered by "Mighty God, Eternal Father, Prince of Peace" (Isa 9:6–7). Judah and Israel will be blessed with an abundance of peace and security (Jer 33:6; Ezek 34:25; 37:26). The proclamation of it will move us like beautiful music (Isa 52:7–8). God's covenant of peace will reign unshaken (Isa 54:10b; Ezek 37:26). Peace will flow like a river (Isa 48:18b). It will extend to those far and near (57:19b). In fact, the word of the Lord proclaims endless peace to all nations, from sea to sea and from the river to the ends of the earth (Zech 9:10b).

Jesus is also steeped in this prophetic peace tradition. The mission for which John the Baptist is to prepare Israel includes "the path of peace" (Luke 1:79d). The message of the angels at Jesus' birth foreshadows "peace on earth" (2:14). Having received the infant Jesus for the temple dedication, the priest Simeon seems to see before him the culmination of his hopes for Israel's salvation. He is now ready to depart and receive the long-promised peace (2:29–30).

The peace shared by Jesus during his ministry is first *personal*. It is received by countless people who encounter Jesus and trust him—the sinful woman who washes his feet with healing oil and tears of repentance (7:36–50), the shy woman with the issue of blood who dares to touch his garment and believe this feeble connection to him will bring miracle (8:43–48)—two among many who not only receive forgiveness and healing, but are given the blessing of peace as well. Preparing his disciples for his death, Jesus gives them the gift of his peace and assures them he will return (John 14:27–28a). His very words bear the promise of his peace (16:33). Fear, however, can invade the received peace, as it does with the disciples following Jesus' crucifixion. The resurrected Jesus appears, however, and his first words are an invitation for them to receive the peace again (20:19–21).

Jesus does not come to launch a political revolution, though over time his movement is to spawn a social revolution. The Prince of Peace seeks no kingdom save the human heart. It is from the heart at peace, however, that the peaceable kingdom of God is unleashed into this world. Ironically, it is these who have received the peace of Christ that terrify this divided, warring world. Peace is a threat to polarizing politics, power alliances, ruthless competition, and winning at any cost—those things that in the mind of most people are what make the world go round. In truth, they are what have the world on a path to destruction.

Only this helps us make sense of those seemingly uncharacteristic words of Jesus recorded in Matthew 10:34–39. Jesus tells his disciples, "Don't think that I've come to bring peace to the earth. I haven't come to bring peace but a sword." He goes on to explain that families will be divided over him. On other occasions he expands the extent of the opposition by explaining that even though God loves the world (John 3:16), the world will largely hate his disciples just as it hated him (15:18–19). The world's hatred of Jesus' disciples arises precisely from the refusal of Jesus' disciples to hate, the refusal to have enemies, the refusal to be drawn into the animosities both overt and subtle that drive and destroy human relationships in a fallen world. The "sword" Jesus is preparing his disciples to be ready to use is the most truly powerful sword, the paradoxical sword carried by those who are at peace, the sword of the Spirit.

The early church was famously opposed to bearing arms. If we follow the history we see that the more the church became associated with the political entities and power structures of the world, the more it approved of, or even participated in, undermining the peace of Christ—and further, the more people like Francis of Assisi or Martin Luther King of Atlanta became rare examples of Christians who actually risked their lives on the peace of Christ.

Disciples of Jesus risk their lives for peace in the world. The personal peace Jesus gives his disciples becomes *social action*. The peace cannot be held in private, else it stales into a hard, tasteless misery. The peace is at home with compassion. It is itself when it shares itself with the world. Jesus blesses not those who are simply at peace within themselves; he blesses those who are actively *making peace*. "Happy are the people who make peace . . . they will be called God's children" (Matt 5:9). The inner peace of Christ goes external. It compels us to make peace at home, at church, in our neighborhood, at work, in the world. It calls us to mend bridges and love our enemies. It calls us to work for social justice by risking the peace where war, exploitation, racial, ethnic, or national terrorism are ways of life.

Sometimes well-meaning people who are not at peace within themselves take on righteous causes. The campaign becomes personal, they widen the divide, and peace is the loser. Disciples of Jesus are called to oppose and sometimes fight evil practices that exploit the vulnerable. Jesus invites us to be at peace and fight with wisdom and love. He is at work in the world around us, the kingdom of God is here. He gives us the courage to speak truth to power and say, "This is wrong!" He gives us the courage to take some action or to refuse to go along with some unjust policy or requirement or action that exploits people.

In late nineteenth-century England my own faith family, The Salvation Army, pressured Parliament to raise the age of consent for girls to make it legally impossible for criminals to lure hundreds of young teenagers to London under the false pretenses of a decent job, then kidnap them, drug them, and ship them in boxes to Holland where they were being forced into prostitution. To prove the ease with which this exploitation was being carried out at the time, an actual scenario of this detestable trade was enacted by The Salvation Army (keeping the unsuspecting girl safe throughout the dealings) and recorded. Then the whole affair was reported to the authorities. The Salvation Army personnel who were involved paid a personal price: they were arrested, put on trial, and sent to jail. This whole affair created widespread publicity and so shamed the government that they quickly raised the age of consent.

Jesus teaches us that social justice is a part of our calling. Injustices are all around us. In spite of our laws enforcing equality and fairness, inequality is entrenched in countless informal ways, as I saw in the traffic court. Most of us have on occasion—probably on more occasions than we have realized—been the benefactors of injustice, discrimination, or exploitation.

Have the diamonds in our rings come to us via cruel de facto slave labor? Has the clothing on our backs been assembled or the food on our tables produced by the exploitation of underpaid workers? Did my reprieve at traffic court have to do with my appearance as white and middle-class? We all might confess our complicity in the injustice, if only by our ignorance, our social insensitivity, or our blindness to how we are profiting at the expense of others. The peace of Christ is not a protective barrier, it is a path leading into a world needing peace-makers who are willing to speak truth and take risks on behalf of others. Disciples of Jesus are called to open their eyes and see what we all are tempted to deny or pass over, to live bravely by naming the injustice, and to ask our Rabbi Jesus when and how to act.

Chapter 55

Living Outside the Circle

The pilgrimage Keitha and I made in Spain along the last 75 miles of the Camino de Compostella (see Chapter 11: "Live Simply") concluded in Santiago. There was a special mass for pilgrims at the cathedral at noon, and we attended. The huge Cathedral of St. James was filled with people from around the world, standing room only. On that day we felt immersed in a gathering of our wonderfully diverse world. Most of the congregants undoubtedly professed a Christian faith. Some probably professed a different religious faith. Still others probably claimed no religious belief, but something drew them, perhaps a need to bring together, understand, or define what their journey was all about. We sensed that everyone there was a seeker after something, Keitha and I included.

For us it began to become clear when the congregation was invited to sing responses to a part of the mass sung in the pure but penetrating voice of a small, slender nun. All was in Latin, as was our repeated response, but we all knew exactly what we were singing: "*dona nobis pacem*"—Lord, give us peace. It was an almost childlike asking of God. It was a flood, voices blending into deeply felt waves of prayer that washed over us again and again with each response. People from around the world—a world of people—praying for peace. I imagine some were praying for peace in their own troubled hearts. Others for peace in their marriages, families, friendships, churches, communities. Peace in their divided governments or in their war-torn countries. Or peace around our globe. Here was the world longing for peace, and the sound of the responsive longing was a clear, penetrating song suffusing the sanctuary, as if the gothic stones themselves were crying out. We were praying for ourselves, for each other, for the world. It seemed the whole world was at prayer.

When the mass was over, it wasn't over. Something happened that doesn't happen at every pilgrim mass, but it happened that day. A huge incense burner was lowered from high above us and swung across the full expanse of the nave, embracing us in a cloud of incense, covering us all with its pungent but sweet palpable blessing, as if to mark us all as called to take the peace of Christ with us, outside our own narrow circles. As if we all belonged now to each other, our very clothing saturated with the aroma of peace. As if our very being had been torn from the bondage of our small concerns, our little circles, our all-too-narrow faith.

ONE OF THE CURIOUS things about Jesus is that his ministry is confined to a very small, outlying area of the Roman Empire: Judea and Galilee, with occasional forays into more extensively Gentile areas (Samaria, Phoenicia, and Decapolis). Geographically, his ministry is Palestinian; but spiritually it includes the world (Mark 16:15; John 1:9; 3:16–17, 4:42b, 8:12, etc.). This worldwide inclusion seems to be a problem for most of the religious leaders: Jesus isn't exclusively "Jewish" enough. Jesus, however, believes he is more Jewish than they are, more faithful to the Old Testament calling of God's covenant people to be a blessing to the Gentiles, even to welcome them into the covenant family. It takes his own followers a while fully to get it. The first hurdle for the church to cross is to reach out to the Gentiles and enable them to find a way to become *Jewish* Christians. The second is for the church, led especially by a strong-willed man named Paul, to insist on the inclusion of Gentiles without their having to become Jews.

Let's remind ourselves of the scope of Jesus' ministry. He sees himself to be called first to Israel. It is sung in the song of his birth (Luke 1:54). Birthed in Israel, he dies there as well. His most poignant lament for a city was for a largely unrepentant Jerusalem (Matt 23:37–39; Luke 13:34–35). He sends out his disciples on a mission that is to focus on "the lost sheep, the people of Israel" and to avoid "the Gentiles or . . . a Samaritan city" (Matt 10:5). When disturbed by a persistent Gentile woman with a very sick daughter, before he heals her daughter he challenges her presumption by confronting her with the first priority of his mission: the lost sheep of Israel (15:24). Jesus is a Jewish rabbi called to the Jews.

Within this first focus of his mission to the Jews is a further refinement. As we have seen, this concentration on the Jewish population of Palestine weighs heavily in favor of the poor and oppressed Jews, who are the great majority. The Pharisees in general seem to look down upon them with varying degrees of contempt for their laxity, never mind that their lack of resources and spare time makes it impossible for them to be fully observant of all the religious laws and ceremonies of the spiritually elite in the Jewish community. Jesus' mission to the Jews crosses a very distinct boundary within Judaism. It is the boundary between the smaller number of law-observing, publicly-pious Jews, and the far larger number of "lax" Jews. And it is clear that Jesus is expanding the narrow circle of those who considered themselves the true Jews to include the whole race of Jews. He does it by honoring the poor Jews (Luke 6:20) and shocking the chief priests and elders by assuring them that "tax collectors and prostitutes are entering God's kingdom ahead of [them]" (Matt 21:31b).

The circle of Jesus' life and mission is further widened when he reaches out to populations who have partial Jewish ancestry, but whose Jewish religion has been influenced by other religions or by independent development. Samaria is a good example. In spite of its history as the main part of the northern Jewish kingdom of Israel, Assyria had conquered it and changed its character by resettling many of its Jews in other countries and bringing in populations from various part of the Assyrian Empire to replace them. Those newly arrived Gentile settlers brought their own religions with them, becoming catalysts for the further evolution of a Samaritan Judaism. Over time the Jews of Judah began to see Samaritan Judaism as more Assyrian than Jewish, and in the time of Jesus Samaria was looked upon by the Jews of Judea as the home of a mongrel Judaism. The contempt was palpable. Judean Jews who had to travel north went out of their way to avoid traveling through any part of Samaria, even if it meant a much longer journey.

Given this prejudicial mindset, when Jesus, a Judean Jew by birth, sets his face to go to Jerusalem for the last time, he strangely decides to go by way of Samaria. Luke gives to this journey through Samaria a major part of his Gospel, from Luke 9:51 through to 19:28! During this journey Jesus sends out seventy-two disciples on a Samaritan mission, shocks Jewish pride by telling the parables of the Good Samaritan and the Prodigal Son, tells many other important parables, expands his teaching about the kingdom of God, continues to debate with scribes and Pharisees, tells a devout man who is also rich to sell what he has and give it to the poor, heals many people, and invites a sinful tax collector named Zacchaeus into the kingdom. John's Gospel gives us one of Jesus' most intriguing encounters with a Samaritan— a woman, who is shocked that a Judean Jew would even talk to a Samaritan, and a woman at that! The circle continues to widen.

It widens further still, to the limit, or maybe there is no limit as far as Jesus is concerned. John's Gospel makes this unlimited expansion a central theme of Jesus' mission. Salvation includes the Gentiles (John 3:16–17). It is signaled in Jesus' response to the pagan centurion's plea for the healing of his servant (Matt 8:3–13) and especially in Luke's version of the story where Jesus is, well, blown over by the man's faith (Luke 7:1–10). Also in Jesus' response to that Syrophoenician woman who barrels her way into his presence while he is on retreat and begs him to heal her daughter. Jesus is clearly shocked by this forced intrusion of a Gentile to ask a big favor of a Jewish rabbi! It almost seems that Jesus surprises himself when he pronounces the healing. In spite of his own culturally and religiously-based rudeness toward her, he can't seem to help loving her, honoring her outrageous faith, and healing her daughter (Mark 7:24–30; Matt 15:21–28). The expanding circle of God's love has Jesus in its grip, expanding even *him* when need be.

Perhaps Jesus' greatest challenge in expanding the circle of God's redemptive love is to convince the leaders of the religious community to follow him and expand *their* boundaries. He does try to reach the Pharisees, Sadducees, and teachers of the law. He meets them on their own turf—the temple in Jerusalem and the synagogues of the Palestinian towns—and as an invited guest at their own dinner tables. Few of them, however, seem willing to move beyond a more confined and legalized version of their Jewish faith. Some see Jesus as a threat to the whole religious establishment, a few even plotting his death. Jesus spends most of his time with the poorer "lapsed" Jews, the people of the land—not, however, as a rejection of the religious establishment, but as a sign and an invitation for them to accept the expanded boundaries of God's inclusive love. The old wineskins of an excluding faith and its religious establishments must make way for the new, inclusive kingdom of God. The true church of Jesus marches to the order of their resurrected Lord: "Therefore, go and make disciples of all nations" (Matt 28:19a)—all peoples, races, ethnicities, economic classes. Everyone.

Let us be clear about what Jesus' expansion of the circle of God's love and concern actually means for his disciples. It certainly means expanding our circle of prayer. Jesus calls us to pray for enlarged hearts and expanded horizons. Pray even for our enemies and those who mistreat us (Luke 6:27–28). For example, we are called to pray for those who attack our country and commit acts of terror. Pray for those near and far. Pray for those we love up close and those God is preparing us to love even though we don't know them personally. The prayers of the saints in heaven include a song of Christ's redemption for "every tribe, language, people, and nation" (Revelation 5:9). It is not, however, only a matter of those for whom we pray. It is also a matter of those *with* whom we pray. All nations are invited into our place of prayer (Mark 11:17a; Matt 21:13a; Luke 19:46a). As disciples we pray both for the world and with the world. And as we pray, and keep praying, we begin to see ourselves for who we are: not just Christians, *world* Christians. True disciples of our world-loving Rabbi Jesus.

In praying with and for the world, we give *ourselves* to the world. We not only pray outside the circle, we *live* outside the circle. As best we can, we imitate our Rabbi Jesus by living in the world, living for the world, giving ourselves to the world. Our lives echo the *dona nobis pacem* of a whole world praying in a cathedral. We refuse to stay inside borders of difference, prejudice, and hostility. We no longer bow or surrender to suspicion and hate. We give up the lie of our superiority. We risk a gospel that encircles the globe. We follow Jesus.

Chapter 56

Inverting the Order

Just a few short years ago an unusual high school football game took place in Grapevine, Texas. The Grapevine Faith High School team was playing the Gainesville State football team. Even though Gainesville State was 75 miles away, there were at least 200 loyal fans who were there to support their team—and they were on fire! When the Gainesville players came out of the field their fans formed a 40-yard spirit line and a crash-through banner spelling in big letters, "GO TORNADOES!"

When visiting Gainesville made a good play, both on defense and offence, their fans yelled and clapped. And when they scored their two touchdowns, the fans exploded. The Gainesville players couldn't believe they were doing so well; they had scored only two touchdowns in their first eight games of the season. What was the difference here? They were playing a 7 and 2 home team who had seventy players, eleven coaches, and the latest equipment. Gainesville didn't have anywhere near those many players, and only one coach. They wore seven-year-old shoulder pads and helmets older than anyone could remember. The final score was 33 to 14. The visiting Gainesville teams lost; but they played their best game of the year. Maybe it was because of their tremendous fan support, those 200 people on their side of the stadium who yelled themselves hoarse.

Oh, did I tell you who those 200 fans were who cheered the visiting team? They were parents, brothers and sisters, and fellow students of the Grapevine Faith High School. Was this some kind of conspiracy? Why would hometown fans cheer for the visiting team? That's not how it's supposed to work in competitive sports.

Well, the person responsible for the conspiracy was the Grapevine Faith High School head coach, Kris Hogan. He suspected the Gainesville team would have few to no fans present. He was right. So he suggested that half the Grapevine fans become all-out Gainesville fans for the night. At first the coach's unusual suggestion did not meet with universal approval. How can we not root for our home team? We go to these games to support our players, to help them win.

But one by one, the Grapevine Faith community began to see the incredible beauty of Hogan's idea. Fellow students, parents, brothers and sisters of the players started getting a little glimpse of something outside the ordinary, a different way of acting, a new way of being. They signed on.

Oh, did I tell you who was on the visiting team? They were teens with convictions for drugs, assault and robbery. Most had been disowned by their families. Gainesville State wasn't a high school; it was a detention center for teenagers. After the game Gerald, one of the Gainesville players, said what a shock this was to the Gainesville team. "When we go to play these games with high schools," he said, "we can tell people are a little afraid of us. You can see it in their eyes. They're lookin' at us like we're criminals. But *these* people, they were yellin' for us! By our actual names!"

When the game was over, both teams gathered at the center of the field for prayer. To the surprise of a few people, Isaiah, one of the boys from the detention center, asked to lead in prayer: "Lord, I don't know how this happened, so I don't know how to say thank you; but I never would have known there were so many people in the world who cared about us." Prayer was followed by every football player's favorite pastime: burgers and fries and a soda—a kind of Lord's supper. When the meal and talk were over, each Gainesville State player received a personal letter of encouragement from a Grapevine Faith player, and of course a Bible. As the Gainesville bus was about to pull out, all the Gainesville players crammed to the side of the bus facing their "opponents" outside, their hands pressed to the window, their faces staring at these strange people they had never met before, their minds trying to comprehend this extraordinary, upside-down evening, their hearts unable to deny that for the few hours of their visit their world had changed (based on Rick Reilly's "Fifty-Second Best Story," in *Life of Reilly*).

And the world may have changed for many in the Grapevine Faith community. There was no questioning they were good Christians. That night, however, it seemed they broke out of the shell of a more protected Christian faith and fell into a holy craziness. In a beautiful way, they signed up to stand the expected on its head, which is pretty much what you have to do to let the gospel loose in this world and to be taken by it where it wants.

What happened on that football field under Friday night lights in little Grapevine, Texas was a far cry from the usual extracurricular activity of autumn nights across America. Friday night is high school football night, the night we're all supposed to be concerned about supporting our team—and if you don't show up, what's wrong with you? There's a town in south Georgia where if you're not at the stadium for the game, you'd better keep the lights off in the house lest your home occupation is noticed and you are exposed to the community as traitors to the team.

Football is a rough sport and kids get injured, sometime seriously, but there's some good in it, too. Kids learn to work together as a team, build on their strengths, implement strategy, practice discipline and fairness. Hopefully, they also learn to win (or lose) with grace. It's also good for the people in the stands to support their team, come together as a community, have fun. All those things can combine to make a team winners, whatever their win-loss record. That's the culture of our land we celebrate and live out on a Friday night in autumn.

On a Friday night in Grapevine, Texas, however, something very, very different happened. A different sports culture was celebrated and lived out that night. Both teams played hard, both sides cheered with noisy passion. No difference there. What turned the whole thing around was that other, bizarre thing. People guilty of inappropriate behavior at a football game. Leveling the playing field. Playing like they were all one family. And both teams having the support of *all* the people in the stands. It was football being played in a way football is *not supposed* to be played. It was the un-football game.

Where did Coach Hogan get the idea for such a thing?

It looked suspiciously like the way our Rabbi Jesus invites us to live. Jesus comes preaching this "upside-down kingdom." (That's what Donald Kraybill called it over twenty-five years ago in his award-winning book of that name.) When we enter *this* kingdom, we learn we have to see and do everything differently, even oppositely. We can't treat our enemies as enemies anymore, because we have to love them (Luke 6:27). We have to bless those who curse us and pray for those who mistreat us (v. 28). We must offer our second cheek to the person who slaps us on the other cheek, and not withhold our shirt from the person who steals our coat (Luke 6:29; Matt 5:39–40). We must volunteer to go the second mile with the person who forces us to go one mile (Matt 5:41). And most importantly, we must treat every person, no matter how disadvantaged, poor, or guilty of breaking the law, as we would treat Jesus himself (Matt 25:31–46).

On that Friday night in Grapevine, the hometown folks treated their opponents from Gainesville with friendship rather than fear, with compassion rather than caution. By the values of Jesus' upside-down kingdom, it will probably go down as their best game ever.

In the Gospels we get a strong signal early on that Jesus is setting out to turn everything upside down—or said differently, turn this upside-down world right-side up. It begins with Jesus showing *how* he's going to bring in the kingdom of God. Remember his forty-day temptation in the wilderness (Mark 1:12–13; Matt 4:1–11; Luke 4:1–13)? Matthew and Luke tell us that over those days Jesus is tempted in three different ways over how he's to accomplish his mission. First option: Put ample food on everyone's table to lick starvation and poverty, and you'll win everyone over. Second option: Take the kingdoms of the world by force and use you great power to gain the upper hand in order to impose *your* kingdom agenda. Third option: Perform spectacular, miraculous feats to get everyone to worship you. These are well-proven ways to get people to build a power base and get everyone to follow you. What Jesus clearly knows, however, is that none of them will open the door to God's upside-down kingdom. Only compassion will. Only the life and death Jesus was to live out. We can only be loved into the kingdom of God.

Jesus turns everything upside-down with his love. The way the early church saw God's love winning out on the cross was extraordinary. (Swedish Theologian Gustav Aulen wrote about it in *Christus Victor*.) Think of Jesus on the day of his crucifixion. Christians came to believe that Satan thought getting Jesus crucified would do away with him forever. What Satan did not understand, in this view, and what is still so foreign to business-as-usual in the world today, is the overcoming power of love. Calvary love turns the tables on sin and death—and wins. Shortly before his arrest and crucifixion, Jesus says, "Now is the time for judgment of this world. Now this world's ruler will be thrown out" (John 12:31). I imagine we call this day we observe annually as the day of Jesus' crucifixion *Good* Friday because the crucifixion wasn't a defeat that was overturned on Easter, as if the real outcome was uncertain. Jesus wins the battle on the *cross*! The resurrection is the confirmation of love's victory on the Friday.

As the story goes, Satan doesn't get it. So sure that a crucified Jesus will be rendered powerless and fully in hand, Satan is poised to close in and claim his kingdom. He thinks that for all intents and purposes, the battle is over. The cross is *his* triumph. Jesus hangs there helpless, a defeated man, his life slipping away. Smacking his lips, Satan is tasting victory. He's won.

What he doesn't know yet is that God has volunteered. The cross is actually *God's* initiative. Jesus says, "No one takes [my life] from me, but I give it up because I want to" (John 10:18a). It isn't Satan's cleverness that gets Jesus on the cross. Jesus, God in the flesh, gets himself there. God chooses to come to our rescue, chooses to give up power and authority, chooses to endure humiliation, chooses to allow himself to be crushed by our sin, chooses to receive every abuse Satan can inflict on the defenseless. God *chooses* Calvary!

Jesus is very intentional when he sets his face steadfastly to go to Jerusalem. And the truth it all reveals is this: There is nothing more redemptive than love giving itself completely, leaving every rightful claim of its own behind and pouring itself out for the ones who are loved—us. The Divine Lover, the Stronger One, becomes the Weaker, and *this, and this only, is Satan's undoing.* It is love God pulls over on Satan, a gift of such disarming value and force as to eliminate all comebacks. It's a surprise ransom that catches Satan completely off guard, weakening his grip on us and robbing him of all but his pretense. It's love's knock-you-over, unbeatable punch-line.

So what does a hell-bent world do with *that*? How do those who aren't interested cope with this disturbing message? Perhaps they reject the folly of it outright: Such extravagant behavior exceeds the bounds of a manageable lifestyle. It suggests, to the dismay of many, that the person who accepts it must then become an excessive lover himself. Radical love is not consistent with a rational, controlled, balanced life. No, it casts us in strong currents that may force us to people and places that call us to take the risk of compassion. It turns our comfortable, cautious lifestyle on its head. It inverts the order of our lives, turns our priorities upside-down.

Disciples of Jesus are those who allow themselves to be claimed by this crucified Messiah, this "wondrous attraction." They allow the crucified Son of God to draw them to himself (John 12:32) like a powerful magnet. They are won over, on board, traveling as the claimed beloveds of God who now give themselves to love's inversion. They swear allegiance to the upside-down kingdom of Jesus' shocking teaching, compelling living, and unselfish dying. And they start living in a way they call resurrection, because death has been defied and the power of sin has been broken.

I like to think that on that shining Friday night a few years ago, the Grapevine Faith High School community got a taste of what that was like. And I hope enough of those students and their families were shaken by the beauty of their own upside-down behavior, the cross-boundary love they discovered God had given them, and by the gracious response of those marginalized teens from Gainesville who will never forget (and might have been changed themselves by) what they were so stunned to receive that night.

Perhaps the biggest and most liberating challenge of Jesus' disciples is to loosen up and let Jesus turn them upside-down, so that his strange and crazy kingdom will seem normal to them (though cock-eyed to some). And perhaps the greatest joy of Jesus' disciples is to share compassion and

community with someone no one else wants to bother with or be threatened by, and to know deep down this is the disciple's deepest fulfillment
(though looked upon by some as wasted effort). To study the Jesus of the
Gospels is to see a way of life counter-intuitive to the present world order.
Over the centuries readers of the Gospels have heard Jesus calling them to
this extraordinary life. Many have chosen to follow it, and their lives stand
as witness to the things that really matter and forever endure.

When you and I have been at *our* best, we have been among those
people. And our best may very well be yet to come in the years we have left
on this earth to live as Jesus' upside-down disciples.

Chapter 57

Taking Holy Risks

Kelly Candaele wrote an article in *The Los Angeles Times* that ran on April 2, 2002 in praise of the stolen base. She lamented that America's obsession with the home run as an act of epic proportions had lessened our appreciation of the drama of the runner on first threatening the steal. She wrote:

> A home run launches the ball on a journey into the ephemeral light. It creates the fantasy that it may never come down, defying nature's basic laws, disappearing somewhere in the distance. The stolen base, though, is of the earth, grounded in the world's gravity and weight. . . .

Candaele said her mother, Helen Callaghan, played four years in the All American Girls Professional Baseball League, immortalized in the film A League of Their Own. She stole 112 bases in 1944 and felt more pride in those steals than in her league-leading number of hits and her home runs. Candaele closes her article with these words:

> Like all great base-stealers, [my mother] was not satisfied to remain on first, so far from "home." In that first crossover step and drive toward second, she asserted her freedom, a kind of personal sacrament and destabilizing jolt against the status quo. By running, she set the world in motion.
>
> I imagine the quick turn of my mom's shoulders, the frantic thrust of her arms and the hunger of her pumping legs. I feel today what she must have felt then. I'll take the mad dash of a great base-stealer over a lazy trot around the diamond any day.

Most of us do not have the gift of a power swing nor of brilliant pitching. But we may have the savvy, adventurousness, and raw nerve of a wiry base-stealer. We may be risk-takers who are not afraid of the possibility of failure or injury. We may be heroes of the small things that win games. The church world of today seems to admire, even idolize, the big hitters and adroit pitchers who populate the pulpits of some megachurches, those who preside over an ever-expanding empire of campuses and publications. We should not become too enamored of the hype. I dare say the church will advance the cause of its Rabbi and Savior more by its kingdom-of-God daredevils than by its high-profile prima donnas. These daredevils are mostly not super-stars; they are the no-name, unknown-by-the-world-at-large disciples who risk something for the Gospel. They take a stand and pay a price for doing so. As best they can, they live by the values of the kingdom of God in a world of raging competitive-ness and self-aggrandizement. They place their lives on the line every day, like base-stealers who move beyond their uncertainty and fear for a holy cause worth the gamble.

JESUS INVITES US TO be risk takers. Not the risk of chance, the blind gamble, a playing the odds. Nor just the calculated risk where we factor everything in and conclude there's a good chance of success. It is an entirely different kind of risk. Simply put, it is the risk we take in following him.

Wait a minute, this doesn't sound very safe and secure. Doesn't Jesus offer us life in all its fullness (John 15:11; 16:24b)? Life abundant (10:10b)? Doesn't he offer us everything he has (17:10)? Isn't he our friend (15:14–15)? Doesn't God promise to be by our side, to walk with us on our jour-ney, never to leave us or forsake us (Deut 31:6b; Heb 13:5)? The answer, of course, is yes.

He also offers us nothing. He does not guarantee that when we follow him we will not find ourselves in a lot of trouble. We cannot live in a way that places us in opposition to the present world order and then expect everyone to welcome us with open arms when they realize where we really stand and what we're really about. That is why in the Gospels the more people are exposed to Jesus the more the crowds become divided over him and the thinner the positive crowd attraction becomes (see, for example, John 7). If we follow the Rabbi who had nowhere to lay his head (Matt 8:20; Luke 9:58), who comes to his own and they do not receive him (John 1:11), who is plot-ted against by the very religious establishment that taught and nurtured him (Mark 3:6), and who is finally done away with by a cruel execution made possible through the partnership of religion and government, why would we expect a life without risks? We can't.

Unfortunately, some decide to follow Jesus in the hope he will keep them safe and their enemies at bay. Opting for a painless life they hunker down in an enclave of protective Christianity, surrounded by other Christians seeking safety from the world. As the enclave continues to maintain itself as a separated community, safe with Jesus, they make their Rabbi into a Christ sufficiently spiritualized, disembodied, and removed from the earth to authorize their own disconnect from the world around them they see as dangerous. Their Jesus, however, is not the one we find in the Gospels, who lays down his life and calls his disciples to lay down *their* lives for his sake and the gospel's (Mark 8:34–37; Matt 16:24–26; Luke 9:23–25).

In the Gospels Jesus guarantees suffering for his disciples. When James and John (or their mother on their behalf) request top kingdom position and privilege, Jesus is shocked by their presumption, not to mention their ignorance of what he is about. Only his heavenly Father bestows glory. The only entitlement Jesus can give them is a cup of suffering (Mark 10:35–40; Matt 20:20–23). In both accounts the story is closely connected with Jesus' prediction of his own suffering and death (Mark 10:32–34; Matt 20:17–19). Mark's account speaks of the disciples' shock and the following crowd's fear over what Jesus is telling them (Mark 10:32). Jesus does not mince words over the risk to be taken and the price to be paid by his disciples.

Thomas à Kempis has penetrating words for those who shun the risk and lower the price of discipleship:

> Jesus has many lovers of His heavenly kingdom, but few bearers of His cross. Many He has who are desirous of consolation, but few of tribulation. Many He finds who share His table, but few His fasting. All desire to rejoice with Him, few are willing to endure anything for Him. Many follow Jesus unto the breaking of bread; but few to the drinking of the cup of His passion (Luke 22:42). Many reverence His miracles; few follow the shame of His cross. (*Of the Imitation of Christ*, 83–84)

There is no place in the Gospels for a discipleship of compromise and comfort. Settled and safe religion is not the religion of Jesus. To be sure, the presence of Jesus brings deep peace, but it is an uncompromising peace that is under attack and must be defended. The fellowship of brother and sister Christians is God's gift of love to Jesus' disciples, but Jesus calls us to share compassionate community with outsiders and enemies as well. The forgiving grace of God frees us from personal condemnation, but it also calls us to risk offering this mercy to the world.

We disciples of Jesus are base stealers who put ourselves on the line by our down-to-earth mad dashes for the world whom God so loves. To borrow Candaele's words, we are "of the earth, grounded in the world's gravity and weight," asserting the freedom of the gospel by giving a "destabilizing jolt against the status quo," defying the weight of our self-imposed imprisonment. We are Jesus' holy risk takers, menacing gamblers whose next steps are unpredictable, except that they will be driven by the outrageous example of our Rabbi Jesus.

Chapter 58

Living in the Patience of God

FRED CRADDOCK TOLD A Christmas story in the *Milk and Honey* newsletter of the Craddock Center (December, 2013, 2). It came from his days working at the general store part time while he was still in school. He lived in a small town where in those days the general store was where you bought just about everything you needed. Here is Fred's story in his words:

> To say it was Christmas at the general store simply meant more of the same. There was one noticeable difference: the tide of war [World War II] had taken a favorable turn and customers dared to say "Maybe before next Christmas." Otherwise, Christmas at the store brought the same inventory, but in larger quantities. Coconuts and pineapples were popular items for Christmas baking. Hardware, feed, and seed received little attention; not now, maybe in the spring.
>
> And Christmas customers were the same. They were of two kinds: cash and credit. For the majority of credit customers, income was seasonal and so payment was seasonal. Except for Will. (I call him Will because that was not his name.) Will walked down the railroad track to the store every Saturday morning, a gunny sack over his shoulder for carrying his order of groceries. His order was always the same; I can still fill it from memory: cabbage, dried beans, corn meal, coffee, salt pork. Total: about $8.00 dollars. On Saturday each month he brought his pension check from the L and N Railroad: $22.40. We cashed his check, he paid $2.00 on his bill, and gave his order which was, as I said, about $8.00.
>
> On this particular Saturday, the owner, who personally kept the record of credit customers, said, "Look, Will," as he held up a stack of weekly bills. "Do you know how much you owe?" Will, looking puzzled, said, "I just paid some of my bill today, like I do every month. You know I never miss a payment. You can count on me."

"Merry Christmas, Will," said the owner as he tore into pieces the stack of bills, letting them fall on the floor. Will looked stunned and hurt. "Does this mean I can't trade here anymore?" "Oh, no, Will. You are one of our most faithful customers." And turning to me he said, "Give Will what he wants," and turning to Will, said, "Will, put some of these peppermint sticks in your bag for those grandchildren. It's Christmas."

Will smiled an uncertain smile. "You know when my check comes, I'll come in to pay you. You can count on me."

The impatience of many Christians is pervasive. Some cannot understand why God tarries as the world seems to be coming apart at the seams. Others, not so anxious for the world to end, wonder why so many Christians and so many churches can't seem to get it right. Why doesn't God just fix things, bring real revival and transform his people, make us a more perfect church? We would love for the church to be a band of believers who have their act together and look like convincing disciples of Jesus. So would Jesus, I'm sure. God, however, allows us to keep bumbling along with our imperfections while he waits and waits, perhaps hoping we'll move on to what Wesley optimistically called "Christian perfection."

The patience of God is frustrating! With Fanny Crosby we may be "watching and waiting, looking above" for God's arrival and the triumph of his kingdom. The evidence of such an arrival, however, is largely not there. What does the church need to do that it's not doing? Perhaps we need to weed out those who don't measure up to the call of Christ. It must mean *something* to be the body of Christ and the bride of Christ without spot or blemish! (Thank you for that, Paul!) So why do we put up with all the imperfections? Why don't we just clean up the place so Jesus can come?

Jesus has something to say about this in a couple of parables about the kingdom of God (heaven). First he tells about the farmer who sows good seed in his field, but while he's sleeping an enemy comes and sows weeds among the wheat. No one knows the difference till the seeds begin to sprout and the problem becomes obvious. The farmer's servants assume he will want them to go through the field and pull up the weeds so that the wheat can grow unimpeded and the harvest can be clean-cut. That would seem to be the sensible and efficient thing to do. The farmer, however, gives directions that surely no farmer in his right mind would give: Let the wheat and the weeds grow alongside each other. At harvest first gather and burn the weeds. Then gather the wheat and bring it into my barn (Matt 13:24–30).

The second parable is about the fisherman who casts his net into the water and pulls in an unusually large catch. Instead of throwing back the inedible fish there and then, he waits till he returns to shore to separate the edible from the inedible fish (Matt 13:47–50). This doesn't seem to be as counter-intuitive as waiting for the harvest to separate the wheat from the weeds, but the same idea of waiting till the end to separate the good from the bad is there.

These parables force us to face our own desire to see matters of the kingdom of God on earth sorted out *now*. So many of us Christians are nervous perfectionists. We want things fixed. We're uncomfortable with a far from perfect church, a congregation that can't seem to get along half the time, the petty squabbles that sour our spirituality. The patience of God is frustrating! How can he put up with our inadequacy and dysfunction?

Jesus tells another parable, this one found in Luke's Gospel. It's about a man whose vineyard has a fig tree that hasn't borne fruit in three years. He decides the tree ought to be cut down to make room for a new and productive planting—a very sensible thing to do after three years of unfruitfulness. The man who takes care of the vineyard has another idea: Wait another year. I'll give it some work, dig around it and fertilize it, and we'll see what happens. If it doesn't produce fruit in another year, we'll cut it down (Luke 13:6–9). What are the chances? Well, we don't know. We don't even know if the owner agrees, and if he does, whether the extension pays off. In our hearts we suspect the owner probably gives in. The vineyard caretaker wants to work further with this fruitless fruit tree, as Jesus always seems to want to work further with these flawed humans of his. This tolerance of God—when will it end?

God's behavior can be frustrating. Why won't he let us help him clean things up now, separate the wheat from the weeds now, get rid of the bad fish now, chop down those trees that aren't producing the fruit they're supposed to? Can't we do something to get this church of his to pull itself together and act like the pure bride and the healthy body of Christ it's supposed to be?

Some of us might judge certain church members as, well, lax in the living of their faith. And we're thinking, "Lord, it's because of *them* that we're not moving forward. Shouldn't they be weeded out now so that a better harvest of good disciples can be achieved?" And the Lord does not answer us. He looks into our face, his eyes piercing us, and if we dare read him we see an unsettling truth: We also are not ready for his harvest. God's patience has as much to do with us, as we may well have reached a level of self-satisfaction that blocks our own spiritual growth, and like many of the Pharisees of Jesus' day, *we* are the great impediment to God's kingdom. God's patience and tolerance has far more to do with us and our need to be stripped of our spiritual arrogance than with those who are humbly aware they are sinners and would be greatly helped by disciples of Jesus who stand by them in humility and confess their own sins too. Jesus also tells a parable about that: The self-righteous Pharisee and the sinful tax collector praying in the temple and God hearing the sinner's prayer rather than the self-justifying bragging of the cleric (Luke 18:9–14).

We can thank God he's incredibly patient, not only because there's a whole world of people he wants to win over by his extravagant love, but also because it takes some of us self-satisfied saints so long to be brought to our knees to confess how much our loveless holiness, our forced sanctity, and our lack of self-awareness and self-honesty have stood in the way of Jesus' saving mission.

When we do recognize and confess that God is incredibly patient with all us Christians, how do we then live with and in this patience of God? First, *we learn to wait expectantly*. Think of the eager watchfulness of the child waiting for grandma and grandpa's visit coming up. Think of sitting on the edge of our seats at a concert waiting to hear our first live performance of Sibelius's Second Symphony, having only heard it over and over on a CD and already having come to love it. Think of waiting for our first child to be born. We know something good is coming, but it may seem an eternity of waiting. We live in the hope that this wonderful thing is going to happen. We wait in eager expectation.

Second, *we learn how to live within the waiting*. God's patience does not call us to be idlers, passive, unengaged waiters-around for the kingdom of God to come in its fullness. It calls us to be faithful stewards and full participants. The child waiting for her grandparents' visit is getting ready to ask questions, tell them what she's been doing, work on the little house she's been building with her brother in the back yard. The concert-goer readies himself for that first live performance of Sibelius's Second by listening to the CD again, researching how the symphony came about and why it was composed, maybe even bringing a score to the concert to follow along. The parents waiting for their first child to be born have made more preparations than they can count.

We, the disciples of Jesus learn to live our lives well within the waiting. We plant seeds for the kingdom and tend the soil. We do our part to reveal the miracle of a kingdom that grows from a seed to a tree of sheltering hospitality and never-ending harvest (Mark 4:30–32; Matt 13:31–32; Luke 13:18–19). We put yeast in the flour, believing it will work its way through and be the catalyst for a delicious, nurturing loaf of bread (Matt 13:33; Luke 13:20–21). We are not the source of the miracle of the tree or the bread. We do not make the miracle happen. We live as if it *is* happening, and will happen, even though we sometimes, even often, do not see it happening. The reality of the hidden kingdom of God has taken hold of us, and we claim the kingdom as the only enduring reality and its Lord as the only God worth worshiping.

We must resist the impatient activism to which we are tempted. Our now-ism lures us. We want completion now, so we set out with our own ideas for achieving it. (How often do we say, "Let's make this *happen!*"?) The problem with this compulsive activism is that God is the one who makes his kingdom happen; we don't.

Whenever the disciples want to rush into peremptory action, Jesus stops them and settles them down. When a Samaritan village refuses to welcome Jesus and help him prepare for his messianic entrance into Jerusalem, James and John suggest that Jesus call down fire from heaven to get these unbelievers out of the way. Their solution is answered with a stern rebuke from Jesus (Luke 9:51–56). The true kingdom of God is not gained by our outward displays of force (Matt 11:12). It doesn't come with signs easily noticed (Luke 17:20). It is advanced by the righteousness of disciples who don't even know they have advanced it through their compassion shared with "the least of these" (Matt 25:31–40). The righteous, not the activist achievers, "will shine like the sun in their Father's kingdom" (Matt 13:43). The child who trusts God's future, not the adult with a long list of past successes, is the greatest in the kingdom of God (Matt 18:1–4; Luke 9:46–48).

Jesus teaches us to live in the patience of God, to be planters of gospel, cultivators of the kingdom, harvesters of righteousness. When we live in this patience we live radically because we let God's initiative set the agenda and override our impatience. The outcome, however, is not inaction; it is mission. We watch to see what God is doing, we wait to discover where he is leading. We look for Jesus in action, using Scripture, prayer, discernment, the wisdom of other disciples, and fasting if need be. Then we exercise the patient activism of a disciple.

The thing is, what comes out of this patient activism is far more sub-stantive and life-changing than the quick fixes or rash actions of our spiritual impertinence. The kingdom of God sometimes breaks in unexpectedly in a transforming moment that startles us. At other times it emerges gradually like the slow growth of a seed into a tree. In both instances it is neither forced by us, nor is it the exact outcome we specifically planned. It is the work of God.

This is why Jesus speaks of our seeing the future as the story God is writing. He tells his disciples neither to live in fear of what is coming nor to live in denial of it. He invites them to prepare themselves to receive it. To complete Fanny Crosby's vision, we do the watching and waiting "filled with his goodness, lost in his love."

Like a small town waiting for Christmas and the end of war, we also wait in hope while sensing the inadequacy of debts not fully paid and efforts falling short. Fortunately, the God of our past, present, and future is patient with us, receiving our meagre efforts and tearing up the insufficiently paid invoices of our accumulated inadequacies. It's enough, he says to us, enough for now, because he knows our future, our becoming, and the glory we will share together on the earth and through eternity. And he invites us to learn from a patient general store owner who looks beyond what people owe, beyond the ways they fall short, beyond their spiritual inadequacies.

God invites us to see his world of debts already paid, grace given, love shared. And in this world of his patience, we find a freedom to become who we are. We discover motivation to move beyond our dissatisfaction with ourselves and others. We give up waiting around for God to appear and fix everything, and we don't set out to fix everything ourselves. God will indeed come and establish his kingdom in its fullness, but—bless him!—he works in and through us. Can you imagine?!

Appendix

The Importance of the Jesus of the Gospels

WHY IS THE STUDY of Jesus so important for those who call themselves Christians? There are a number of reasons, and I want to describe them as best I can. I think this background will help us prepare for our study of Jesus. I'll begin with a look at the church itself.

Sickly Bride and Broken Body?

The church today is a complex mosaic of races, ethnicities, and nationalities. Its corporate worship ranges from the most spontaneous and Pentecostal to the most traditional and ordered. Though most, if not all, Christian communities agree on a common confessional core, expressed simply, for example, in the Apostles' Creed, there are still differences in doctrinal expression and emphases, and some doctrinal viewpoints are held as sacrosanct in some traditions and not in others.

All this diversity, however, sometimes morphs into divisiveness, which causes many Christians to become dismissive of other Christians. Some churches may see other Christian traditions through the eyes of their own racism, ethnic hatred, or xenophobia. Some congregations look with disdain on the worship of other Christian traditions, describing them as a formality too captive to dead tradition or, as the opposite case may be, an unfettered spontaneity too vulnerable to human excess and manipulation. And some Christian groups claim an unquestioned doctrinal purity and keep a safe distance from other groups seen as theologically compromised, sometimes even consigning them to eternal damnation for their doctrinal error.

Such a picture of the church today is not pretty. The church, Christ's holy and blameless bride (Eph 5:27c), is too often looking sickly, and the church, the body of Christ (chapter 12 of both Romans and Corinthians), is too often looking broken. We all should confess our own sin in this dereliction. We don't, however, help the church by endlessly reciting woes over its failures. We certainly ought to expect that God can do something to answer Jesus' final prayer in John's Gospel that his church be one as he and the Father are one (John 17:11, 22, 23). And we ought to pray to that end. The last of those verses brings the church's divisiveness into the larger perspective of her credibility and witness. Jesus is addressing the Father:

> I'm in them and you are in me so that they will be made per
> fectly one [brought to complete unity, NIV]. *Then* the world will
> know that you sent me and that you have loved *them* just as you
> loved me. (italics added)

I think we should also recognize and accept the uncomfortable answer God gives to such prayers—namely, *we* are the answer to them. How could that be? Well, the answer is there staring us in the face. It comes from Jesus our rabbi, inviting us to know him, learn from him, live like him, imitate him. The answer is: study Jesus and follow his call. The answer is to go back to the basics by engaging the Jesus of the Gospels rather than the adapted and compromised Jesus of cultural and sectarian Christianity.

The Gospels are not a Sunday School primer for children from which the mature Christian is supposed to graduate in order to move on to the presumably more important cerebral matters of doctrinal discourse and endless theological debate. The Gospels get at the heart of who we are as Christians. They ring with the call of a radical, kingdom-of-God revolutionary, extended to those who are ready to lay down their lives for their Rabbi Lord and embark on his course of authentic living. They throb with the life of our incarnate God, now with us, shaking us up and turning us in the right direction—promising us his empowering Spirit so that we can begin to look like our rabbi. If we didn't have the Gospels, we wouldn't have a gospel to live by.

I believe Christian churches are being called to serious study of the Jesus of the Gospels—the person himself; the life he lived; the priorities he espoused; the things he said, taught, and did; and the values of the kingdom of God he inaugurated and demonstrated. This, I believe, is the doorway inviting the church into a unity around Jesus in one household of disciples focused on their rabbi rather than the maintenance and defense of their differences.

The Divisiveness of Our Treasured Opinions

All Christians are part of one tradition or another, each of which has its own treasures. I realize there are some Christian groups who claim their beliefs and practices are an accurate replication of the New Testament church and draw nothing from subsequent reflections or traditions. Since we see change and development within the New Testament church itself, I find it hard to see their claim as sustainable. Within my own denominational tradition, I have seen much change that was actually necessary in order to keep our church faithful to its Scripture-based calling. Most denominations are birthed as a movement to reclaim some lost treasure, some crucial part of what it means to be the church of Jesus Christ. The Lutheran Reformation, for example, was an uprising within the church to reclaim, among other treasures, the doctrine and practice of salvation by grace through faith. Such reclaimed treasures, as restorative and enriching as they are, however, often subsequently evolve into dead dogmas and practices to which that tradition clings all the more possessively as the way it defines itself. The dogmas and the practices are finessed, and further qualifications are added. The outcome is an elaborate and sophisticated product, a doctrinal and performance wonder, elevated as proof of supremacy. The vibrancy is lost as the treasure becomes a weapon for debate and sometimes ugly verbal warfare with other Christians over biblical faithfulness. Much of the church of Jesus is loud with these battles.

John Wesley saw how distractive and divisive doctrinal differences and debates in the church had become in his day. Here are quotes from a couple of his sermons on the subject (Note: Wesley's reference to "opinions" has to do largely with certain theological positions and traditional practices that divided Christians and Christian groups.):

> And I beseech you, brethren, by the mercies of God, that we be in no wise divided among ourselves. Is thy heart right, as my heart is with thine? I ask no farther question. If it be, give me thy hand. For opinions, or terms, let us not destroy the work of God. Dost thou love and serve God? It is enough. I give thee the right hand of fellowship. (*The Character of a Methodist*)
>
> I will not quarrel with you about any opinion. Only see that your heart is right toward God, that you know and love the Lord Jesus Christ; that you love your neighbor, and walk as your Master walked; and I desire no more. I am sick of opinions: I am weary to hear them. My soul loathes this frothy food. Give me solid and substantial religion; give me a humble, gentle lover of God and man; a man full of mercy and good fruits, without partiality, and without hypocrisy; a man laying himself out in

the work of faith, the patience of hope, the labour of love. Let my
soul be with these Christians, wheresoever they are, and whatsoever opinion they are of. "Whosoever" thus "doeth the will of
my Father which is in heaven, the same is my brother, and sister,
and mother." (*A Farther Appeal to Men of Reason and Religion*)

Over the last almost one hundred years, endless discussions have tak-
en place, organizations formed, conferences held, books and papers written
about the great need for the churches around the world (as well as that "different" church down the street) to affirm and begin to realize its unity in
Christ. These efforts have been undertaken largely to take seriously Jesus'
prayer for the unity of his followers, a prayer which has been undermined
again and again in the church over its almost 2,000-year history.

Without a doubt, our disunity and factionalism—not to mention actual physical violence and warfare between Christian camps—have been the
cause of continuing grief on the part of our Lord. He surely dances with
delight over his church's rich diversity, but he cries over her dangerous
pathological divisiveness. Threatened by our diversity, unable to handle our
differences, addicted to the comfort of our more familiar ways of thinking
and doing, we build ugly, self-protecting walls around our own traditions.
And people wonder how followers of the one and same leader can be so
intolerant of each other. Our divisiveness undermines our credibility, and
therefore our witness. Years ago a Christian missionary in India was having
a private audience with Radhakrishna, the President of India. The missionary was explaining to the President that Christ could do so much for the
people of India. The President referred to the often hostile relations between
the Christian denominations in his country. He then asked, "If your Christ
has done so little for you, how can I expect he'll do more for us?"

What, then, can unite us? Certainly not a merging of our ethnic, racial,
or national cultures: these differences stand as blessings to the whole church.
Certainly not attempting a sameness in styles of worship: these differences
will, and should, always vary depending on the culture and character of
the worshiping group. Certainly not consistencies in theological interpretations: theological discussions tend to become debates, and they can get ugly;
in fact, many of the major breaks in church unity have been precipitated by
doctrinal warfare. And certainly not in some kind of forced institutional
merging that blends our rich diversity into bland sameness.

I am convinced that the crucial starting point for genuine Christian
unity is for Christians to study Jesus and seek to live the way of life he taught
and demonstrated as simply and as plainly as they can. The starting point is
not to attempt to create a unifying social culture labeled "Christian"; not to

get agreement about worship style; not to achieve the impossible by trying to construct a common theology every article of which all churches embrace; and not to force a merger. The starting point is to go to the Gospels and find our common rabbi, our one teacher. Learn him. Become intimate with him. Act like him. Be him. That's what disciples of their rabbi do.

What we will see very quickly is that Jesus did not teach concepts, he told stories—stories that invite us in different ways to enter the big Story of God's love affair with us and to become a part of that Story. He used metaphors from everyday life that people could relate to and draw their own conclusions and applications from—metaphors like finding a lost coin, getting ready for a wedding, planting seeds, harvesting crops. He did not teach much doctrine, he taught a way of life fleshed out in very straightforward sayings. He taught us to live life in a way that makes our claim to be his followers credible and opens a door to what God is doing in the world. In the Gospels we meet a Jesus who calls us to live as we were meant to live in order to become who we were meant to become.

Rediscovering the Jesus of the Gospels

Cyprian (d. 258 CE) was a pagan convert to Christian faith who became bishop of Carthage. His writings about the church became very influential in the Christian world of that time. One of his helpful analogies of the church was to see her as many streams flowing down from one source. Let's take Cyprian's analogy and ask, "What, then, is this source?" Is it God? Well, yes, but the word "God" is so broad and general, and open to many different (and even conflicting) interpretations. Then is it Scripture? Though Scripture is essential to identifying, preserving, and providing the historical basis of the source, it is a record and not the originating source. Is it correct theology? As important as theology is in the life of the church, it lives largely in the mind, and over the 2,000 years of the church's history it has lent itself to differing views and even conclusions. What, then, *is* the source of the many streams that comprise the church? *It is Jesus*, an actual human being, a person, the incarnation of Alpha and Omega, God himself in flesh, our Savior and model, our Lord, and the whole church's only marriage partner. And the Gospels have the details!

As Christians we believe that the man Jesus is the Christ (the one anointed by God to save his people). On the face of it, that was not so difficult for many people in his day to accept, or at least entertain, since Jews thought the Messiah would be a man. But we Christians also believe he is the Son of God. That was far more difficult for people in his day to get their heads around. How could one person be both God and man? It was enough to cause riots, which it did.

Over a relatively short period of time, however, followers of Jesus came to believe that "*God* was in Christ, reconciling the world to himself" (II Corinthians 5:19a). And of course we have the testimony of Jesus himself, who for good reason did not announce his divinity from the housetops; it would surely have precipitated a premature end to his mission. But he calmly owned it when he was pushed. He not only prayed as a son to a father, he claimed a oneness with the Father (John 10:30). When we call this person Jesus Christ, we are actually making a statement, "Jesus is the Christ." We are claiming that Jesus, the man, is God.

What we know from church history is that there were some who had difficulty with the divinity, and others who had trouble with the humanity. Consequently, there were some who decided to embrace only the humanity of Jesus, others only the divinity. Some scholars wonder if the apostle Paul's statement to the Corinthian church that "no one says, 'Jesus is cursed!' when speaking by God's Spirit" refers to an early heresy that claimed that the human Jesus had somehow been superseded by the divine Christ (I Cor 12:3a).

We do know that the four Gospels were written in the latter half of the first century CE, while the New Testament letters, which contained a good deal of Christology (doctrine of Jesus as the Christ and Son of God) were written earlier. In other words, the witnesses we have about Jesus' life and ministry on earth were written down later. The earlier material in the New Testament, therefore, gave testimony to Jesus the Christ as the Son of God, Savior, Redeemer, Lord, and to his continuing presence in the church and the world through the Spirit. It also gave helpful guidance in dealing with life issues in light of Christian faith and belief. Obviously, congregations in the earlier part of the first century, populated primarily by the uneducated, did not typically engage in intellectual conversations about the exalted Christ to the exclusion of the human Jesus. They were steeped in the stories of Jesus, passed down orally by first-hand witnesses. They memorized, recited, and passed these stories on to new generations and congregations. (Memorization of sacred stories was a carefully honed skill in those days, especially since few could read.) As Jesus proved again and again, stories are what engage the majority of us, who prefer not to dwell for long in the realm of intellectual discourse.

As the church expanded and the oral tradition (the stories and teachings of Jesus) could not keep up, and as questionable versions of and additions to the story appeared, the need arose for reliable evangelists to write the story down. These witnesses either had first-hand knowledge of what they wrote or were themselves well acquainted with certain witnesses. Four of these Gospels endured over time, emerging in the judgment of the church as inspired word.

These four Gospels enable us to keep in touch with the human Jesus, the rabbi who taught us how to see, think, and live. They invite us not to get lost in our illusions and trapped in our dead ends. They help us avoid the spell of a dehumanized Jesus, an exalted Christ/Savior/Redeemer with no real grounding on earth, to the diminishment of the rabbi Jesus who for three intense years taught and demonstrated a kingdom-of-God way for us to live on earth, a way he actually intended us to follow. The Gospels keep the radical Jesus up front, in our face and demanding a response. They help us spot and avoid a cheap grace that demands too little of us because we perceive the exalted Christ as so far removed from the dust and grind of our daily lives. Rabbi Jesus does not allow us to miss the truth: the down-to-earth costly grace of discipleship.

Perhaps some of us have too eagerly and easily embraced certain phrases in the New Testament letters suggesting we claim some kind of Christian closeness to Christ as a vague assurance that we are secure and healthy spiritually. But what does Christian assurance mean if we are not steeped in the Gospels, studying the actual man Jesus in whom God was incarnate, measuring our lives by his? Is our preference a cozy Christ rather than a jarring Jesus? Of course it is! It is much safer to get close to a disembodied Christ than to the incarnate Christ. The incarnate Christ (Jesus) confronts us with a life that is far from safe and about as down-to-earth as you can get.

The Gospels give us the story of the real Jesus. Apart from this real-life story, "having the Spirit of Christ" (Rom 8:9) is so vague as to be meaningless; being "one body in Christ" (Rom 12:5; I Cor 12:27) is a sentimental, idealistic dream with insufficient foundation; claiming to have "the mind of Christ" (I Cor 2:16) is arrogance; being "in Christ [and therefore] . . . part of the new creation" (II Cor 5:17) has no concrete point of reference; testifying that "Christ lives in me" (Gal 2:20; Col 1:27) is presumption; asking that "Christ may live in [our] hearts by faith" (Eph 3:17) is asking for a permanent dweller we don't know and withholding from ourselves information we *need* to know; seeking "the fullness of Christ" (Eph 4:13) is to have no standard by which to measure progress into this fullness; to seek to be "partners with Christ" for life (Heb 3:14) makes little sense as our partner is obscure; and our willingness and attempts to "share in Christ's suffering" (I Pet 4:13) will go down wrong paths if we don't understand the innocent suffering of Jesus in the Gospels, the utter lack of self-centeredness in it.

Maybe we need to hear the voice of God from the cloud on the Mount of Transfiguration, and prostrate ourselves like Peter, James, and John when they heard God say, "Listen to him!" (Matt 17:5–6) Listen to Jesus! Take seriously what he tells you to do. Yes, allow yourselves to get caught up in Jesus' glory—but not to the exclusion of living in his story and living out his story. Not to the exclusion of hearing and believing what he has to say, watching and imitating what he does, risking and following where he goes—like a true disciple. As a matter of fact, the glory of God *is* most profoundly encountered in the humble carpenter-rabbi from Nazareth. The most shocking glory is in the earthly story.

During the week leading up to his crucifixion, Jesus makes a curious statement. He has just criticized some of the Pharisees and the legal experts of religion, pointing out that they "place heavy packs [of teaching] . . . on the shoulders of others," which neither they nor anyone else are able to live by. Impressed by the astuteness and confusing complexity of their own teaching, they love to be honored at banquets and addressed as "rabbi." Having pointed this out to them, Jesus then turns to his own disciples, future leaders and teachers in his movement, and hits them with this:

> But you shouldn't be called *Rabbi*, because you have one teacher, and all of you are brothers and sisters. Don't call anybody on earth your father, because you have one Father, who is heavenly. Don't be called *teacher*, because Christ is your one teacher. (Matthew 23:8–10)

Jesus is obviously speaking in hyperbole. He doesn't really mean we are to call no one rabbi, father, or teacher. He seems to be reminding his disciples that *he* is the one who has "the words of eternal life" (John 6:68b), he is the source from which flows fullness of life (John 10:10b; 14:6), he is the full measure by which they are to mark progress in their own journey (Matt 10:24–25; Luke 6:40; John 8:31–32).

Yes, we have the benefit of spiritual fathers and mothers, pastors, mentors, teachers, and counselors. We would have been lost without them. None of them, however, is Jesus. None is perfect, and none merits our absolute allegiance as disciples. Those leaders who claim they possess absolute truth and deserve our total obedience are deluded imposters. And even those of us who have a good teacher or mentor, a person worth admiring and listening to, can make the mistake of becoming a full-blown disciple of that person and failing to see beyond him or her to *the* rabbi, Jesus. Or, we may think we can see the way of Jesus only through the way of our teacher or mentor. What inevitably seems to happen when we lose the real Jesus of the Gospels as our reference point for discipleship is that factions of differing Christian lifestyles and doctrines spring up. Each faction believes they have the corner on the way of life and teaching of Jesus. Each thinks it owns doctrinal purity.

When we immerse ourselves in the Gospels, however, we come to understand the gospel is a real story, not polished concepts or doctrines. Jesus knows that doctrine and theology have their place among his disciples. The Gospel leads us to conclusions about who God is; what his intentions in the world are; how he reveals himself; how we are saved; how we are called to live in his world; and who Jesus is. Its story does beg for conclusions (we call this doctrine) and guidelines for living (we call this ethics). Jesus also knows, however, that bringing the gospel to the world is not really a matter of getting people to buy into a set of doctrines or ethical standards; it is a matter of our living Jesus' life in the world by what we do, what we say, and how we think.

In a private meeting with his disciples recorded in Matthew, Mark, and Luke, Jesus asks them who people think he is. The answers range from John the Baptist, or Elijah, to one of the other prophets. Then he asks them to answer for themselves. Peter blurts out, "You are the Christ." Jesus immediately orders them not to tell this to anyone. He then goes on to say that he would "suffer many things and be rejected by the elders, chief priests, and the legal experts, and be killed, and then, after three days, rise from the dead." Peter, who was obviously enamored by his earlier correct answer, now demonstrates that he *doesn't* get it. He strenuously objects to what Jesus has just revealed. He sees "the Christ" as a conquering, all-powerful Savior of the Jewish nation, a *proper* Messiah. Suffering and death don't fit into his Christology. The Messiah is supposed to be a conqueror, not a victim.

Jesus responds with a rebuke of surprising harshness: "Get behind me, Satan. [Peter], you are not thinking God's thoughts." Jesus then goes on to say his true disciples are those who follow his earthly example by taking up their cross and following him, because only by losing their life will they find it (Mark 8:27–35). The only way for Peter and the rest of us to see and begin to understand the truth of this mystery is for us to see and study the life of this singularly different rabbi and to pay the price of following him. Our doctrines, as brilliant and correct as they may be, will not bring us there; our ethical standards, as admirable and good as they are, will not do it. We begin to understand when we join the circle of Jesus, our rabbi, and follow him.

Important to discovering the Jesus of the Gospels is to realize that Jesus does not promote himself or a doctrine about himself. He tells his disciples not to trigger a bombshell by proclaiming his messianic identity—not to mention his divinity! He orders his disciples not to tell anyone he is the Christ (Mark 8:27–29; Matthew 16:13–20; Luke 9:18–22)! It will not be doctrinal statements that draw people to the kingdom of God Jesus is inaugurating; it will be the radically compassionate life that Jesus and his true followers embody and their straightforward witness to the world of how a disciple's relationship with their rabbi Lord shows, teaches, and empowers them to live this way. The life and words of Jesus are God's lure. In the Gospels Jesus does not promote himself or a doctrine about himself. He promotes the kingdom of God, and himself as the way into it, and the teacher and demonstrator of it.

I sometimes wonder if we misunderstand and even over-emphasize the "impressiveness" of Jesus. To be sure, he did initially impress a lot of people, but as time would eventually prove, many of them were either only momentarily curious about this very different rabbi or they came with high expectations for the establishment of a new and powerful Jewish kingdom. Over time they left, unimpressed according to their own standards, perhaps unaware of their own Scriptures which spoke of a messianic figure who "possessed no splendid form for us to see, no desirable appearance" (Isaiah 53:2b). Eugene Peterson says many people had trouble with the ordinariness of Jesus, and they still do (*Christ Plays in Ten Thousand Places*, 34–36). Jesus doesn't locate himself above the level of ordinary people; they are the ones he hangs around the most. He doesn't set himself apart and demand to be served; he serves. He doesn't manipulate the admiration and love of others; he loves. He doesn't preserve his life and cultivate his power; he gives his life and surrenders power. To be sure, something extraordinary comes out of all that, but the extraordinariness happens in real life, with common people like you and me—as we follow a lowly rabbi, who happens to be the Christ, the Son of God, our savior and our teacher.

Re-framing the Kingdom of God

There was a very powerful belief in operation among most Palestinian Jews in the early first century CE. Biblical scholar N.T. Wright calls it a "second-Temple" theology which saw the soon-to-be-completed new temple in Jerusalem as the center point of a long-awaited new Jewish kingdom which God would establish. Jews, including Jesus, believed that the salvation of this fallen world would come to and through Israel, God's chosen people. The great majority of Jews believed it would come when a messiah, whoever he was, drove out the oppressors and set up a political, as well as a social and religious, kingdom of God. And then, over time, all the nations would flock to Jerusalem, where true worship of God would take place. In other words, the center of gravity for the new kingdom would be *the temple*, and the political power would be centered in *Jerusalem*. (This view was based on such Old Testament texts as Isaiah 2:1–5.) As the centuries-old center of

Jewish faith and life, the temple would be at the heart of a new order for the Jews (Wright, *The Challenge of Jesus*).

Now consider Jesus' relationship with the temple. It is not by accident that whenever Jesus goes to the temple, he always seems to get into trouble, challenge the teachers there, cause controversy, or do something violent—he, a Jewish rabbi! He just doesn't seem to fit into what the temple represents to the religious establishment. He proclaims the coming of the kingdom of God, but he has no place for the temple in it (John 4:21–24). *His* kingdom is not temple-based; it is based in a community of disciples which anyone can join.

The rabbi Jesus does believe the Old Testament prophecies that salvation will come to the Jews first (John 4:22) and then to the rest of the world through them. But that's where the similarity ends. Jesus says it will not be centered in the temple in Jerusalem. It will be centered in *him*: "I am the way, the truth, and the life"(John 14:6a). Furthermore, it will not be a political kingdom: "My kingdom doesn't originate from this world" (John 18:36a). And further still, it will come about by his suffering, death, and resurrection: "The Human One (Son of Man) must suffer many things and be rejected by the elders, chief priests, and the legal experts, [in other words, the very leaders of the Jews to whom salvation was supposed to come first!] and be killed, and then, after three days, rise from the dead"(Mark 8:31). Jesus believes *this* is the true fulfillment of Old Testament prophecy (Wright, *The Challenge of Jesus*).

I mention all this because when we really get acquainted with the Jesus of the Gospels, we come to see that, as he didn't fit the common messianic profiles of his day, *he is also quite different from many of the views of who he is that are going around today, even within the church.* Often his words and his actions are an offence to our polite Christianity. We've tried so hard to tame him and domesticate him that we are sometimes unprepared for the Jesus we meet in the Gospels; he is so at odds with the Jesus we've constructed. We may well need a clarifying of our view of Jesus, a correcting of our distortions—as innocently as we may have come by them. And we may, as well, need a correction of some of the compromises we have made as Jesus' disciples because of these misunderstandings.

Our misunderstandings and distortions of Jesus are reason enough for Christians to keep studying Jesus, reading the Gospels with open minds— open to their witness and to the Spirit's insight—seeing the life and teaching of Jesus for what it *is*. The Gospels will show us that what Jesus was up against back then is not that different from what he is up against today, both within the circle of his followers and in the world at large. Still he calls us to be with him, to watch him, know him, follow him, live him. Still he calls

those who comprise his church and those who do not, to be his disciples—
and that's the whole point of the Gospels!

Jesus offers a radically different way of seeing God, ourselves, the
world and how to live in it. We can call it a huge paradigm shift. Jesus comes
to introduce this new paradigm, to model it, and to open the way for us
actually to live in and by it. He introduces it by teaching a stunningly different way of life; he models it by his many surprising actions of compassion,
humility, confrontation; he opens the way for us by inviting us to be—not
his admirers, his supporters, his advocates—but his *disciples*!

Believing Jesus is Following Jesus

The metaphor of God as our Shepherd appears more than once in the Old
Testament. In Psalm 23 the psalmist David uses the metaphor to demonstrate that we are God's people by virtue of coming under his guidance "in
paths of righteousness for his name's sake" (v. 3b, NIV). The point is that we
stay in those paths by going with the Shepherd who goes before and prods
from behind.

Jesus adopts the metaphor to describe his relationship with his own
flock. The word that described a divine Shepherd now takes flesh in the very
person of Jesus: "I am the good shepherd," says Jesus. "I know my sheep and
they know me, just as the Father knows me and I know the Father" (John
10:14–15a). There's intimacy and love here so deep the shepherd is willing
to "give up [his] life for the sheep." (v. 15b) At this point the metaphor is
being stretched beyond what literally makes sense, all the more drawing our
attention. And then we learn the shepherd is actually one of us, his sheep.

There is an account in John's Gospel of Jesus visiting the temple in
Jerusalem at the time of the Feast of Dedication when Jews commemorated
the last miraculous deliverance of the Jewish nation from an oppressor in
165 BCE (John 10:22–30). Thoughts of a new deliverance are probably in
the air, and on seeing Jesus Jewish leaders gather around him and again
push the messianic question: "How long will you test our patience? If you
are the Christ, tell us plainly." Jesus replies first by saying he did tell them,
as well as demonstrate God at work through him with miracles, but still
they did not believe. Then he tells them why: "You don't believe because you
don't belong to my sheep" (v. 26).

This may sound strange to us. Many, if not most Christians tend to
think that being a Christian requires, first, a confession of faith in Jesus, and
then, having committed ourselves to that belief and having accepted Jesus
as Savior, learning how to follow him. Now there is certainly truth in seeing

conversion in this way. Jesus, however, in his response in the temple, seems to be inviting us to see yet another dimension of faith. An initial conversion, as powerful and as genuine as it may be, sets us on a journey with Jesus where we discover much more than we knew when we began. We may find we have gotten ourselves into far more than we knew! As with the twelve disciples who left their occupations to follow this compelling rabbi, we, also, learn very quickly that we are a long way from coming to terms with what he is asking us to believe, how he is asking us to live, and what he is asking us to do. It seems we have to go through a series of "conversions" or changes before we are personally prepared to continue what he started in us.

How does this help us understand Jesus' response to those in the temple that day, to whom he said: "you don't believe because you don't belong to my sheep"? Is he saying that belief in him is a process that comes to fruition only as we follow him? That he becomes our good shepherd only as we experience his shepherding and learn to trust him? That faith is not simply the agreement of our minds, but more fully the trust of our hearts, deepened and strengthened over time by seeing what he shows us, doing what he commands us, and being who we really are as he reveals this to us? If this is true, then we discover what this conversion really means as day by day we actually seek to *follow* this counter-cultural Jesus—this rabbi who continually shocks us with the breadth and depth of his compassion and the radical nature of his mission, all the while calling us to let his Spirit mold us accordingly. When we do follow this rabbi, when we, like rescued sheep, trust the good shepherd and learn his ways, then our *faith* has the real substance of *life*. It is solidly grounded in a person we are getting to know and a way of life we are allowing to challenge us the more we see it and are willing to give ourselves to it and risk our lives for it.

Only as we follow Jesus can we fully believe in him. Jesus says, "You do not believe because you do not belong to my sheep. My sheep listen to my voice. I know them and they follow me" (vv. 26–27). Following Jesus, actually being his disciple, is not a separate thing from believing. It *is* believing, in the truest and deepest sense. A person may simply believe the truth of a doctrine or a package of doctrines. His mind is agreeing to believe. That alone, however, is not the belief Jesus asks of us, though our minds are a part of our faith—how could they not be? Our faith doesn't require we check our brains at the door. It does require that we *belong* to Jesus, and doing that requires that we *follow* him, that we become a part of his community of disciples where together we learn how to live his life in our lives.

Going back to the story, we read that at this point his questioners are so angry about what they are hearing, they pick up stones to pummel him for blasphemy, for claiming the right to be followed and believed, as if he were God Himself, as if totally trusting what he says and living as he lives is exactly what God has in mind for the human race. Their anger is understandable. Unless we become his disciples, unless we "belong to his sheep," what he says, does, and claims—everything written about him in the New Testament—makes no sense to us. In fact, for those who don't accept Jesus' claim, it *is* blasphemy.

One thing that has diluted our discipleship is our tendency to reduce Christian faith to the acceptance of certain doctrinal propositions. "I am a Christian because I believe in the divinity of Jesus, the Trinity, this or that theological concept." Jesus never asks his disciples to believe in the doctrine of the Trinity, and when he asks them who they believe he is, he is clearly not asking them to articulate some doctrinal concept about him; he is asking for their commitment to him as Messiah. In all three Gospel accounts of Peter's confession at Caesarea Philippi, the confession is followed by Jesus' prediction of his own cruel death, and then his revelation that being his disciple means losing *our* lives for his sake (Mark 8:27–38; Matthew 16:13–26; Luke 9:18–25). To confess that Jesus is the Christ (the Messiah) of God is much more than a mental assent to a doctrine; it is a life surrendered to a person. In the Gospels—and the entire New Testament, for that matter—there is no believing Jesus without following Jesus. What makes those early disciples authentic is that they leave their nets, tax booths, political revolutions, begging—or whatever their line of work—to join the company of Jesus and follow, wherever he takes them.

Imitating Jesus

As the rabbis of Jesus' day were both teachers and models of righteous living for their disciples, so Jesus both taught and modeled the new kingdom of God for *his* disciples. As it was then, so it is now: To be a disciple of Jesus is to be both a learner and a follower. To "follow" in this sense is more than hanging around our rabbi, more than listening to the music of his words, bathing in the refreshment of his presence, getting inspiration from the charm of his metaphors and the incisiveness of his stories. Being a follower of Jesus *is* all this—and much *more*. What is the "much more"? It is actually *the main thing*. Thomas à Kempis had the nerve to say it and teach it when he wrote a book about it called *Of the Imitation of Christ*, a book that caused a backlash from many leaders of his church before it became a spiritual classic many years later. The main thing, the bottom line in the gospel, is to learn from Jesus how to live our lives.

Now "imitation" can be a tricky word here, and easily understood in wrong ways. Jesus doesn't call us to follow him around like the besotted fans of some rock star, desperately seeking to capture their own identity through association and proximity. Nor does he call us to drag our weak selves after him like grace-fed parasites who choose indulgent grace over enabling grace. Imitating Jesus is not finding personal significance through image affiliation and a vicarious attempt in style and manner to act like some star or any much-admired person.

Nor is it a perfectionist desperately straining to acquire the personality profile of Jesus—trying to come across, for example, as a copy of "gentle Jesus meek and mild," or any other stereotype of Jesus (the muscular Jesus, Jesus as the perfect CEO, Jesus as our cozy buddy, etc.). Such a gesture may well be seriously attempted, but we really can't pull off any of it successfully. It is doomed ultimately to fail. We can't *make* ourselves Jesus. Jesus had his own unique personality; otherwise, he would have been a stereotype of humanity and not truly human. We, each one of us, have *our* own unique personalities. Imitating the personality of Jesus is imitation only on the most superficial level. The imitation of himself to which Jesus calls us is the imitation of a life and all that life brings to God, to our relationships, and to the world—whether we are a decorous deacon or a crusty dock worker.

If believing Jesus means following Jesus, following Jesus means imitating Jesus, his way of life not his personality profile. Over the course of his public ministry, Jesus is teaching and living the way he wants *us* to live. He is modeling our discipleship for us. We are lifelong learners with him, perfecting the art of imitation, growing into his likeness. We never fully perfect it, never "arrive" at a place where there's nothing more to learn or act on. The fact is, like those first disciples in the Gospels, just when we think we fully understand what it means to be a mature disciple of Jesus, and just when we think we're living so well the life he calls us to, Jesus moves on ahead, forcing us to *keep* learning—always disciples, never masters. "Call no one rabbi," says Jesus.

One further caution about how we approach this matter of imitating Jesus. Some of the things he said and did do not call for our imitation. They are words that can be said and actions that can be done only by the messianic Son of God. The Gospels are replete with them as well. They are the words and actions of the Word of God in action. We cannot say them of ourselves or do them of ourselves. They belong to the Divine, incarnate in Jesus. They can be understood as what only the Messiah can claim for himself or presume to do—and we are not the Messiah.

Garry Wills refers to this in the excellent foreword to his book *What Jesus Meant* (xv-xxxi). He begins the foreword by saying that using "What

Would Jesus Do?" as the formula by which Jesus' followers can decide their *every* action is misguided as an all-encompassing approach to imitating Jesus. Obviously, some of what Jesus said about himself was not something we dare say or claim ourselves. For example, when he said he had come to bring not peace but a sword and to set family members against one another, he is realistically predicting the divisions that his mission would inevitably bring; he is not inviting us to be self-consciously divisive (Matt 10:34–36). Some of what Jesus did was a living parable not meant for imitation, and it would be presumption and insensitivity if we tried it. Jesus' treatment of his mother, brothers, and sisters when they sought him out because they were concerned about him is a living parable of the *inclusiveness* of the Kingdom family *he* is inaugurating; it is not a way for Christians to treat their parents (Mark 3:33–35)! The destruction of some farmer's herd of 2,000 pigs to dramatize an exorcism of demons, an act that may have also impoverished a number of people is not a way for us to treat someone else's property or livelihood (Mark 5:13)! Jesus telling a would-be follower to choose between following him and fulfilling his urgent filial obligation to bury his father is Jesus illustrating the primacy he must have in the lives of his disciples; it is not a choice we ourselves have the right to require of anyone (Matt 8:22)! Jesus was more than the model for his followers to imitate; he was also God in action, presuming to do what only God can presume. His followers must discern between his invasive, sometimes outrageous actions as their messiah and his teaching and exampling as their rabbi. One leads us to worship, the other to imitation.

Let us all confess we have a tendency to mold Jesus into our own image or profile him by the culture with which we are personally identified. I have tried not to do so in this study, but of course such pure objectivity is rarely achieved (if ever). The reader will need to exercise his own discrimination in such matters. Furthermore, there is so much in the Gospels left for us to "fill in" for ourselves—and that is not all bad. We, all of us, must contextualize Jesus in *our* life setting. What we disciples who read the Gospels must keep in mind, however, is that there is a border beyond which our self-contextualizing becomes a caricature, a fictional shaping of Jesus to fit our personal profile or cultural comfort level.

In this journey we are taking together, perhaps we can see ourselves as those who, like the apostles Peter, James, and John on the Mount of Transfiguration, recognize the importance of Jesus in a new way and hear the voice of God loud and clear: "This is my Son, whom I dearly love. *Listen to him!*" (Mark 9:7b, italics added). In our study together and throughout this book we listen in many dimensions. We listen to what Jesus says, listen to the shocking themes of the kingdom of God he describes, listen to the extraordinary meaning of his actions, listen to his compelling call to reck-less action for his sake and the gospel's, and listen to his calling us to follow him wherever he goes and wherever he is. And in the listening, we begin to see life.

Works Cited

Auden, W.H. "For the Time Being." In *The Collected Poetry of W.H. Auden*. New York: Random House, 1944.

Aulen, Gustav. *Christus Victor*. Translated by A.G. Herbert. New York: Macmillan, 1961.

Blackburn, Thomas. "No Single Station of the Globe." In *Selected Poems*. London: Hutchinson, 1975.

Bonhoeffer, Dietrich. *Letters and Papers from Prison*. London: SCM, 1953.

Buechner, Frederick. *Listening to Your Life: Daily Meditations*. Compiled by George Conner. San Francisco: HarperSanFrancisco, 1992.

Candaele, Kelly. "On Opening Day, a Call for the Return of the Stolen Base." *The Los Angeles Times* (April 2, 2002). http://articles.latimes.com/2002/apr/02/news/lv-basesteal2.

Dunne, John S. *The Reasons of the Heart: A Journey into Solitude and Back Again into the Human Circle*. Notre Dame: University of Notre Dame Press, 1978.

Episcopal Church. *Hymnbook 1982*. New York: The Church Hymnal Corporation, 1985.

Gregory the Great. *The Book of Pastoral Rule*. Translated by George E. Demacopoulos. Crestwood, NY: St. Vladimir's Seminary, 2007.

Guy, David. "Abraham Lincoln, Shakespeare, and Frederick Coutts." *Salvationist* (September 19,1998) 7.

Hunter, George G. *Radical Outreach: Recovering Apostolic Ministry and Evangelism*. Nashville: Abingdon, 2003.

Jordan, Clarence. *Sermon on the Mount*. Valley Forge, PA: Judson, 1952.

à Kempis, Thomas. *Of the Imitation of Christ*. Springdale, PA: Whitaker House, 1981.

Lawrence, Brother. *The Practice of the Presence of God*. Grand Rapids: Fleming H. Revell, 1958.

Lazarus, Emma. "The New Colossus." New York: Statue of Liberty National Museum.

McNeal, Reggie. *The Present Future: Six Tough Questions for the Church*. San Francisco: Jossey-Bass, 2003.

Peterson, Eugene. *Christ Plays in Ten Thousand Places*. Grand Rapids: Eerdmans, 2005.
———. *Tell It Slant*. Grand Rapids: Eerdmans, 2008.

Reilly, Rick. *The Life of Reilly The Best of Sports Illustrated's Rick Reilly*. Kingston, NY: Total Sports Illustrated, 2000.

Sehgal, Parul. "Power Play," *The New York Times Magazine* (July 19, 2015) 11.

Slater, Philip. *Pursuit of Loneliness*. Boston: Beacon, 1970.

Smith, Martin L. "The Spirit of the Lord is Upon Me." *Sojourners Magazine*. https:// sojo.net/.

Tickle, Phyllis. *The Shaping of a Life: A Spiritual Landscape*. New York: Doubleday, 2001.

———. *Wisdom in the Waiting*. Chicago: Loyola, 1987.

———. *The Words of Jesus: The Gospel of the Sayings of Our Lord*. San Francisco: Jossey-Bass, 2008.

Wesley, John. "The Character of a Methodist." In *The Works of John Wesley*, VIII. Grand Rapids: Baker, 1996.

———. "A Farther Appeal to Men of Reason and Religion." In *The Works of John Wesley*, VIII. Grand Rapids: Baker, 1996.

Wills, Garry. *What Jesus Meant*. New York: Viking, 2006.

Williams, H. A. *The Joy of God*. London: Continuum, 2002.

Wright, N. T. *The Challenge of Jesus*. Downers Grove: Intervarsity, 1999.

CPSIA information can be obtained
at www.ICGtesting.com
Printed in the USA
BVHW041835010321
601411BV00025B/295